THE FILM DIRECTOR PREPARES

A PRACTICAL GUIDE TO
DIRECTING FOR FILM & TV

MYRL A. SCHREIBMAN

THE FILM DIRECTOR PREPARES:
A Practical Guide to Directing for Film & TV

Lone Eagle Publishing, a division of
Watson-Guptill Publications
Crown Publishing Group,
a division of Random House Inc., New York
www.crownpublishing.com
www.watsonguptill.com

Cover design by ZekeDESIGN
Book design by Carla Green
Edited by Steve Atinsky

ISBN-10: 1-58065-067-8
ISBN-13: 978-1-58065-067-0

Library of Congress Cataloging-in-Publication Data

Schreibman, Myrl A.
The film director prepares : a practical guide to directing for film & TV /
By Myrl A. Schreibman
　　　p.　　cm.
ISBN – 1-58065-067-8
1. Motion pictures—Production and direction. 2. Television—Production and
direction. I. Title.

PN1995.9.p7S344 2006
791.4302'33—dc22　　　　　　　　　　　　　　2006045155

Printed in the United States of America
10 9 8 7 6 5 4

Directing is an art form that is one of the foundations for telling stories. It deals with compromise, staying calm, creative and focused while confusion and imposing deadlines materialize limitations. It requires a love for actors and being their pal, confidant and trusted best friend. It demands an understanding of the human condition and knowledge to communicate it visually to affect an audience. It is not just what someone learns in a film school program but also what someone needs to know, feel, and understand about the practical side of telling stories. Myrl Schreibman's *The Film Director Prepares* does exactly that and more. Schreibman has been there as a director and producer and educator. While there are many books written about directing, only one is able to provide practical directing wisdom. And this is it! No doubt it will be the canon of film directing books for years to come.

—Maggie Murphy, President, Kiefer Sutherland Productions

Myrl Schreibman makes a giant leap forward in the world of "how to" books for directors. While lovingly acknowledging and supporting the creative process that all directors must have and use to realize their visions, he also bluntly and necessarily introduces the real-world problems and shows you how to deal with the challenges that can conspire to crush these visions: producers, studios, budgets, etc. He gently reminds us that the "business" and the "art" are inextricably linked and that that knowledge can only help the visionary director get his project made.

—Phillip Charles MacKenzie, Cable Ace Award-winning director

What's a director do, you ask? Read Myrl Schreibman's *The Film Director Prepares* and you'll never ask that question again. So concise! Schreibman's book covers it all—from the importance of fully understanding the text, through pre-visualization, to the motivation behind still shots and shots that move. Every director, no matter the level of experience, will get something fresh from this thorough, nicely written text. The Table of Contents alone is impressive. The section on understanding actors and the chapter on "Directing the Actor" are essential reading for any good director/actor relationship. The read is deceptively simple. And Schreibman takes the complex work of a director and breaks it down into a thoroughly readable text.

—A.P. Gonzalez, Award-winning writer/director

Myrl Schreibman is one of the people who gave me the encouragement and confidence to go out there and direct films. He was a true inspiration while I was a graduate film student at UCLA. This book proves to be a breath of fresh air as the mysteries of directing a film are clearly explained from a very down-to-earth perspective. They're the same professional techniques and directing precepts that he taught me. I use them in both my fiction and documentary work.

**—William Tyler Smith, Writer/Director, *Kiss Me Again*;
Director, *Imagine a School: Summerhill* (Documentary)**

To my mentor, legendary film director Jack Arnold,
and my dear friend Carolyn Haber, who always has
unfailing faith in me, this book is dedicated . . .
and to Danny and Janet

CONTENTS

FOREWORD

I first met Myrl when I was president of the Directors Guild of America. He was an active participant who attended meetings and was supportive of the Guild's goals. To become a member of the DGA one had to be sponsored by other members, so I knew Myrl was a capable director.

When I became the founding Dean of the UCLA School of Theater Film and Television, Myrl became a colleague of mine and one that I admire greatly. Myrl Schreibman is an excellent teacher and administrator. The knowledge that Myrl brought into the classroom inspired the likes of Justin Lin, Patricia Cardoso, Dan Angel, and an entire generation of directors and producers making their mark in our profession. His "industry skills" and friendships also provide the school with a professional faculty and administrator who understands the many creative elements that are required of a director, actor, writer, and producer. During his time at UCLA he continues to direct (and produce) achieving the acclaim of his peers and winning awards for his direction.

Now Myrl has written a book about the practical and creative issues that face film and television directors everywhere. Myrl's book focuses on the realities of the directing process and the need for directors to plan and to think creatively on their feet when faced with the real problems and limitations that productions often present. The book is full of examples and excellent methods of understanding and handling problems of both talent and camera coverage. Based entirely on practical experience, it demonstrates that it is not only what you do as a director but also how much love you put into the doing. This has been Myrl Schreibman's approach to his work and continues to be the substance of who he is. You will see it in this book and be moved by it as well—*The Film Director Prepares: A Practical Guide to Directing for Film and TV.*

—Gil Cates
Producer, Director
Past President, Directors Guild of America

PREFACE

During my thirty-five year career, which includes over forty feature films and hundreds of commercials and television shows, I have worked with not only experienced directors but also many first-timers. Early on I realized that directing is an art that is not easily learned. It takes the experience of understanding the pragmatic approach of the directing process and its correlation to the creative result of storytelling. It takes knowing how coverage works in telling that story and working with actors to understand what the camera does to interpret their work. And most importantly, it takes thinking on one's feet in solving problems to get the results on screen while at the same time maintaining the focus that the art of directing demands.

Learning the art of direction can take years of costly trial and error. Well, the learning curve has just been shortened by this no-nonsense book that you are holding in your hands. It comes from a realistic approach based on years of experience from a director who not only directs in various mediums but also produces and understands what a director must do to tell a story.

The Film Director Prepares should be required reading for students of directing, screenwriters, producers and, believe it or not, seasoned directing professionals. If you don't believe me, just ask the director of my next film.

—Tom Denove
Cinematographer

ACKNOWLEDGMENTS

I want to thank the many people who I have met in the entertainment industry who, in their own way, have encouraged my passion for images, actors and storytelling and to Dean Robert Rosen of the UCLA School of Theater Film and Television for his words, understanding and assistance. Many thanks to Gil Cates, Tom Denove, and Eyan Schreibman for their contribution and compassion. A special thanks to Delia Salvi for her brilliance and camaraderie. And a particular thank you to Lionsgate Films, Cathy Schulman, Paul Haggis, Bobby Moresco, and Lee Kramer for making it possible to use excerpts from the screenplay *Crash*. A loving thanks to Robert Fiveson for his contribution and friendship through the years. To Herb Stein, Nathan Amondson, and Barry Zetlin for letting me gather from their individual creative knowledge. And a warm gratitude to Steve Kaminski, Will Gotay, Patsy Lake, and Adrian Morales for their ongoing friendship. And of course gratitude to the smartest attorney/ confidant in the world, Steven M. Stein of Stein and Greene, who is always there at the drop of a hat. I am deeply grateful to Ben Peyser for his genius, dedication, conscience and creative contribution to the book, to Carla Green for her layout genius, and to Betsy Ahlstrand for her commitment. Of course a big thanks to the creative brilliance of Ken Schafer, and to Gabriele Meiringer, Dan Douma, Jesse Douma, and Ethan Markowitz of FrameForge 3D Software for their support, as well as appreciation to the folks at Watson-Guptill. But I cannot go on without my heartfelt gratitude and appreciation to my insightful, soft spoken but relentless editors, Steve Atinsky and Brian Phair, and of course to the most amazing publisher in the world, Jeff Black, who really should have been a movie producer or was in another life! His wisdom, vision, and energy have been one of the driving forces. But most of all, to the hundreds of students and professionals throughout the world who inspired me and gave me clarity and insight into the concepts and knowledge that is offered in this book. Finally, to the many others who have so freely given, I thank you.

INTRODUCTION

Directing a motion picture is an artistic activity unlike any other. It requires embracing and turning to advantage two core contradictions that pull you in opposite directions.

The first is a seeming paradox. The best films have characteristically been an oil-and-water combination of a single director's personal vision and the intimate collaboration of a broad range of creative artists. Unlike art forms such as poetry or painting that can be created by an individual working in isolation, motion pictures are at once personal modes of expression and acts of community building—a complex interlacing of inspired leadership and social engineering. To tell a compelling and memorable story on screen, a director must have clarity of vision but at the same time must be able to communicate that vision to a team of talented professionals, all of whom are visionaries in their areas of specialization. To be a director is to have at once a strong ego and a profound sense of humility, an overall knowledge of all the many skills that go into a production and an acute awareness that, in the end, it is others who will be involved in putting your vision onto the screen. To be a director requires being on top of a thousand decisions made by a small army of diverse collaborators working in a hectic environment without ever losing sight of the only objective that ultimately matters: the effectiveness of sound, images, and performances in telling a story that is compelling and memorable.

The second contradiction is equally daunting. A director's task is to be at once rigorously practical and expansively utopian. On the one hand, the material realities of making a film require its creative leader to be ever vigilant of seemingly mundane matters of due date and bottom line and to make decisions within the constraints of finite and often severely limited resources. The director must know how much coverage is needed and how to get it, how to work around bad weather or noisy locations, how to cheat a shot or use music or sound to enhance a scene, and how to solve a thousand other knotty problems.

But all of these practical decisions are mobilized to achieve a remarkable objective that transcends the prosaic, i.e., to seduce broadly diverse audiences to suspend disbelief and to accept flickering images on the screen as a reality capable of evoking feelings, provoking reflection, and expanding our sense of the possible. Pragmatic knowledge and practical skills are absolutely essential to a director, but they are only means to an end. A director must be at once an artisan and an artist, a pragmatist and a dreamer.

Thanks to this publication, future generations of directors will come to know what students at UCLA have known for the past twenty years, namely that Myrl Schreibman knows how to guide and train filmmakers who are at once knowledgeable and inspired. His presentation is clear and accessible. His wise advice is empowering to and for all directors, but particularly those working within limited budgets. And his dogged practicality is matched by an acute awareness of the power of film to transform the human spirit.

—Robert Rosen
Dean, UCLA School of
Theater, Film, and Television

> *"I think our job as artists is to bring to light things to talk about, to constantly say that debate is not disloyalty."*
>
> — **George Clooney**, director,
> *Good Night, and Good Luck*

SO YOU WANT TO BE A DIRECTOR?

Directing! Directing! Directing! This is the war cry for every young filmmaker I come across:

> *"I want to be a director!"*
>
> *"I can direct better than that."*
>
> *"Directing is easy. There is nothing to it, if you are used to being a leader."*
>
> *"I am a visual person, so I know I can direct."*
>
> *"I have stories to tell and an independent voice."*

I hear statements like that every week from anyone and everyone, and especially from students at the university. They are full of wonderful dreams, passions, energies, and imagination. Their voices speak volumes while in school but oftentimes barely speak at all when they leave. They discover that directing is much more than what they learn in school. It's about life, about the world around them. It's about the human condition, social consciousness, social awareness, and humanity. It's about tears and laughter. It's about joys and sorrows. It's about budgets and deadlines. It's about limitations and restrictions. It's about studios and networks. It's about collaboration and vision and a whole lot more.

Many books have been written about directing for the screen, and they will continue to be written. But they mostly talk about the mysteries of working with actors and other on-screen talent. They delve into the intricacies and secrets of the actor's psyche and *finding the key* that opens their performances. They speak of the analysis of text and "actor speak." They discuss *method acting, technical acting, theater games, the Meisner technique,* or other systems in the hope that the reader will totally comprehend everything there is to know about actors. Or, if they detail the camera, they are full of graphs and diagrams that show camera placement and they talk about types of lenses, cameras, depth of field, framing, film stock, editing, and other technical issues. They go on and on about aspects that relate to directing while preaching what directors need to know and do to instantly and automatically become a director. And as soon as the readers have turned the last page of one of these books, they are ready to direct their first feature and run to their closet to pick out their wardrobe for next year's Oscar ceremony.

A director has an obligation to tell a story and to do so with the skill of a master storyteller, using the tools that directors use while working with and recognizing the collaborative team that shades the story as it is being told. Directing is a thought process, just as producing and cinematography are thought processes. From my experience, you either think like a director or you don't. Books like this one can provide you with knowledge, some practical and some theoretical, which you take with you when you direct, but none of them will make you a director. Directors must be visionaries. They must be passionate about knowledge and discriminatory in knowing their own limitations. They must know a little about everything relating to the process of what they do so they can be discriminating with the people they work with and speak the individual languages of the art director, the costume designer, the property master, the editor, and so on. Some calling themselves directors are writers, some are producers, and some are even cinematographers. *And they think like directors.* They come in both genders, all sizes, and, thank goodness, all colors. *And they think like directors.* They bring their own identities and voices to the screen as well as the voices and identities of others. *And they think like directors.* Being a producer and a directing member of the Directors Guild of America for thirty years I have encountered hundreds of them, and being an educator, I have trained many of them, giving them the foundation for a very successful career: *to think like a director.*

Schools all over the world have curricula that teach about directing. Some even teach people how to think like directors. But there is more to directing than what is taught in schools. Directing involves knowing and understanding the actors' techniques and being able to communicate to each and every one of them. Directing involves the collaborative process of production and understanding how it works with postproduction. Directing is about good planning, collaboration, trust, and delivery. Directing involves telling a story, not in the broad strokes but in the minutiae and knowing how it will impact the vision. Directing involves knowing about camera placement, coverage, and the production process and its relationship to the creative process of the actor. Directing means being able to juggle the relationship of time to creativity and getting a day's work completed as scheduled. Directing entails knowing how to work with producers, studio and network executives, editors, and writers. Directing requires knowing about budgets, negotiations, and the pitching of projects to get them made. Directing involves writing, language, and a passion for the human condition and characters and their emotional state of mind from moment to moment. Directing takes someone who knows when to be forceful and when to stand back and let the world unfold in front of the camera. Directing requires knowing the pop and the intellectual. It requires patience, creativity, and an inner visual skill that is based in an artist's instinct. Directing demands seeing something before anyone else and knowing how to pull the strongest elements together to tell the story. Directing requires knowing how to earn respect from others and willingly stepping into the stressful fray of leading egos and tempers. Directing involves knowing the business of *the business* and knowing when creativity and business must be looked at independently of one another. And above all, directing is intuitive!

Directing is much more than what you think it is. Hopefully, this book will show you what you *think* you know about directing, what you *need* to know, and what you *must* know if you want to call yourself a director.

"The husband and wife story was the soul of the movie. It was the Everyman's side of things. It wasn't an idealized relationship, it was this real palpable love they felt for each other. That love was the foundation of their survival and that love was the foundation (and theme) of the film."

Ron Howard, director, *Cinderella Man*

CHAPTER 1

THE WRITTEN WORD— THE SCRIPT

WHERE TO BEGIN?

Most books on directing begin with a discussion of the text. And this book is not the exception, since the foundation or the map that a director works with is text. It sparks the creative imagination of the director and fans it until the text becomes a reality.

Directors have three basic responsibilities. *The first is the responsibility to their creative self.* They must be honest in what they believe regarding the material they are working with and allow it to absorb into their creative being whether in development or during the directing process. They must, before anyone else, feel the human condition and see the details of the story unfold in their minds and imagination. They must be attuned to the characters and who and what they are. Their creative research leads them to understand the soul of the material and the nuances that are either indicated or explicit in the material.

Their second responsibility is to their producer, who either brings them to the material or develops the material that they brought to them. The producer is paying the director's salary, so it is important that directors realize that the producer is the first of many with whom they must collaborate and the nearest one to see the vision of the material. It is a foolish director who thinks of the producer as only a source for money or putting together deals and not one who can collaborate on the creative nature of the material. The producer must share in the creative vision of the work which must be simpatico with the director. Or to put it another way, the director must share in the creative vision of the work which must be simpatico with the producer. This shared vision is the glue that holds the project together, prevents any creative differences from creeping in between the producer and the director, and strengthens the foundation of the project as it picks up steam during the process of getting it made.

A project is not a project unless it is seen by an audience. *A director's third responsibility is to that audience, since, after all, the movie business is a business.* The director's job is to interpret the screenplay and take the material on the written page and heighten it to its glory on screen. The director's creativity and contribution to the project begins where the writer's creativity ends; the actors' creativity and contribution begins where the director's task ends; and of course, the audience's contribution, their involvement with the story, and hopefully their money at the box office, begins where the actors' creativity ends, completing the entire cycle of the creative process which begins with the text!

READ, READ, READ

A director must read the script many times, with the first three times being the most important in terms of understanding the text. *The first time is for knowing where the story is going.* The director needs to see what the author's intention is, discuss it with the producer, and look inside their own creative self to see if they can contribute something in interpreting the story. Certain directors are better at directing certain types of projects. Martin Scorsese, for example, directed social and character-driven pictures of great significance and scope, such as *GoodFellas, Raging Bull, The Aviator,* and *Gangs of New York.* These have made him a legendary filmmaker. But his movie *The Age of Innocence,* a smaller, more intimate and beautiful picture, did not really enhance his reputation. You expect a certain type of picture if it is directed by Tim Burton, whether it is *Batman* or a remake of *Willy Wonka*. And you know that when material is based on a play or has dialogue concerning the interpersonal relationships and complexities of people, Mike Nichols will handle it beautifully, as he did in *Closer, Angels in America, Biloxi Blues, The Graduate, The Birdcage, Silkwood*, and *Who's Afraid of Virginia Woolf*.

The second time a script is read it should be read with a view towards the characters: who are they and what do they think about each other? While reading the script, the director should be determining what is motivating the individual characters while trying to "feel" the emotional thread that ties them together. The director must be clear about these motivations and get into the characters by accessing their thoughts and know when they need to be revisited with the writer. If the director is not clear about the relationships as they develop in the story, then actors will not be clear about who they are and what they think about one another. Writers create dialogue and dialogue should be the result of impulses that the characters are feeling from moment to moment. But oftentimes they are not. And the director must see past those words to find the honest motivations to strengthen the characters and their relationships—because, let's face it, a good story should always be character-driven.

The third time the script is read the director should read it from the gut. In other words, the directors' third reading should be an intuitive one in an attempt to link his or her internal instincts to the material and become closer to it. By the time actors are brought on board and the project is shooting, the director must know every little intricacy, nuance, and microcosm of the story. This third reading is the beginning of that journey and the most important reading. During each of the readings the director must also be visualizing the story, and with each read the visualization becomes clearer. Through this technique of *at least* three specific readings a director will see problems with the story and be better prepared to guide a writer down a path to solve them and ultimately make it a better, more fulfilling story.

THEME

Theme underlies the elements of character and plot in stories. Determining the theme or themes is the foundation from which any director must work, as theme evokes an interpretation or a message that is intended throughout the story. It may not necessarily be the primary message that the screenwriter intended, but it might be the message that is substantially at the center of the vision for the director and producer. *"All scripts contain ambiguities, unresolved questions, and therefore, possibilities. Understanding (or determining) theme is not a matter of understanding exactly what the writer meant. It's about the director arriving at an interpretation of the author's work."* [1] In order to clearly keep the analysis of the text in perspective, directors should determine themes and try to identify them in one or two words, as themes become the visual driving force around which the directors' interpretation moves. Is it *privacy,* as in Coppola's *The Conversation,* or *discovering oneself,* as in Alexander Payne's *Sideways?* Is it *succession,* as in *The Godfather?* Or is it *schizophrenia,* as in David Koepp's *Secret Window?* By focusing on a one- or two-word theme, a director maintains focus throughout the direction of the project. These words are carved in their psyche, and creative decisions that are made (and there are many that a director is asked for) may at some time come back to that theme.

When Coppola was asked by his wardrobe designer what raincoat Gene Hackman should wear in *The Conversation,* he referred to his theme of privacy and looked to the best type of raincoat that could express some aspect of that theme. So in that specific case and for that specific character they determined that a transparent raincoat would be best. In *Secret Window,* touches of schizophrenia crept into the cinematography, staging, and unusual camera positions throughout the direction. In *The Godfather,* Coppola was attracted to the succession theme by the story of a father with three sons *"like a king and his three sons and each one got a particular talent of his but each did not get all of them. Michael was cunning, Sonny got the big Rabelaisian energy and Fredo got his sweetness."* [2] This is a somewhat classical theme in drama and certainly in Shakespeare, so when Coppola looked for a visual style to his movie he focused on one that was classical, without a lot of moving camera shots, and cinematography and design that dealt with a lot of light and dark elements. Focusing on the theme prevails over every aspect of the vision and keeps it on the right path. A skilled director will keep it in the forefront of creative thought and let it be a useful guide through the myriad decisions that are made.

---

[1] *Friendly Enemies, Maximizing the Director-Actor Relationship,* Delia Salvi, page 60.

[2] Francis Ford Coppola Master Class, UCLA, October 20, 2004.

When looking at the text, the director should read each scene with an eye toward the theme and determine its direct or indirect relationship to that theme. Does it relate at the moment the scene exists in the story? Or does it have a relationship to other scenes that, when joined together, develop the theme? One good way to look at the text and see when it follows true to form is to read the screenplay backward: from the end of the script to the beginning and *feel* how the linkage connects to the theme of the story. Does it connect through character, through plot, or through the subtleties that join the two together? This method of examination will clearly show the director the connective tissue that joins the theme to the story.

THE TEXT

Analysis

Some directors go through and analyze the script from several perspectives. Certainly by the time the director is brought into the picture there is an understanding of what the story is about—but it is the director who must go through it and do an analysis on several levels. What is the *dramatic history* of the story? Does the story take place over a few hours, a few days, a few years, or over decades? This will have an impact on the characters and what they say and feel. Not all screenplays are fully developed or realized, and certainly unless you are directing a screenplay that is fully developed, deep analysis in terms of the purpose of each scene or the characters' embodiment of the scene may not be realized. In that event, the director (and/or producer) works closely with the writer to further develop the characters and plot. This often takes the form of script notes that are discussed with the writer during various phases of the writing/development or rewriting of the screenplay. The director's job at this juncture is to point the writer in the right direction so the characters can become more fully developed and the screenplay will appeal to actors. Producers especially need this, since they are concerned with the financing and marketing of the project, and often, having an actor who has marketability becomes important to getting the project financed. The key to getting an excellent (and marketable) actor is to have a screenplay that is driven by characters that are well defined and multidimensional. A tight, character-driven screenplay will always appeal to the actor's ego, and it becomes a project that they *must* do no matter what! A director can be the guru who is able to guide the writer in that direction.

There are good script notes and bad script notes, and the way in which script notes are given to the writer can cause the difference between the two. Script notes should be constructive and not destructive. They should not be offered in a dogmatic way but *suggested* so that the writer will feel that the story and script is still his or hers. In this way, the script notes massage the writer's ego while strengthening the story. Script notes should never be given in writing but instead during a meeting with the writer. If they are given in writing, the writer often interprets them negatively and sometimes finds them offensive since they do not understand clearly where they are coming from. I learned this the hard way on a project when the network, without any explanation, handed me notes to give to one of my writers—a talented but challenging writer. It included instructions for deletions and insertions of dialogue that came from the opinion of a story editor or network reader that no one had met. Story editors and script readers are often frustrated writers themselves.[3] When I gave the network notes to the writer, he sneered at them and then threw them away, letting me know with a few expletives that he didn't take notes from people who didn't have the courage to face him.

Script notes should include words to the writer phrased in such a way as: "What do you think about . . .?" or "Do you think the character should say . . . in the scene?" In this way the director will be implanting his or her idea into the writer's creative mind that will usually shape the idea and consequently make the idea their own. Through this technique, the collaboration between director and writer becomes stronger and brings the writer into the directors' previsualization process without the writer realizing it.

Writers invariably rewrite their scripts from the beginning to the end, and experience has taught me that the end (the last twenty minutes or so)

---

[3] On one project that I produced, the writer was to have taken a novel that was optioned and write a screenplay that came very close to the novel. It was to include the same plot, action, characters and storyline. When the writer turned in the first draft of the screenplay and came in for his script note conference, I turned to him and said, "Did you get this out of your system?" He replied, "What do you mean?" I said, "The screenplay is nothing like the novel, and it is the novel the studio bought. You have invented characters, combined characters, and changed the plot. May I suggest that you go back to the original novel and write what is in it, please?" He looked at me and smiled and said, "This is the most constructive script note conference I have ever had. Thanks. I learned a lot. Will do! Give me a week please." I thanked him and a week later we had a draft of the script close to the novel.

often gets the least amount of attention. So directors should examine the *end* of the script very carefully. This is often the most important part of a film since it is the last thing the audience sees and the first they remember when they come out of the movie theater asking "what did you think?" What they are really talking about is how it all summed up at the end. By looking at the end of the script, so much of what happens before becomes clearer because you know where you are going; you are able to see any trouble in the structure and can collaborate with the writer to resolve those problems. Of course, when the writer and director are the same person that becomes more difficult.[4]

Dialogue

Structure of the script is one thing, but the true nature of a good story lies in the characters and what they say to one another through the use of dialogue. Dialogue is not the impulse itself but should come out of the impulses happening to the character causing them to say the words. Dialogue must pattern real life, in which people say things at a certain time in a certain way because of the urges which motivate them to say the words. Words don't happen just to happen. There is always something behind the words. Or should be! Some may call it the subtext. Writers should be writing with that thought in mind, and for that to happen they must completely understand the life of their characters.

The structure of the dialogue will provide clues for the director as to what the impulse may be. One of the first clues is what the *author indicates for the actor to do in the text and the structure of the text that comes after it.* For example, in scene 57 of *Crash*,[5] written by Paul Haggis and Bobby Moresco and directed by Haggis, the character Christine (Thandie Newton), visits her husband, Cameron (Terrence Howard) on the studio lot to apologize for her behavior from the night before, when they were pulled over by a police officer.

---

[4] I remember leaving the movie theater after seeing *Syriana* written and directed by the same person and I heard a woman in her sixties comment, "This is way over my head!"

[5] The Lionsgate picture *Crash*, produced by Cathy Schulman and Paul Haggis, received three Oscars in 2006 from the Academy of Motion Pictures Arts and Sciences, including Best Picture and Best Original Screenplay. Writers Paul Haggis and Bobby Moresco also received numerous other awards, including the Writers Guild of America Award for Best Screenplay.

57   EXT. STUDIO LOT - DAY
      She meets him and they walk together.

                    CHRISTINE
            I tried to call, it sounded like you
            were having a hard day.

                    CAMERON
            Yeah.

                    CHRISTINE
            I got scared, Cam. I mean, it's not
            like I haven't been pulled over
            before. But not like that. And I was
            a little drunk and I shouldn't have
            been mouthing off, it was stupid.
            But when that man put his hands on
            me…I just couldn't believe you'd let
            him do that. I know what you did was
            the right thing, I know that, but…I
            was humiliated…for you. I couldn't
            watch. I couldn't stand to see that
            man take away your dignity.

                    CAMERON
                (coldly)
            Yeah. That's what happened.

                    CHRISTINE
            Don't do this.

                    CAMERON
            You're right. Leave it at that. I've
            got to go.

      And he walks away.

                    CHRISTINE
            Do not walk away from me. You
            bastard. I apologized! Don't walk
            away from me!... Cam!!

      He keeps going, she fights back tears and rage.
      Turns on her heel and…

      END OF SCENE

In Cameron's second line of dialogue, the writers indicate *(coldly)* before he says, "Yeah that's what happened." The impulse for the line comes from a cold, withdrawn place within Cameron, based on the events from the night before and Christine's reaction to those events. The impulse results in the line, "Yeah. That's what happened," which, depending on the direction and choices by the actor, will provide the shading or depth of emotion for the character. In addition, the subsequent interchange of dialogue, based on Cameron's reaction to his wife in the scene, results in him walking away, leaving her in tears with her emotions unresolved. If Haggis and Moresco had indicated that Cameron should be *shouting* or *crying*, the impulse would have been different and the line of dialogue would have had a different intent. Dialogue is the result of impulses, and impulses between characters result in character relationships, and character relationships are the basis of good storytelling.

A second clue rests with *what the character says about himself or herself at any moment in the dialogue.* It is obvious when a character has lines such as "I'm angry," "I'm embarrassed," or "I'm hurt" for a director to discover the impulse that motivates the line. But in a skillfully constructed screenplay, in which the characters are brilliantly and fully developed, it can be more difficult, as in scene 39 of *Crash*, when officer John Ryan (Matt Dillon), hearing someone groaning in the middle of the night, gets out of his bedroom to find his father (Bruce Kirby) in the bathroom.

```
39   INT. RYAN'S BURBANK DUPLEX - HALLWAY - NIGHT

     Ryan wakes with a start, thinking he heard
     something. Bleary-eyed, in T-shirt and boxers,
     he steps out of his bedroom and walks toward
     the sound of someone groaning. He stops at the
     bathroom door, which is slightly ajar.

               RYAN
     How you doing, Pop?

               POP RYAN (O.S.)
     If I could piss I'd be doing a lot
     better.
          (keeps himself from crying out)
     Jesus. All right. I'm done, give me
     a hand.
```

Ryan pushes open the door. POP's in his 70s,
but frail and in pain, which makes him seem more
frail. Ryan holds out a hand. Helps Pop up.

                POP RYAN (CONT'D)
          Wait a goddamn minute.
              (reaching for his pajamas)
          Okay.

Ryan pulls his father up. Pop pulls his pajamas
up at the same time.

                RYAN
          You're okay. You're okay.

As they head out:

                POP RYAN
          Stop, stop. I gotta go back.

They turn around. Pop grabs hold of the sink,
pulls down his pajamas and looks at his son.

                POP RYAN (CONT'D)
          You gonna stand there and stare at
          me?

Ryan moves off as Pop eases himself onto the
seat, the pain obvious on his face.

ANGLE ON RYAN

Leaning against the hallway wall, staring off at
the window, the first rays of dawn breaking on
his face.

END OF SCENE.

Ryan's first line of dialogue, "How you doing, Pop?" prompts his father to say, "If I could piss, I'd be doing a lot better." This line of dialogue tells Kirby how the character should be feeling at that moment. He does not come right out and say how he is feeling but instead, through the line, tells his son the pain he is feeling physically. Further, the indicated physical reaction to his pain (keeps himself from crying out) provides a further clue for how he is feeling. This is then followed up with an exclamatory "Jesus" to emphasize his feeling. And then resolved with "All right I'm done, give me a hand." In those few lines of dialogue the character tells his son exactly how he is feeling.

A third clue as to intent within the dialogue *comes from what one character says to the other character in a scene.* Dialogue such as "Don't cry," "Stop yelling at me," and "Can you speak up please?" tells an actor how they are to play a moment. From that bit of dialogue, they can determine what impulse they are to play that will result in a specific response from another character. In scene 26 of *Crash*, again between Cameron and Christine:

```
26    INT. CAMERON AND CHRISTINE'S BEDROOM - NIGHT

      Christine drops her purse and snatches up the
      phone.

                    CAMERON
            Who are you calling?

                    CHRISTINE
            I'm gonna report their asses. Sons
            of bitches...

                    CAMERON
            And you actually think they're going
            to take you seriously?

                    CHRISTINE
                (slams the phone down)
            Do you have any idea what that was
            like to have that pig's hands all
            over me? And you watch him do it and
            then you apologize to him?? What the
            fuck was that about?

                    CAMERON
            What did you want me to do, get us
            both shot?

                    CHRISTINE
            --They were gonna shoot us on
            Ventura Blvd??

                    CAMERON
            So, you would have been satisfied
            with just being arrested.
```

                    CHRISTINE
You're right, Cam, much better to
let him shove his hand up my crotch
than get your name in the paper.

                    CAMERON
Yeah, that's what I was worried
about.

                    CHRISTINE
It wasn't? You weren't afraid all
your good friends at the studio were
gonna read about you in the morning
and realize you were actually black?

                    CAMERON
You need to calm down here.

                    CHRISTINE
No, what I need is a husband who
won't just stand there while I'm
being molested!

                    CAMERON
They were cops! They had guns! Where
do you think you're living, with
mommy and daddy in Greenwich?

                    CHRISTINE
Go to hell.

                    CAMERON
Maybe I shoulda let them lock your
ass up. I guess sooner or later you
should learn what it's like to be
black.

                    CHRISTINE
Fuck you, like you know. Closest
you ever came to being black was
watching the Cosby Show.

                    CAMERON
At least I wasn't watching it with
the rest of the equestrian team.

```
                  CHRISTINE
        You know, you're right, Cam, I got a
        lot to learn. 'Cause I haven't quite
        learned how to shuck and jive. Let
        me hear it again: "Thank you, Mr.
        Poh-liceman. You sure is kind to us
        po' black folk. You be sure to let
        me know next time you wanna finger
        fuck my wife."


                  CAMERON
        You know what? Fuck you.


                  CHRISTINE
        Oh that's good. A little anger. A
        bit late, but nice to see.

   He slams out of the room.

   END OF SCENE
```

The third clue of *what one character says about another character in a scene* is clearly in the dialogue when Cameron says to Christine, "You need to calm down here." That line would indicate that Christine is upset and angry [6] and not calm by any stretch of the imagination. Thandie Newton, working with her director Paul Haggis and her partner Terrence Howard, needed to find the sequence of impulses within her that prompted Howard's character to say, "You need to calm down here." And what does the last line that Christine has in the scene tell you about how Howard is to play the line before it?

Any scene is a scene of relationships between the characters. And when the characters discuss another character they each have a relationship to but who may not be in the scene, it is important for the actors to play the relationship not only to one another but also to the character about whom they are discussing.

A fourth clue rests with any *physical activity that exists along with a line.* In the scene above, Christine "drops her purse and snatches up the phone" which is indicative of her feelings at that moment. The writers didn't write, "drops her purse and *picks up* the phone" but "*snatches* the phone" which has a different connotation. They also wrote "slams the

---

[6] Note: Anger is protest and comes from another emotion causing someone to be angry. Actors should be encouraged to play the source of the anger rather than the anger itself.

phone down" toward the beginning of the dialogue between Christine and Cameron, which helps her motivation on the line, "Do you have any idea what that was like to have that pig's hands all over me?" The physical activity of slamming the phone helps the actor find the impulse for that line, since physical activity will always cause an impulse to occur in an actor. And what about the physical action that Cameron does at the end of the scene where he "slams out of the room"? What does this tell you about the impulse of the character at that moment?

Again, the way the dialogue is played is decided by the actors and the director in conjunction with the physical action that is written in the script. For example, if the phone is slammed down *after* saying, "Do you have any idea what that was like to have that pig's hands all over me?" the line may be said differently and the subsequent lines affected. Or what would it be like if Cameron "slams out of the room" *after* he says his line, "You know what? Fuck you." What would that do to the impulse that motivates Christine's last line, "Oh that's good. A little anger. A bit late, but nice to see"? These subtleties relate to subtext that has been discussed previously.

Finally, the *word structure and author's punctuation* gives the director a hint as to the characters' intent in a scene. In scene 26, above, Cameron has a line that says, "What did you want me to do, get us both shot?" The phrasing on this line puts Cameron and Christine on opposite sides of the incident because Cameron is attacking Christine's judgment of how he should have behaved. But the line would not have the same personalization if it were, "Did you want me to get us both shot?" "What did you want me to do" makes it a direct criticism of Christine.

In this scene, the writers also italicize the words *apologize* and *you* on the lines, ". . . and watch him do it and then you *apologize* to him??" and "Fuck you, like *you* know," both spoken by Christine. This indicates that the writers wanted those words emphasized in the speech, which immediately puts a certain spin on the line. Of course, when the scene is rehearsed, the director and actors may find other subtle ways to shade the moment, but the italicized words are clues for the director in terms of the impulse for the character. The same holds true for punctuation, as in this case when double question marks are used at the end of a question. Remember, dialogue is created in the minds of writers, who have strong ideas about the impulses the characters should feel. The writers put these clues on the page for the director to look for.

Examining the choice of words, their intent, and their structure in the line offers directors (and actors) the prospect of seeing the rhythm (if any) in the dialogue and opens up the possibility of multiple shadings for the characters. The director may even make suggestions to the writer to enhance the dialogue once they get into the soul of the character. Many directors, when studying a script, note the possible shadings of the characters in the margins of their scripts so they can work with the actors on their performances.

Directors look for these five basic clues (as well as others) to help them understand the text and the characters. The clues are in the structure of the dialogue; a skilled director links all of those clues together to help tell the story.

The Character Arc

The process of directing single-camera narrative, because of production logistics, is a process in which scenes of a movie are shot out of sequence of the story. Because of this, actors look to the director as their barometer to keep them on track in terms of their emotional peaks and valleys, their inner struggles, their momentary values and principles, and clarity towards their relationships throughout the story. This faith and trust means that the director must not only clearly understand these character traits but understand the character's *arc* developed through the story and where each scene falls on that arc.

The arc of a character is what attracts talented actors to a role when they read a script. The discussion with the director, before they commit, is primarily to see whether they can trust the nuances of their performance to that director. So, the director must know the arc of each character backward and forward, up and down. They must know who that character is at the start of the story (or their introduction into the story) and what happens to the character to make the character change. They must know how the character changes and of course know who the character is after the change is made. They must know precisely when the character is affected and by what in the story they are affected.

Rarely is character development considered when laying out a schedule for production. The middle scene of a character's arc may be shot on the first day along with the ending scene of the arc. And the scene that introduces the character may be shot on the last day. In order for the actor's performance to be true to the story, the director must be clear and concise in knowing the character's development throughout the script. This is one of the most important aspects of directing and the only aspect that is entirely in the hands of the director. It is somewhat easier when the story takes place over a few hours, a few days, or a few weeks, as in George Clooney's *Good Night, and Good Luck,* but it becomes much more difficult when the story takes place over decades of the lives of the characters, as in Ang Lee's *Brokeback Mountain.*

The Visual Arc

The creation of a visual arc to a movie begins with the director's ability to read and visualize the script. They must not only see the characters but also begin to find a visual presentation and interpretation to the script that is in sync with or can be convincing for producers to agree with. Although the director has developed and explored a theme and understands the characters and what they saw and how they feel, he or she still must find the visual arc to the storytelling.

The director must know what it will look like when it starts off and where it will go as the story unfolds. The director must know the individual visual pieces as they fit together to the whole and be able to allow that visualization to subtly tell the story.

Brad Silberling, in telling the story of *Lemony Snicket's A Series of Unfortunate Events,* knew he wanted to appeal to an adult audience and felt that the movie needed a dark tone of visual shading to make that appeal. When he was reading the script while developing the visual arc and attempting to delve into and understand the characters, he wrote a narrative in first person for the character Olivia that spoke about herself and her brother and their life. Once the picture was cast, he used the narrative as a voice against the visual look of the characters while doing wardrobe and cinematography tests for the picture, as well as searching for the right visual look of the characters: one that showed the dark but mature visual approach he wanted to take with the film. He then made a little trailer of this test and showed it to the producers so they could see the visual arc that he wanted to take with the project. They fell in love with it. In fact, he points up for his audience this visual approach by opening Lemony Snicket with a Technicolor cartoon of a little elf and the happy life he is leading and then stops and immediately switches to the dark look that the picture finally takes in the telling of the story.

It is the visual arc to a picture that puts its distinctive mark on the project and usually has the first impact upon an audience. *Good Night, and Good Luck*, shot completely in black and white, visually looked like a 1950s television show, and George Clooney approached it with that in mind. The visual arc in Martin Scorsese's *The Aviator* paralleled the historical development and changes in color cinematography as the story unfolded through the 1930s, 40s, 50s, and 60s. Although subtle within the story, the visual arc that a director should work toward while reading the text and visualizing the project is at the heart of what the director does.

GUIDING THE SCREENPLAY

When working with some screenplays, and especially when working with a writer who is working on the screenplay, the director may need to do some research to be able to bring more to the story than just intuition and ideas. Research might give the director an image that might drive a creative idea that can be incorporated into the story or the characters and thereby enhance the text. The director's ability to work with a writer along many lines is important, since most of the time a director will not be directing his or her own script. It is important that you make a writer feel safe. If you are a writer/director, that will be easy, but if you are a director and *not* a writer, your approach is very important. *Never tell a writer directly what is wrong with the script.* That will do damage, and it is probably best to just talk about the story at first. If you bring the conversation back to a discussion of story, you will be able to describe and implant in the writer's mind the story you want to do. And through some element of trust you can begin to gently steer the story around. Understand that many writers like to use a lot of words in the form of dialogue to tell the story. But some of the best stories are told without a lot of words. In working with the writer try to explore the screenplay from the standpoint of what is not being trusted in the story. The imagery! Where is it not allowing for this wonderful aspect of movie magic? Brad Silberling worked with Dana Stevens for six months on a draft of *City of Angels* while waiting for Meg Ryan and Nicolas Cage to finish projects they were doing. In that period of time he built trust with

Stevens, and in his communication with her, he would sketch out a scene and ask her to improve on it a thousand times, letting her know that the scene came from his storytelling instinct.[7] Could we ever forget the shot of the moment the angels stand on the beach looking at the glorious sunset in *City of Angels*? The magic of movies!

Collaboration across the board is key to a successful project, and it includes the collaboration between director and writer. As long as the project is still in the screenplay stage and working toward becoming a locked shooting script, the project should remain in the writer's lap. It does not truly become the director's until the director begins preproduction on the project.

CHAPTER ONE SUMMARY

➤ Directors are responsible to their creative self, their producer and their audience.

➤ Directors should read a script many times and the first three times are strategic.

➤ Themes underlie the characters and the plot in any story.

➤ Directors must analyze a script from many perspectives.

➤ Directors should provide writers with constructive and not destructive script notes.

➤ Directors must allow writers to feel safe about their material and gain their trust.

➤ The true nature of a good story rests with good dialogue.

➤ The structure of the dialogue provides clues about the desires of the characters.

➤ Directors must clearly understand the emotional arc of each of the characters.

➤ The visual arc begins with the director's ability to read and visualize the script.

➤ Directors must work with the writer so that imagery is important to storytelling.

---

[7] Brad Silberling Master Class, UCLA, March 4, 2005.

CHAPTER **2**

PREVISUALIZATION, PLANNING, AND ACTORS

Directors have a vision of a project in their heads. But they must break that vision down into pieces and carry it through. When a director is stuck seeing only the forest and not the trees, the trees never stand out to define the intricacies, depths, and mystery of the forest—all the things that make it a desirable and wonderfully intriguing place to visit.

STORYBOARDS AND SHOT LISTS—THE FALLACY

Storyboards

A storyboard consists of hand-drawn or computer-generated still images of individual shots within specific scenes. One needs only to look to the funny papers or comic books to see storyboards that inspire the imagination of readers. Teachers of film production emphasize to their students the need to construct storyboards in interpreting the visuals of the narrative. Although they don't require their students to do anatomical drawings and detailed images of each frame of the movie, they encourage them to be as meticulous as possible. This technique often starts at the very beginning of their learning process and establishes that the basics of directing rests in storyboarding the project from start to finish. This approach produces directors who are impulsive about using various cinematic techniques but who understand neither the importance of the actors' performance to the story nor the directorial process to get to any storyboarded image. It also develops directors who think image first and actors' performances second. These directors spend more valuable production time creating the image than focusing on the performance, and when that happens they lose the trust of their creative team and their actors.

My cinematographer and colleague of twenty years, Tom Denove, tells the story of a director he worked with who storyboarded every scene of the movie they did together before he got to the set. During preproduction, he was able to show anyone who asked exactly how he was going to shoot the movie—regardless of the inspired, spontaneous performances that actors give during the production. In one shot, he had storyboarded an actor to enter the scene through a door from camera right, and on the day the scene was to be shot, the director walked onto the set, stopped in his tracks, and froze. The door in the set was on camera left. He was stunned, flabbergasted, and couldn't figure out how to stage the scene according to his storyboards because the door was on the left side of the frame and not the right as he had drawn it. He sat down and for three hours was at a total loss as to what to do. It wasn't until Tom took the director's storyboarded image and held it up to the light and reversed the paper that the director realized how to stage the scene. By turning the paper over he was able to see the door on his storyboard in the exact spot that it was on the set and was thus able to block the scene. His creative planning was locked to something he had imagined: his preconceived storyboards. And he was unable to see the trees for the forest.

A storyboard is a single image. In narrative directing, that image should be fluid to the structure of the scene and not an image that a director preconceives, stages, shoots, and then figures out how to stage the actors in the scene to fit the storyboarded image. Storyboards are single images that do not move, and motivated movement is the fuel a director uses in framing the narrative.

Actors must be motivated by the staging and not by an image on a storyboard. On one movie that I produced, the director created copious storyboards predetermining certain images that he wanted to see in the movie—even though he had no concept of what the locations were to be. In one scene he had envisioned and storyboarded a five-shot[1] that contained a rack focus.[2] The scene was one in which ten characters interacted with one another, and it was pivotal to the movie as it was the scene in which the good guys met the bad guys for the first time. The first shot he did in the scene was the five-shot; he put the actors exactly in the position that was in his storyboard and did the rack focus on the precise line that he had planned. After he completed several takes of the shot, he set out to stage the scene with all ten actors. But since the five-shot was in the middle of the scene, he did not know how to dramatically motivate the actors and the camera into the position that would logically allow the five-shot to be cut into the scene. In fact, after he had completed the scene and was working with the editor, he realized that he did not have the camera coverage for the nuances in this pivotal moment in the story. He had no reverse angles, and the audience never knew who was where at any moment in the scene. And this because of the need for the storyboarded preconceived five-shot.

If the director's entire foundation is the storyboard and they are unwilling to see their work unfold on the set, they generally see things only one way: how they created it in their imagination. On set their eyes are closed to the story unfolding in front of them: the story that must be told by the actors in what they say and do and how they feel. The actors must always motivate the camera, never the other way around.

Storyboards *are* necessary, however, because they provide the opportunity to help directors think visually through concepts and ideas that may be germinating in their heads. But they must not be used as the map for the *entire* project, unless the concept of the project is totally dependent on the visual image, as in comic strips, animations, TV commercials, music videos, or multimedia designs. They will become an impediment to the narrative when a director shoots only the storyboarded images. And why? Because by shooting (directing for) individual preconceived shots without seeing the movement or the motivation that brings about those shots, the editorial fluidity suffers. The thought process for the director is to look at

---

[8] A five-shot is an image that has five characters in it.

[9] Rack focus is a cinematic device in which sharp focus within the image moves from one subject to another.

only one image at a time—not the linkage that connects the images (shots) through direction of the actors and motivated staging![3]

Since the earliest days of moviemaking, filmmakers have relied on storyboards to aid the understanding of certain scenes and to give the cast and crew a visual interpretation of what the finished result should look like. Movies with key action sequences use storyboards to allow stunt coordinators, special effects supervisors, and other creative units, such as set design, to visualize their creative contributions to the sequence. The images created are discussed ahead of time with the production designer, the director, and a storyboard artist who translates the image into a series of drawings for the sequence. This can easily be seen below in a series of storyboards created by production designer Nathan Amondson for Wim Wenders's film *Land of Plenty*.

In the motion picture *The Cooler*, director Wayne Kramer and a storyboard artist carefully worked through the opening montage sequence, giving us the setup of a very sad lead character, played by William H. Macy. The character is so negative about himself that he generates energy that makes him the saddest and unluckiest guy in the world. Nothing goes right for him, not even having enough cream for his coffee in the morning. He works for a casino as its "cooler" to cool off anyone

---

[3] Students studying directing in film schools are occasionally trained this way. Their films often lack fluidity because they cannot see the tissue connecting the shots, resulting in reshoots, pickup shots, and extended budgets.

who is *hot* and winning at the games. His presence near them automatically causes them to lose. Kramer and his storyboard artist repeat the montage later in the movie, after Macy meets a cocktail waitress. They fall in love, and his attitude about himself changes. And so does his luck: it is reversed, causing people to win. The storyboards for the movie [4] provided Kramer and his set designers, costume designers, and cinematographer the ability to discuss and determine how they were going to do the details of those two sequences. When you see the montages in the movie it is clear that the storyboards were used as a *guideline* in telling those aspects of the story and not as a bible.[5]

Since narrative projects are actually made during the preproduction process and executed during the production process, storyboarding during previsualization for this purpose is used extensively—and digital technology has introduced us to digitally-created, animated storyboard computer programs. Through CGI they create a series of images that are then animated and given movement to see how they will work together in the sequence. Once the sequence is developed and approved, it is then shown to the creative production team, who determines how best to create and marry the production's elements to replicate the animated storyboarded sequences. Again, these animatic storyboards are a guideline toward the end result of the sequence, which may be continuous or cut in with other dramatic action in the storytelling. This technique was used in such movies as *Secret Window,* the *Spider-Man* and *X-Men* movies, and Peter Jackson's *King Kong* and is being used more frequently, especially when other creative departments must contribute to the sequence. The results may be simple or complex. A sequence may need elements that are designed, built, and shot during production and then include elements created in postproduction by the visual effects supervisor. Storyboards, whether animated or not, get everyone on the same page working towards the same visual image.

There are, however, directors who like to storyboard a movie as a way of helping their own creativity understand even the simplest of sequences. And there are computer-generated programs that help the director not only visualize the shots but also see the camera positions in relation to the staging. One such program is Frame Forge 3D, which includes not only

---

[4] The storyboard sequences can be seen on the DVD for *The Cooler* under special features.

[5] Referring to being unfailingly precise and beyond question to each and every storyboard.

the shot as seen through the camera but also the overhead set layout with camera setups and all the relevant camera information such as height of the camera and lens millimeter. Such storyboard software tools deliver a high degree of previsualization elements and creative exploration that directors can work with personally as they visualize their projects.

But these directors keep their storyboards for themselves and a few other people. They do not show them to anyone as the *only* images that will be shot. These directors recognize that the staging must motivate the camera and that the storyboard images only help them (and others) to see where the story *might* be headed! More important, these directors don't force these storyboards into the staging but rather look for (and refine) them as they stage the actors during rehearsal. They forewarn everyone that the storyboards may change so that it does not become a hindrance to what they may discover when they work with the actors on the set. However, working this way brings up another issue that can strap the fluidity of storytelling by the director: the use of *shot lists*.

Shot Lists

According to legend, Alfred Hitchcock storyboarded every shot in all of his films. This was understandable because it was at a time when technology was limited; the camera of choice was large and heavy, and it was impossible to move the camera quickly during production. In addition, Hitchcock was known for giving his actors very little freedom to experiment with the characters they were portraying. As we have already discussed, today it is very time-consuming and possibly detrimental to storyboard every shot of a movie, so generally, with the exception of helping directors with their own visual ideas, storyboards are used primarily for more challenging scenes such as action sequences, extreme camera moves, and any scenes that may require a complicated setup and/or mechanical or visual effects. So instead of storyboarding, directors may create a list of shots detailing every camera angle, move, and sometimes even the lens of choice. Such a list is intended to help the director in advance of the shooting days. A shot list is a list of all the camera angles for a scene and should (but rarely does) include all the coverage[6] and cutaways.[7]

---

[6] Coverage is a sequence of shots that are needed to allow the editor to make choices in a specific scene.

[7] A cutaway is a shot that does not relate directly to the characters within a scene but may be a shot that is devised to allow for editorial changes, e.g., if there is a scene with two characters talking and one of them is cooking at the stove, the cutaway would be a shot of what is being cooked on the stove.

Shot List Example

SCENE#1		EXT- CEMETERY
Shot Number	Type	Description
1	Wide	Master of mourners at burial
2	Medium	Rabbi reading the Kaddish
3	Medium Close-up	Esther as she puts a rose on the casket
SCENE #2		INT- COURTROOM
1	Dolly	Counter dolly along the row of judges
2	Medium Close-up	Lead Judge-low angle "This court will ...."
3	Medium	Ann (Def. Attorney) "Your honor I wish..."
4	Medium	Bill (Pros. Attorney) "But your honor...."
5	Three-shot	All judges
6	Medium	Ann
7	Four-shot	Ann approaching the bench
8	Close-up	Bill
SCENE #3		INT- ANN'S HOUSE
1	Steadicam	Ann wanders through the house to kitchen
2	Close-up	Ann at stove
3	Wide	Children enter kitchen
4	Close-up	Ann "Do you have your things for...."
5	Two-shot	Nancy and Lily (kids) "Yes but..."
6	Wide three-shot	Kids fight
7	Close-up	Profile of Ann "Stop that I can't"

Direction includes deciding which shots will best tell the story and involve or elicit an emotional reaction from the viewer. Today, shot lists are often the norm and not the exception, as many producers require shot lists from their directors before they start a day's work. A producer colleague of mine requires her directors to give her shot lists. She went to this practice several years ago when she discovered that most new young directors cannot think on their feet during production and do not know how to focus on the performances. She believes that many of them have little or no knowledge as to what is needed in telling the story without a discussion ahead of time. She believes that many directors do not know how to prepare and is unsure whether they even have a sense of what the story is about and thus are able to cover the scene appropriately. The shot list provides her with information to build her trust in the director, and she hopes that they will, at the very least, deliver what was discussed.

When directors study the script, they are expected to see certain moments in shots: for example, the close-up on a character at the height of their confession. So planning shots to some degree is unavoidable. However, whereas a director's planned shot list should be only a blueprint, many beginning directors consider it a bible and attempt to do the list of shots they preconceived before seeing the actors, the locations, or the logistics that affect time management during production.

Some film educators do a disservice to their students by teaching them to create shot lists and predetermine the amount of time they will take to do each shot.[8] When working this way they discover that they have planned too many shots, and the direction of the actors suffers because they are unable to get the utmost performances and multiple-camera takes of a shot. They also again find out that when shooting *only* their preconceived shot list they lose the connecting visual tissue needed for an audience to understand the spatial relationships of the sequence. For example, the shot list may call for a close-up shot of a character in a store as he is speaking to someone else and who crosses away from camera, and then another close-up shot of the same character in the second area of the store. If only these two shots are part of the sequence and the shot list does not have a shot that shows the relationship of the character to the second place in the store, the audience will be confused as to where the characters are in physical relation to each other *in* the store.

(2-1a) (2-1b)

Shooting *only* the shots listed (and preconceived) and *only when* they are preconceptually used in the scene is called "editing in the camera" and causes another major problem. For example: the shot is preconceived for

---

[8] e.g., 10:00 A.M. – 10:20 A.M. the close-up, 10:20 A.M. – 10:40 A.M. the two-shot, etc.

a specific line of dialogue. A director (and especially students of directing) will shoot *only the specific line of dialogue* for that preconceived shot. This is wrong. This not only limits the editorial choices and prevents the director from spontaneously creating based on the actor's performance, but it also works against the actor's instrument in creating the character from a logical emotional or transitional moment in the scene. I see it time and again with beginning directing students. When they work this way, I know they are pre-editing the project (cutting in their head) before they have finished shooting.[9]

Another problem that arises with a preconceived shot list is that the director may have a tendency to shoot the shots in the sequence of the list. This will cause the production to work inefficiently as directors conceive each shot as the scene develops rather than consider the choreography and efficiency of production needed to achieve each shot.

Many of these and other issues arise when shot lists are used inappropriately. A written shot list is important as an organizational and conceptual tool but should be kept in the director's back pocket when working on the set. The list can be given to the assistant director and the script supervisor so they have an idea of what is in your mind, but you, the director, should keep it in your back pocket. It is there to remind you of what your plan is if you need to get focused when all the people on a production set are swirling around you doing their jobs. And if the preconceived and pre-visualized shots are embedded in your head while working with the actors, they will unconsciously happen as the scene is being staged for camera. As we will find out in the chapters on coverage, the shot list should be kept as a backup, as it is a guide for you in visually understanding the scene. You must keep yourself open and spontaneous on set for visualizing your project. You must never lock yourself down to the list just in case you come up with something more creative or practical. In this way your actual list of shots will constantly go through revisions on the set. Beginning directors use shot lists as a crutch because the camera doesn't talk back if it doesn't understand its motivation. Actors, on the other hand, do. And to a new director that can be intimidating.

---

[9] This results in editing not making sense in relation to the story and the need to shoot pickup shots because the director was cutting in his or her head at the time of production.

PLANNING—THE DIRECTOR IN COLLABORATION

Models

Many times directors need to use constructed multidimensional models of locations and sets to help their previsualizations, as Susan Stroman did for the movie version of the musical *The Producers*. With these models, directors use small figures of people as actors much like they are used in a child's dollhouse. Like storyboards, they provide you with the ability to collaborate with a group of people to get your vision across. You are also able to try out ideas for camera positions and discuss them ahead of the production period with your cinematographer, producer, or production designer. These models are not to be photographed as a miniature set used in the project but as a tool for the director to collaborate with others and get everyone on the same page. Therefore these models do not have to be very detailed to get the point across.

The Production Board

In preproduction the director must learn how to read and use a production board which is the production's roadmap for the creative logistics of production, its relationship to the budget, and the ability to achieving success during the most volatile stage of the filmmaking process—*production*. If Murphy's Law is going to happen on a project, it will happen during production. The director's input in the layout of the production board is key to the success of completing the project on time and on budget. The board consists of individual strips representing each of the scenes in the movie. The strips contain important information that tells everyone who is in the scene, where and when the scene takes place, how long the scene is in the script, any mechanisms that must be considered in order to shoot the

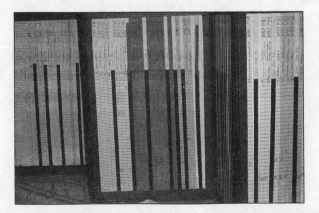

Production board

scene, and the specific dramatic or emotional action of each scene and how it relates to the story. You have an obligation to your producer to complete the day's work within twelve hours (including setup and wrap), and the production board helps you focus in on what your production crew needs to do to allow you to plan out your creative directing decisions. Early in the planning stages, your first assistant director will prepare the board with that in mind, either manually or by using one of several types of organizational software for that purpose. As you get closer to the first day of production—and during production—your input to the board will be most important. This will be discussed further in Chapter 8.

The Budget
In preproduction the director must be able to read a budget and understand what he or she is reading. Many producers do not give the director access to the project's budget. This is not a good idea, since it is the director who is the quarterback of the production, has a responsibility of completing each day's work during production, and, along with the producer, keeps the project within the guidelines of the budget while preserving creativity in telling the story.

The director should have input in the budget or at the very least be able to make suggestions to the producer about where money needs to be allocated during production. But a bit of forewarning: you need to be knowledgeable in the many areas of production in order to provide reasons for your suggestions, since a creative producer who is on the same wavelength as you will always *want that information before making decisions.* It is not enough to say "I think we need more money in wardrobe" without saying why. Or if you need a camera crane or another technological device for the project, you must make sure that you won't end up using it for just one shot. Having knowledge of budgets and how they work in correlation to creativity makes you a more informed and valuable director. It gives you the ability to collaborate with not only your producer but also the other members of the creative team. Chapter 9 will discuss the director and budgets further.

Locations
Locations are a key part of any project and involve many people once the director has determined the locations that are right for the project.

Locations are a large part of the previsualization process since the location (or set) is most important for directors so they can do their homework before working with actors.

Location managers are given the task of working creatively with the director (and producer) in getting an idea as to the look of a specific location. Since the right-looking location is a major part of the texture of the story, the director's ideas are discussed in detail with not only the location manager but also the producer, the production designer, and the art director. The location manager will present several suggestions for locations, taking into account the logistics and fiscal limitations of the project. The locations are then scouted during preproduction with a group of people that will include not only the director, production designer, cinematographer, and location manager but also the assistant director, production manager, gaffer, key grip, and production sound mixer. Even before that a wise director will take into account how and when the location will be used and scout the location accordingly. For example, if the scene calls for a magic hour shot,[10] you should scout the location around magic hour. On one movie I produced I asked the director to scout a specific woodsy location both in the daytime and at night since the picture had many scenes that called for both. He and the scout crew scouted it only in the daytime. The first night shoot in the woods location was costly in both setup time and cast and crew creativity. The scenes to be shot had twelve actors in them with an artificial moonlight established with extra lighting, generators, and crew personnel. After everything was set, the first assistant director called for quiet, getting the camera ready to roll on the first shot. In the brief silence that occurred on set before the actors spoke, a sound came from the woods: "croak," then another "croak," then another and another "croak," and then many others—"croak, croak, croak, croak, croak"—and in a short period of time there was a cacophony of frog sounds coming from a stream near the location, making sound recording impossible for the scene. This of course impacted the actors' performances, as they could not concentrate. We had to rerecord the dialogue in postproduction, and the performances suffered since automatic dialogue replacement (ADR) never sounds as good as actually doing it during production. Had the director scouted the location at night, he would have heard the frogs and would have thought about finding another location. So the collaboration on finding the right

---

[10] Magic hour is the time of day just before the sun rises or sets.

location is very important. It must not only work logistically, efficiently and fiscally but also create the environmental truth for the actors so they can deliver the performances for the story. Planning for the right location will only enhance your previsualization for the movie.

Although you are the quarterback for the movie, your ability to collaborate and work with your team will determine the effectiveness of your plays. The collaboration begins in the planning phase of the project and continues through production and into postproduction. The sooner your collaborators understand and get excited by your vision, the easier time you will have as a director. You must always show respect and integrity and you will get that in return. A lot of that comes from your passion, understanding of the material, its themes and its characters, and how and what others have to do for you in their roles. It all must be there when it comes time for you to bring the actors into the game so your focus can be primarily with them. You must become the in-the-trench collaborative driving force and romance many egos to deliver the goods. Once you do, you are on the road to thinking like a director!

UNDERSTANDING ACTORS—YOU GOTTA LOVE 'EM!

Actors Talk Back!

Your actor will talk back to you if you don't know what you're doing. Your actor will talk back to you if you don't understand the story or its characters. Your actor will talk back to you if you don't understand what they are all about in bringing to life the character they are playing. So make sure that you understand the text, the characters, the theme, the content, and most of all: *the actor*. Acting for the screen requires the actor to work much more quickly in finding the essence of the character and using themselves to portray the role than they do for the stage. As many film project budgets do not allow for rehearsal time you must be able to get performances from your actors quickly during the shooting process. In order not to be intimidated by your actors—because many of them do talk back—you must first generally understand what an actor is all about.

Actors are basically like children. They like to dress up and be other people. They want and crave attention, and they respond to words of praise or disapproval. They look at you after they have done a scene to see whether you want them to do more, and then nag that they are doing too much. They are complex, creative people. They have a life away from the script, the stage, or the studio, and that life sometimes gets in the way of their life as an actor. Knowing how they think, how they approach their craft, and what they are about and understanding the separate levels of what makes up the person we call an actor can be useful to your success in working with them. Although many books are written about acting—and one or two about directing of actors—this section should give you a brief glance at the makeup of actors.

Actors work on three levels at the same time, especially as it relates to acting for the screen; it is just the nature of who they are as actors. Those three levels function with one another in various intensities from the time they audition through the time they complete their work in front of the camera. Actors spend years in classes developing those levels. Meryl Streep once said that acting is so simple that it is difficult. Simple because actors use who they are and difficult because they have to show who they are and their own vulnerabilities to bring life to the roles they play. Three levels make up the basis for an actor's ability to create a character and are constantly at work as actors act: the *conscious level*, the *subconscious level* and the *unconscious level*. They should be thought of as three levels of one's layered traits. Simply, they make up the actor's psyche and affect how they approach the shading of their roles.

The Conscious Actor

The first level is that of the *conscious* actor. It refers to the facet of a person's or actor's behavior that is closest to the surface on an immediate day-to-day and moment-to-moment basis. It pertains to the little voice inside of the person/actor that asks *How does my hair look?* or *What does she (the director, casting director, etc.) want me to look like when I audition?* or *Damn, I had a flat tire getting to the set, how am I going to get it fixed before going home?* It manifests itself as emotions or feelings that may affect the focus actors need to get into character unless they are trained or directed to work from other levels of their experiences; it certainly is true when actors audition and sometimes is true when they are working in front of the camera. On one project that I directed, a well-known actor had to do a "breakup" scene with his female costar. The scene took place at night on the rooftop of a high-rise apartment building, and it was three pages of dialogue. During the course of the film, this actor was always letter-perfect with his lines each and every take of a shot, so I devised this particular scene to be a continuously moving dolly shot during the interchange of dialogue between the two actors while bringing the night skyline of Los Angeles into the scene. When we went to shoot the scene, he could not remember one line of his dialogue and was continually flubbing through his speaking lines, making the long take impossible. I was baffled and, because of our schedule, needed to change the shooting concept on the spot and revert to shorter takes, breaking the scene up with a fixed camera position for each shot and working more slowly with this actor to get a performance. Not as visually effective as the planned long continuous take, but for some reason the actor could not remember his lines in the relationship of the scene. Even then, the actor never maintained dialogue continuity from take to take. The next day my second A.D. told me what had happened the previous morning. The actor had broken up with his live-in girlfriend of twelve years. I knew then that the breakup scene in the movie was too close to what he had experienced that morning before coming to the set. It was on the surface of his working consciousness and therefore affected his ability in performance.

The conscious facet of the actor often has the strongest impact and can cause the biggest problems with the inexperienced or untrained actor, not only because it can affect the performance but because the emotions that happen only on a conscious level are portrayed mechanically and without meaning. Actors doing this are playing it safe. This is what directors refer to when they tell an actor that they are being mechanical and "playing *at* the emotion." Actors bring meaning to emotions when they bring other parts of themselves from other levels. Working just from the conscious level is untruthful. And the camera records only the truth.

The Unconscious Actor

The life experiences that frame the foundation of the person/actor are found at the *unconscious* level. To some degree life experiences affect and determine who we are and how we might behave in certain situations since we learn something from each experience that life offers us. And it is from those life experiences that a trained actor can call upon to help create a character.

When I produced the play *On the Waterfront* and was auditioning actors, Burt Young[11] read the role of Johnny Friendly, the boss of the union who controlled the labor on the docks. In the film written by Budd Schulberg and directed by Elia Kazan, Lee J. Cobb played the role as a strong, threatening, loud, and brash union leader. Threat and the powerful unpredictability of the character were for Cobb couched in his brashness. When Burt Young read for the Broadway production, his reading was understated, deliberate, and quiet but with the same (if not more) threat and power that was called for in the role. Burt Young grew up and survived in the tough New York neighborhood called Hell's Kitchen. Growing up in this neighborhood—and because of his size—he developed tough-guy mannerisms, through understated, direct, and deliberate behavior. His life experiences developed within him unconscious characteristics that he was able to bring to the John Friendly character. The brashness that was very much Cobb was not in his performance, but the power of the character was evident in every line of dialogue that he read. Life experiences that mold us into who we are cannot be changed. When they are used, it is these life experiences that actors draw upon to shade their character. Thus, Brian Dennehy's performance as Willy Loman in *Death of a Salesman* is different than Dustin Hoffman's Willy. It is the skilled actor who is able to recognize those experiences and can isolate any aspect of them to breathe a soul into the foundation of the character they are portraying.

The Subconscious Actor

For the intimacy that acting for the screen requires, the basis for the actor's performance is at the actor's subconscious level. An actor must always remember that *the closer the camera gets, the more truth it tells.* I will mention this many times throughout the book because it is one of the tenets to remember when telling a story through the camera. And the closer the camera gets to the actor, as in the close-up or the extreme close-up, the more truthful the actor must be with his or her performance. The close-up will show an audience one level of truth, and the extreme close-up will take them further into understanding the truth of the character. That truth must come from the subconscious portion of the actor. This involves the actor's own instincts and emotions that are brought to the role as it relates to the momentary discoveries that are true to the character being

---

[11] Burt Young played the role of Paulie in the *Rocky* movies.

portrayed. As we have already stated, when these emotions are intellectually understood but only "played at," then they are on the surface (*conscious*) of the performance. The audience will not believe the actor in the close-up. But if the emotion is experienced, the audience will believe it in both the close-up and the extreme close-up. In order to do that, actors must be in touch with and bring their own emotions to the character. Directors must always remember that *the closer the camera gets to the actor, the more truth the actor needs to tell*. Directors must carefully make sure they are using these emotions at every moment of discovery on every shot, on every take of every scene when the camera is rolling. A daunting task for any director, but made easier when actors are vulnerable with their emotions. It is the most difficult part of acting for the camera since actors must allow themselves to be vulnerable in order for the camera to see their honesty. The subconscious portion of the actor allows the true portrayal of such fleeting moments as embarrassment, passion, flirtation, shyness, disappointment, disgust, fear, surprise, and so on.

Bringing It Together

Dialogue should be the result of these emotions that the characters feel in a narrative. And as people are complex, the emotional moments can be complex, since one links to another as the characters discover things about themselves, their surroundings, and their relationship to the story. Actors are at the center of this because it is with their acting in the moment and playing the emotional discoveries that the audience is pulled into the story. Can anyone forget the moment at the beginning of *The Constant Gardner* when Ralph Fiennes is told that it might be his wife and her driver who were killed in an accident driving home? In that one close-up, shot out of continuity to the scene, Fiennes very subtly shows surprise, fear, love, hurt, hope, and despair as he absorbs the possibility of it being true. This often becomes easier for actors when they are working in the theater or in television soap operas or situation comedies. These forms have something in common: they allow the actors to play out the scenes without having to go back to the micro-moments of their performances. Directing the visual portion of the presentation is an entirely different process than single-camera narrative directing of movies; these are discussed in Chapter 10 of this book.

As in the case of *The Constant Gardener,* actors directed for individual shots may do many takes before the performance is right. In some instances they spend many hours on a tiny moment of a scene. Directors focus on and use the camera for the moments of a character's emotional discovery that link to other moments that may be shot out of context of the scene. So keeping actors focused on the nuances and gradation of the emotions of their characters is what directing for the camera is about. To be able to do that, actors must be in touch with and use that subconscious level of who they are while recognizing that they have an unconscious level of life experiences from which to draw for the character. When truthful, it will manifest consciously in a truthful performance. Honest moments are developed when the actors are working with their moments of discovery. Keeping it there each and every time it is needed is the difficult part. Actors need to be comfortable and feel safe with their directors, safe in being able to show themselves to the world.

The Objective and the Super-Objective

Much is written about actors playing the objective and the super-objective in their performances. An actor's *objective* is what he or she may want in a scene, their action, their desire, their goal. The objective of each individual scene is connected to the super-objective, which is the driving obsession of the scene. It is the force that pushes the character through the journey of the film and causes the action to take place.

The *super-objective* is the road that the writer provides and thus the road that the screenplay takes. Actors who study "the Method" learn about objective and super-objective. They work diligently in classes analyzing scenes they are working on or the entire material to determine the elements that are necessary for their performance. And they are! But not totally as it relates to the process of acting for the movie director. Although actors and directors must understand the journeys the characters take in the story and see what the objectives and super-objectives are, they must be more cognizant of the arc of their character and what takes the character on the journey.

It is more important for actors in single-camera narrative to play the discovery of the moment and not concern themselves inherently with the objective of the scene. Why? Because the nature of single-camera directing, which you will see throughout this book, focuses time and again from shot to shot on the micro-moment. With this process, a scene may be three pages long and may take a twelve-hour day to shoot. The front end of the scene may be shot and covered in the morning and the last section of the scene may be shot and covered in the afternoon, or vice versa for one reason or another. The movie process involves multiple takes from different angles. The focus that an actor must maintain is therefore difficult. An actor who plays only objective and not discovery will always get confused, and there is little likelihood the performance will be honest. An actor who always plays discovery will be successful, and an actor who can play discovery while maintaining the objective is the most successful of all.

Each actor has his or her own method of working. As mentioned earlier, Meryl Streep once said that "acting for film is so simple that it is difficult." The actor must learn to use who they are when they play a role, not someone they *think* they are. I once asked Anthony Hopkins how he prepares for any of the characters he plays. His answer was uncomplicated. He said "I learn the text!" He said he had a photographic memory and he learns the dialogue. His instinct tells him what emotions to feel to motivate the words he memorized after listening to the words that his partner in his scene throws to him. He is vulnerable and in the moment, and when put into the scene doesn't think about it; he just does it. And in so doing uses himself to create the characters. *Acting (for movies) is so simple it is difficult!*[12]

Actors Are Vulnerable

Actors should be vulnerable in order to bring out a performance. They must be able to elicit emotional intimacies, often at the drop of a hat. They are people who must gain the trust of their director and learn to take risks. A wise director will encourage those risks, since from risk emerges inspiration. During a park scene in *Finding Neverland,* actor Johnny Depp was inspired to play a game with his dog that wasn't part of the scene and to use this activity for his character of J.M. Barrie. It worked so well that director Marc Forster left the business in the story. Actors use their imagination and intuition to bring life to the characters. However, intuition as the character is one thing, and intuition as an actor is another. Since actors have egos, they sometimes do what they *think* is intuitive to the character but in reality is an action that they do to stand out in the

---

[12] When Anthony Hopkins was asked at the 2006 Golden Globes award what advice he had for actors he said "learn the text and be professional."

scene, such as an unscripted kiss or a slap. They will tell you that it felt right to do it. Perhaps. But felt right to whom? The actor or the character the actor is portraying? The director must recognize the difference and know what is true for the character—and if it is not, correct it without damaging the actor's creative ego.

Directors look for talent in their actors, but that word *talent* is a difficult one to define. The best teacher, coach, and innovator in training directors in how to communicate to actors is Delia Salvi. In her brilliant book on directing the actor, *Friendly Enemies: Maximizing the Director-Actor Relationship,* she says that "the components of raw talent are unreliable and will be wasted unless the actor develops a conscious awareness of how to selectively arouse them during the creative process. Artists cannot fully utilize their talent without complete mastery of their instruments . . . and that instrument is their bodies, minds and souls." Salvi goes on to say that it is therefore incumbent upon the director to understand how to play the actors' instrument.

Actors learn technique to build their talent and continue to work and study to do exactly that. But talent for acting in film and television is not always the issue since directors, casting directors, and producers cast actors based upon qualities they project as people that are suitable for the character in the script. Having talent enhances the actor's ability to fully develop the dimensions of the characters; it is not what is necessarily needed for them to get the role.

Actors Are Like Children

Actors are like children. If they weren't they wouldn't be actors. They like to dress up, pretend and make believe. Like children they need constant assurance that they are doing well. On stage they get an immediate reaction from an audience who reacts to their performance. When working in front of the camera they look to their director for approval. Just like audience applause and laughter enforces the ego of the actor in the theater, a word of praise, a laugh or even applause from the director when the shot ends enforces an actor's ego.

Norman Jewison, when directing *Fiddler on the Roof,* stayed very near the lens of the camera on each take. When doing a close-up shot of Molly Picon for the song "Anatevka," he was so tuned in to the performance that Molly was giving as Yente, the matchmaker, that a tear rolled down his cheek, and when he said "cut," he walked over to Molly and hugged her. That little hug boosted Molly Picon's ego and supported her contribution to the scene. Norman was her director and audience, and she performed for her audience. On an episode of a television series, I witnessed a wonderful actress playing the recovering alcoholic mother of the female lead. In the final scene, she walked over to a window on the set and supposedly saw what we later find out to be the man who is her last chance for happiness being arrested for drug dealing. She immediately broke down and sunk to the floor, letting out a Medea type of painful cry. When the camera stopped rolling, the crew and actors in the scene applauded with echoes of "bravo!" The actress beamed from ear to ear and basked in the praise.[13]

Actors, like children, have a burning desire to please others. If not, they wouldn't be actors. Actors, like children, have a major desire to prove themselves and succeed at what they do. And actors, like children, need a creative environment and energy to nurture their work. If not, they struggle to deliver honesty in their performance. The creative environment and energy comes in many forms: wardrobe, makeup, direction, ensemble playing, and everything that pertains to telling the story that must be told. That creative environment and energy starts with you, the director, who must keep the needs of your actors in your mind at all times.

Actors Have Crutches

Some actors do not like to take risks but use crutches to support their character. A crutch is an impulse or an emotion that an actor plays on a line of dialogue in a specific way that is not the intention of the text. It is an impulse that they are comfortable in showing because it has been preprogrammed as part of their acting psyche by some kind of acknowledgment, usually in the form of applause or someone noting that a line of dialogue they once said left a positive imprint. These positive reactions from observers reinforce the impulse (subconscious) in the actor's psyche and they use it instead of taking a risk and showing deeper vulnerability. Acting coaches work with actors to get rid of crutches, but they can creep into an actor's performance during the sometimes exhaustive process of film acting. Directors need

---

[13] On a side note: The shot was an elaborate moving master that ended with the actress at the window. The crew was so into the performance that the dolly grip missed the final marked position of the dolly requiring the shot to be done a second time. Her performance was not as strong as the first take, and it was the first take that was finally used in the episode. Actors' performances will always win out over the shot!

to be on the lookout for these crutches and, when they see them, try to find a way to instill in the actor the right way to discover the moment and to intensify their vulnerability. One way is to alter the emotion of the moment. Another is to discover it through the rehearsal process. When actors are rehearsing a scene and there is a moment that does not quite *feel* right, it is because an actor went for a momentary crutch rather than look deeper inside themselves to find a suitable vulnerable impulse for the moment.

Actors Have a Syntax

Believe it or not most actors should have an understanding of certain words as it relates to their work. They speak about the inner uniqueness of the character and the physical characteristics of the role. The *inner characteristics* involve the psychological and emotional makeup of the character, and the *physical characteristics* refer to how the character moves, dresses, speaks, and relates physically to other characters. The inner being of the character may come from an examination of the text combined with the actors own unconscious and subconscious experiences, whereas the physical characteristics are affected by other people's contributions to the film. For example, a character's moves may be suggested by the author through the description of the character or the structure of the dialogue, the clothes by the wardrobe or production designer, and the physical relationships to other characters by the director, who must merge all these collaborative elements toward the vision of the project.

Conflict is another word that actors use with the director. Conflict is the heart of drama. It is what the actor and director discuss on a large scale, such as the story, and on a smaller scale, such as the inner thoughts of a character and his or her relationship to the other characters. Actors look for conflicts in scenes, since without them there is no drama. It can be as simple as the character deciding whether to get dressed before getting the children off to school or to get them off to school and then get dressed.

Actors like to speak in terms of *subtext,* or the inner struggle that motivates a line of dialogue. Again, dialogue is the result of impulses that happen to the character, and those impulses are part of the subtext of the moment—the thoughts and feelings that the character is having *before* deciding to express them through dialogue or action. It refers to the story that is going on below the dialogue. The strength of the subtext colors the dialogue with specific impulses that affect the delivery of the words. Those impulses must be honest to the actor if they are to be truthful to the character.

The subtext is very important to an actor, as it "communicates that more is going on in the character than they are sharing, that an inner conflict is present, that the person is thinking or feeling something other than what they are saying or doing."[14] Subtext can affect the moments of discovery for an actor in a scene, but only if the director has put the subtext in the right context for the actor. The thread of subtext must be very clear in the mind of the director in order to communicate it to the actor, especially through the disjointed process of single-camera film directing.

Actors should understand the term *beats* and what it means to the process. A beat is defined as a change in situation or action. Beats have beginnings and endings, which is why they are called beats. This becomes very important for the director, since the process of single-camera movie directing involves using beats to find the moments for camera coverage. In addition, a beat allows the actor's psyche to find a safe point in the scene to go from since it is usually the beginning of a new emotional or psychological moment for the actor. This will be explained in detail later in the discussion on coverage.

A director's eyes and ears work together and independently of each other. Therefore, the director's ears help to hear the believability of the impulse in each beat (since words must be the results of impulses), while the director's eyes see images that assist and support the moment of the story.

This now brings us full circle, since if you are focusing only on your preconceived shot list and/or storyboards, your ears will not hear the believability of the impulses, and your eyes will not see all the possible images based on your actors' performances—which is the foundation for telling the story.

---

[14] Salvi, page 45.

CHAPTER TWO SUMMARY

➤ A storyboard consists of hand-drawn or computer-generated still images.

➤ Actors must be motivated by the staging and not by an image on a storyboard.

➤ Storyboards help directors communicate concepts visually.

➤ Shot lists are an organizational and conceptual tool that directors must not lean on.

➤ Directors use models for previsualization, the production board for production visualization, and the budget for planning.

➤ Previsualization involves knowing your locations or sets in preparation of working with actors.

➤ Actors work on three levels simultaneously.

➤ The actor's language includes subtext, objective, super-objective, conflict, and inner and physical characteristics.

CHAPTER **3**

DIRECTORS AND ACTORS

THE DIRECTOR'S INSTINCT

All people are creative artists. You only have to think about the time when you were a child drawing little pictures with your paper and crayons. Then you got some education, and for some of us that creativity became suppressed. But it is still there, and as we grow older it becomes a little voice inside of us: it is called *instinct*. But it becomes difficult to hear or listen to as more and more people tell you what to do. This is inevitable, as filmmaking is a collaborative art form. As a director you are impacted by many different voices and hear many people around you, some of them—such as the producer or the distributor—holding the purse strings of your project. But you *must* listen to your instinct and cultivate that little voice inside of you. By cultivating it you will find that the voice is telling you to take risks, and risk-taking is part of being creative. *Risk-taking is nothing more than following your heart.*[1]

---

[1] Francis Ford Coppola Master Class, UCLA, October 20, 2004.

Animals use their instincts all the time. We have that same ability, that same instinct, but it is a higher form of instinct, which we call intuition. Intuition is a very important part of the creative process and is connected to that little voice inside of you. But you need to listen to that voice inside of you, and not just to be stubborn about getting your own way to the detriment of others or the project. A director's intuition is never wrong. I repeat: your intuition is *never* wrong if it is truly your instinct and not stubbornness or a decision made from the subjective influences of other people. It is a fine balancing act, since directors must not only work with many people but also within the realities of time, budget, and other restrictions that may affect your decision. Your intuition is your greatest tool in making artistic and directorial decisions, and you must never be afraid to use it. By using it, you are taking risks in your directing, and by taking risks you are being creative. That is your investment, no matter how diverse the story may be.

DIRECTORS AND CASTING

Initially, things begin with casting. All the great cinematography, special effects, and production elements won't mean anything without the right cast of performers. They must create and tell the story and imbue the entire project with credibility and intimacy. Look for life in your casting session. When actors audition for you, they come in nervous, scared, or anxious, and once in a while you will find someone who comes in and is just alive—full of life. It is those people you want to see more of.

When directors cast actors, they often work with a casting director. Casting directors are people who know acting talent: they comb theaters, workshops, and acting schools, as well as watch movies of all kinds looking for new talent. Directors must talk to their casting director for as long as it takes in order to impart to them the essence of the characters as they imagine them. Avoid speaking about physical characteristics, because they limit the scope of the search. The author may write the role as someone who is short and dark in appearance, and a tall strawberry blonde actor may walk in who could be better for the part because he has the essence you seek for the character. But also recognize that in some instances it is impossible to avoid speaking about physical characteristics if it makes it easier to explain your vision.

Understand that the casting director will have spent time with the script and will have his or her own ideas but will not act upon them until both of you are on the same page. This may lead to your casting director sending you tape on actors or asking that you visit a theater to see someone's performance.[2]

Once you start a casting session do not read the actor right away but instead sit and talk to them. Talk about the material, about their family, about their life, about music, about movies, or simply share your life with them. Just get to know them, all the while watching their face and eyes, since your camera will be photographing their eyes. Be very interested in them when talking to them that first time. You will know how quick they are with you if you just ask them a question and you see from their response whether they are very engaging. Look for a truthful quality and an essence that is right for the part. Try to distill the salient qualities of the person you are speaking with. Is it someone you can imagine as the character? Do they have the key tenets of the character they may portray? Can you see them in your mind and trust them as the character? Eventually you may read the actor for the role, watching how their instinct tells them to play a nuance of a moment. But understand that actors are put on the hot seat when you do that and they are usually reading the scene with the casting director while knowing that everyone watching is sitting in judgment. This could make them very nervous. Eventually you will have to listen to your intuition which will tell you whether they are right or not right for the role.

If you are meeting with known actors, try to imagine spending several weeks if not months with them. Will they hate you? Will you hate them? They want to know how attuned you are to the story, to the characters, and specifically to the character you are speaking to them about. They are casting you in the role of their director—someone they will put their trust in for the days, weeks, or months they work on the project. They will be sniffing you out as a person and your passion about the project. They may tell you why they like the project and discuss their excitement with their character. This may get you to discussing the character traits, and you will begin to align your ideas with theirs. These sessions can be stressful for you, especially when you know that casting a recognizable actor will secure

---

[2] Norman Jewison was trying to find the right Tevye for *Fiddler on the Roof* and it wasn't until he saw a production of the show in London in which Chaim Topol appeared as Tevye that he knew he had found his Tevye.

the funding for the project. It is common today that well known actors will not take the job without meeting and approving the director, so it is important for you to just be yourself.[3]

Once you work with them, you will find that they are as nervous about the role they are playing as you might be in directing them. So don't treat them any differently or be bashful or keep a distance from them because of their name or stature. They want the same communication with you that you have with your other actors. So give it to them!

Robert Altman says that casting is 70 percent of the success of a project. Whether that is true is debatable, but what *is* true is that consistent casting excellence in an acting ensemble of a project signals a talented director. You only have to look at the memorable films to see that. For example: John Huston's *The Maltese Falcon* (1940) had Humphrey Bogart, Mary Astor, Sidney Greenstreet, Peter Lorre, and Ward Bond; in Michael Curtiz's *Casablanca* (1942) Bogart, Greenstreet, and Lorre were joined by Ingrid Bergman, Paul Henreid, and Claude Rains; Arthur Penn's *Bonnie and Clyde* (1967) had an ensemble of Warren Beatty, Faye Dunaway, Gene Hackman, Estelle Parsons, Gene Wilder, Michael J. Pollard, Dub Taylor, and Denver Pyle; while Coppola's *The Godfather* can be pointed to as another hallmark of a great film, in part due to the strength of the great acting from Marlon Brando, James Caan, Al Pacino, Diane Keaton, Robert Duvall, and John Cazale, as well as the performances in the smaller roles played by actors such as Sterling Hayden, John Marley, Abe Vigoda, Talia Shire, and Richard Conte.[4] Can there be any doubt that the cast of Paul Haggis's Oscar-winning *Crash* is not made up of wonderful ensemble acting, with the names of Sandra Bullock, Don Cheadle, Matt Dillon, Brendan Fraser, Terrence Howard, Ryan Phillippe among its seventy-two cast members? And of course ensemble casting is a priority in television. It is seen time and again with such shows as *Cheers, Friends, Everybody Loves Raymond, Law and Order, CSI, The Sopranos,* and many others. So initially things

---

[3] I was hired to direct a production of Kahlil Gibran's *The Prophet* that was to star Richard Chamberlain, who had just completed a season with the Old Vic in London. Richard had director approval, and knowing this when I met him, I was very nervous. But we talked about everything except the project and soon found that we had something in common: the love of the theater. When I left the meeting, he made me quite happy by telling the producer that he was excited to work with me.

[4] Sofia Coppola played Michael Francis Rizzi, the baby being baptized with Michael Corleone as his godfather.

begin with casting, and making sure that you are secure with your vision of the characters is the first step towards that beginning.

DIRECTOR-ACTOR RELATIONSHIPS

The relationship between the actor and the director is unique, and no other relationship on a project is like it. The better directors are those who have acted themselves or been trained in acting at some time in their career, or have grown up around actors. The reason for this is that they understand acting, while most directors without that exposure are uncomfortable with actors and, in some instances, don't like them. They are intimidated by them. Sometimes they are the proponents of the digital technologies that provide for virtual characters through CGI[5] or animated features such as *Shrek* and *Toy Story*. But even virtual characters and animated features need to be directed at their origin, and even then an actor is needed. So the actor-director relationship is unavoidable.

As mentioned in the previous chapter, the guru on helping directors understand what actors want is Delia Salvi. Her book *Friendly Enemies: Maximizing the Director-Actor Relationship* sums up that the job of an actor is "to open up the most fragile areas of one's being. But exposing oneself like this requires trust, and most actors find it impossible to trust someone who may not understand how to effectively communicate ideas to them. Directors sensing distrust protect themselves by becoming immersed in the technical issues of the shot. The actor may be ignored completely . . . directors often don't understand what actors want and need from them."

There are many schools of acting techniques that help to train actors, and they run the entire gamut from Group Theatre method (Adler, Strasberg, Meisner) to scene study to improvised theater games, and it is up to the actor to find a way to gain that training and up to the director to know the language that training uses to communicate to actors. But putting that aside, first you have to look to yourself as a director and really ask yourself whether you love actors. Deep down inside, do you really have an affection for actors and who they are? And why? That's simple. They are unique artists. They, like dancers, create art out of their own self. When you speak to an actor, they will tell you that their body and their psyche

---

[5] Computer generated images

or soul is their instrument, some of which we have addressed in Chapter 2. If you have this affection for actors you must, if not for anything else, have it for their courage and dedication. Dedication because with acting comes rejection, and courage because actors have to be dedicated to keep coming back time and again after that rejection. So the first notion in a director's relationship with the actor is to love them, because by loving them the director will have the advantage in working with them because he or she will understand them. Any problem you would ever have with an actor will come from understanding that until the camera rolls and you say "Cut! Print that!" actors often have a tremendous feeling of fear or insecurity when they are about to approach a role or play a scene. They might come at you with a troubled look, asking, "What's my motivation for this?" Or they might rip the dialogue apart in front of you while you are trying to defend the honesty of the script. It makes no difference whether they are a major star or an unknown actor, as they will usually be coming from that insecurity and self-centeredness. And if you know that, then you don't have to argue with them but come at them with understanding and compassion, which will always turn them around.[6] Since the single-camera, out-of-sequence process of shooting a movie results in the actor relying entirely on the satisfaction of the director, actors must turn themselves over completely and implicitly trust and respect their directors.

One of the first obligations for any actor is to play relationships, and one of the first obligations for the director is to make sure that those relationships are being played honestly. It makes no difference whether it is the relationship between two main characters or between a waitress and a patron in a coffee shop. Where there is an actor or a person speaking or not speaking, there is always a relationship that is being played.[7] Characters relate to other characters even when they are discussing them within the dialogue. The actors having the conversation as the characters

---

[6] Sometimes you just have to be rude. I directed a well known actor in a musical and during one ensemble rehearsal when he messed up a note in a quartet, he being the best known of all the actors, asked to immediately do it again. I gently said "no" to him and let him know that we needed to move on. He pouted a minute and literally stamped his feet but he stayed in the scene and worked harder to be convincing in the role.

[7] Even atmosphere or extras in a scene should be playing relationships to one another. By playing those relationships they become convincing characters to the story. For example, is there any doubt that the wedding guests in the opening scene of *The Godfather* are not relatives or friends of either the bride or groom?

have to play not only their relationship with each other but also their characters' relationship to the characters they are speaking about. And it is the obligation of the director to make certain that those relationships are being played and being played honestly. In order to play relationships you must help actors know who they are and what their history is with other characters. Once they know that history then you must make sure that the actors believe it. Without suspension of disbelief your actor is unable to elicit truth.

Since actors in movies look to the director for judgment on truth with their performances, directors need to watch for certain shortcomings that can be prevalent in a weak or unbelievable performance. *First*, make sure that actors are not pushing in their performances or indicating. This refers to resorting to external and physical ways to show what their character is experiencing rather than allowing their subconscious to provide the motivation for the character. Sure giveaways of this are affected facial and vocal expressions, gestures, and body language (which are often played away from camera), and lack of eye contact or eye focus.

Second, actors are geared to play action, since discovery of the emotion comes from the action of the moment. It becomes useless to talk to the actor in terms of what you want as the emotional results. Salvi's book suggests that "instead, talk to them in terms of specifics they can use to deliver results (such as) get that wallet from the man, to make that person love you, to get that cigarette, to break up that relationship without causing too much pain. Don't (ever) talk to your actors in terms of results such as 'be angry here' or 'you are happy there.' Realize that emotions are the results of actions, interaction, and conflict."[8] And from a previous chapter we know that dialogue is the result of those emotions or impulses.

Third, you need to encourage actors not to play it safe but to take risks with their performances. Generally, actors who play it safe lack emotion in their performance as they wind up performing on one level and are never in the moment nor playing discovery of the moment. Salvi says that "actors have not fully lived through what their characters are experiencing. They have not made the character's needs important to themselves and, therefore, they lack energy."[9]

---

[8] Salvi, page 20.

[9] Ibid., page 21.

Fourth, you must also have an engaging relationship with actors and be aware of certain of their characteristics that can affect their performances. This comes from and is related to casting, as certain actors are known for playing certain types of roles that mesh with their own personalities for the role. Joe Pesci is an example of that, as he is always playing "gangster"-type roles, whether in a drama such as *Casino* or *GoodFellas* or a comedy such as *My Cousin Vinny* or an action movie such as *Lethal Weapon*.

Finally, the director must always know when an actor is in the moment and is listening, being engaging, and paying attention to the other actors in the scene. This is when the director's barometer takes over. If you find that you get itchy watching the actor in the scene, then realize that you are not emotionally engaged with the actor because the actor is not emotionally engaged in the scene.

Although you may know what you want from an actor's performance, it behooves you not to tell the actor explicitly what to do. Skilled directors find a method of planting the seed with the actor so that the director's idea becomes the actor's. Once the actor thinks it is his or her idea, they work with it and make it their own. If they think they are doing otherwise, there is a danger of the performance being unbelievable as they try to mimic the direction to please the director. Actors for the screen will always do as the director requests; you just need to find a way to have them believe that what you want them to do is their own idea.

No one on a project must come between the director and the actors. Not the writer, the producer, or anyone else. That is to say, no one should give actors comments on their performances except the director. And a *dialogue director* must only rehearse dialogue with actors and never comment on performances once the director has taken over or after they have been shot.

There is an emotional link that occurs on a shoot between actors and directors: in the single-camera process the director is the direct recipient of the performance. In single-camera narrative, the actor's process to get to performance is painstakingly slow; sustaining the character may be needed only for a few seconds or a minute or two while the camera is rolling and then not needed again for an hour or two while the technical crew is setting up for the next scene or shot. Actors working in this style may need some time to themselves away from the set to focus on what they need to do. You should allow them to do this, while keeping your antennae up as to what they are doing.

An actor's psyche as the character also needs constant reinforcement during the shooting day. So you should talk to actors using personal pronouns such as *"you had a terrible day at the office and the argument you had with your boss is still on your mind when you come in to this scene."* Or, *"just before you run into the scene you are painfully hurt because you just caught your lover kissing your best friend."* Additionally, when actors are discussing their characters' relationships and motivations with one another they should speak to one another in the first person as much as possible. This brings the actors' and the characters' psyches closer together. You can also talk to your actors this same way when they are in rehearsal because the more you can reinforce their psyche, the more they will maintain the belief of the characters they are portraying. If they maintain that belief then the camera will believe it, so you need to do whatever you can do to help that belief—the suspension of disbelief! On a movie I produced I went further to help the director by giving the actors double wide trailers for dressing rooms and made sure they were assigned to the actors playing a father and son relationship, and a brother and brother relationship. The camaraderie the actors had with one another off the set helped to reinforce the character relationships on the set.

Rehearsal

Is there time for a rehearsal period when doing a low-budget movie or an episode of a television show? The short answer is no! The longer answer is: only if your producer has budgeted funds for rehearsal time with your actors. In teaching directing students, film schools stress the importance of rehearsals outside of the day of production. But unless your project has a big budget or your producer agrees to budget funds for you to rehearse with your actors, you will find that the likelihood of a separate rehearsal time becomes a luxury rather than the norm. The Screen Actors Guild says that actors get paid from the time they go to work and rehearsal time is work time, so most producers of low- and medium-budget movies and episodic television shows do not budget funds for actors to rehearse separately from the days of production. Of course, this does not forgo the possibility if not the probability of you going to lunch or dinner with your actors to "discuss" the project, its characters, and their contributions to the roles. Your budget and producer may not have allowed for rehearsals, but actors will and should crave this little bit of informal ego-massaging in getting a jump on the movie.

Multiple-camera film formats such as situation comedies and soap operas[10] rehearse on a set, which lets an actor develop some sort of environmental truth to help them with their imagination. But the single-camera narrative film style of production is disjointed, so rehearsals for these types of projects should be handled a specific way, recognizing that many actors don't really begin their journey as the characters until they are on a set. Belief sets in for many of them when they are in wardrobe and moving in and around the set or location used for the scene. This is especially true if the set or location is significant to their character and further defines who they are, because the creative reality of the space that actors work in helps to manifest a reality to their performance that elicits truth for the camera. But there are certain aspects of character and relationships that can be worked on during a rehearsal away from a set that can help.

First, there is a read-through of the script around a table, with each actor playing their assigned roles while you guide them, through suggestions, toward elements of story, character, and relationships. But you must remember that the rehearsal is for your actors and not for you to assert your directorial authority over them. Listen carefully to the read-through and feel what each actor's instinct tells them about a scene. You will find out a lot and begin to craft the sound and rhythm of the dialogue at this rehearsal. This will probably be the only time that you will have all your actors together at the same time with all of them focusing, sharing and discussing the dramatic characteristics of the story. That in and of itself is valuable.

The use of improvisation and getting the actors away from the text during rehearsal may free your actors up and allow you to get their take on what the scene might be about. For example, if the relationship of the characters is about a couple who have been married for many years, you might discuss with the two actors what it might have been like the first time they met. Or perhaps you set up a small table and a couple of chairs and tell them to act out the first time they met in a crowded coffee bar when they were forced to sit with each other. By using this improvisation technique you are depositing into your actors a series of memories that reflect the kind of memories a married couple might have at the foundation of their

---

[10] Situation comedies and soap operas are detailed in Chapter 10.

relationship. It may not be relevant to any of the scenes in the movie, but that is not important—the honesty of their relationship is. Or you set up an improvisation with the same two actors that somewhat resembles but is not exactly the same as what happens to them in the movie. Perhaps it is an argument when they first broke up before they got married, and they improvise that action. In a sense, through rehearsal improvisation, you are giving memories to the actors as though they are deposits in a bank account of shared memories and emotions. Memories that they will take with them to the shoot and make the element of disbelief stronger and your job easier with them on the set. If they are halfway there, your job on set is halfway done!

This improvisation technique in rehearsal can also be beneficial to the dialogue in the script as it is being finalized. If you have a safe relationship with your actors and understand the use of improvisation, you can go pretty far in exploring the dialogue in the script. If the actors know the dialogue in the scene and are comfortable, there is a technique that Francis Coppola has used on projects that he is writing and directing. He makes sure that he has developed a comfortable rapport with his actors so that when he snaps his fingers once, they are free to improvise, and when he snaps them twice they go back to the text of the scene. Using this technique, improvisation can help make dialogue truthful, because sometimes dialogue may not be truthful from a character's point of view, prompting the actor playing the role to say "I would never say this!" And very often the actor is right. So by using improvisation this way, you have a chance to see what is and isn't truthful and work out what isn't truthful in the dialogue. What starts to happen is that from the text (script) and the new text (improvised dialogue) you and or the writer are able choose the dialogue that works for the characters by merging the two together into the script. You have to know the difference between the improvisation and the original dialogue and make sure that they work together and do not develop because of one actor's ego changing the dynamics of the scene. Exploration through improvisation often changes the color of the scene and makes it richer—which is, after all, what you are after.[11]

---

[11] Several years ago I employed this technique with a screenplay that I wrote and found that the improvisational dialogue was more intense and stronger than the written dialogue. It was immediately incorporated into the script.

Rehearsal on the Set During Production

Having rehearsal time in a professional situation is a luxury. So directors have learned a technique of rehearsing on set during production. The process is logical and can be broken down into stages:

1. Using a floor plan, map out the basic choreography, or blocking, of each scene you will stage before you get to the set. In planning out the choreography of the scene you must take into account your coverage, camera placement, and the motivation of the actors.

2. On the day of production, recognize that your director of photography, assistant director, continuity person, and production crew must *see* the choreography before they can provide their individual contributions to the scene. So stage the basics of the scene with your actors as soon as you can. You should not try to rehearse towards performance but simply make sure the choreography is motivated and comfortable for your actors so they can elicit a performance later when you will refine the nuances of the staging and their relationships. It is at this time that you and your director of photography determine the first shot of the sequence. Once this is done, the stand-ins[12] replace the actors while the technical crew goes to work to set up for the scene and the shot.

3. The actors go off to makeup and wardrobe while you discuss the visual concept of the scene with your director of photography to make sure you are on the same conceptual page. If the actors are already in makeup and wardrobe, allow them to go off and be by themselves, since the staging experience they have just had will begin to sift into place for them—they will be working on their lines and dialogue among themselves to ensure that when they are called back to the set they will be ready to work within the constructs of the staging map. This will also help solidify their relationships for the scene.

4. If you need to, you can rehearse with your actors off to the side while the crew is setting up. These rehearsals should concern the interpretative aspects of the characters so you can make sure that the actors are clear about who they are in the scene and what the scene

---

[12] Stand-ins are extras who watch where the actors are staged and replicate those positions so that the director of photography and his/her crew can light the scene and get the set ready without using the actors for this purpose. They are referred to as "the second team."

is about for them. Since they are away from the set, they will not feel the reality of the scene, so you should not expect a performance—in fact, you don't want one. You want to make sure that the performance they give is done when the camera is rolling and not before.

5. Your first assistant director will tell you once everything is ready on the set for you and your actors: the location/set is lit, the camera is in place, and the crew is ready to see the staging and the scene in front of the camera.

6. Now, you and your actors go to work. All eyes are on you as you take the time to refine the staging and the nuances of the scene in front of the crew, while at the same time allowing the camera crew to rehearse the shot, the sound crew to rehearse for sound, and the other crew members to double-check to make sure that what they did during the setup is now in place. It also allows the actors to get used to the technical environment while having all eyes focus on them and to be the only people concentrating on getting the performance for the specific shot.

7. It is important that you do not over-rehearse the actors at this point. Once you feel comfortable that the actors and the camera have been rehearsed enough, you are ready to do a take.[13] The little bit of adrenaline and energy that the actors are feeling at this point is important. It is akin to the feeling they get just before the curtain goes up on a play. It is creative energy waiting to be released! It usually results in strong performances and is exactly what you want as you get into the scene. You might take a moment just before the camera rolls to double-check the choreography of the staging if it affects the camera movement or something else technically. After all, once you say "action," the actors begin their internalization in bringing the characters to life—you don't want to say "cut" in the middle of the scene because of something technical that could have been avoided with a last minute check.

This rehearsal process during production always works if you adhere to the procedure: plan, choreograph for crew to see, excuse the actors to work alone or with you, come back to the set and refine rehearsal for the shot, and shoot the shot. It saves a lot of time, gets the crew and actors all on the same

---

[13] Roll the camera for picture.

creative page quickly, supports the actors' egos and their performances, and keeps you in creative control the entire time—the conductor of the orchestra! It also allows you great latitude to be inventive with the scene and the actors' performances since all is ready when the actors are called back to the set to do final rehearsals and shooting of the shot. Your actors will become very comfortable working this way and be able to improvise performances within the parameters of the choreography (staging).

In the movie *The Score*, director Frank Oz permitted Marlon Brando and Robert De Niro to improvise in several scenes and to play with the relationship that the characters have with each other. One scene in particular is in a bar that was shot with two cameras in which Brando is convincing De Niro of doing one more "score" for him. Brando and De Niro are sitting next to each other and talking while enjoying a drink. De Niro is listening and responding to Brando's pleading. Oz allows Brando to improvise on each take, knowing that Brando will somehow work the cue line for an actor to enter into the scene when he can say "cut" at the end of the shot. Each time Brando does the scene, he keeps the same intent of the words but changes the pleading slightly, giving little nuances to each take. Both De Niro and Brando are skilled actors who speak the same acting language and are comfortable working this way.[14]

Above all, you must make sure that you create a safe environment for your actors, one in which they can concentrate and be focused. You are setting this work atmosphere, which is one that affects the actors' truth.

Environmental Truth and the Actor

It is the director's responsibility to elicit true performances from actors when working on the set in spite of the technical equipment and crew members present. Therefore it is imperative that you work toward maintaining an environmental truth for the actor when it comes time for the camera to roll. Actors need elements that help their imagination achieve that truth. It can be their wardrobe, the setting, the lighting, or their imagination, which in many instances the director must continue to stimulate.[15] Actors will work on their dialogue with one another, but

---

[14] Although Brando and De Niro appeared in the *The Godfather Part II* together, *The Score* is the only movie in which they have actually played scenes with one another. Both are members of The Actors Studio.

[15] Salvi's book is excellent in explaining these techniques.

only when they can *feel* the environment in some fashion will they truly deliver the performances. The movie *Dogville* is a stylistic film that was shot entirely on a soundstage, with the walls of the sets drawn out on the floor of the soundstage. Actors moved from one area to another when telling this highly dramatic story. But to help the actors maintain the environmental truth of who and where they were, director/writer Lars Von Trier made sure that the wardrobe, props, and sparse furniture were accurate to the time and place of the story. This helped Nicole Kidman, Ben Gazzara, James Caan, Lauren Bacall, and others give performances that were focused and true to the story.

Maintaining an environmental truth for actors sometimes gets difficult, especially when actors are required to perform in front of a green screen or digital effects stage, as in movies such as *King Kong* and *Sin City*. In those instances, directors must appeal to the actor's imagination (which is of course one of their greatest tools) and use a storyboard technique (still or animated) to appeal to their imagination before they perform on a green screen or effects arena.

When directors work from the perspective of establishing an environmental truth for their actors to work within, the result will help the camera find its place in the scene. The camera never lies, so the truth must begin with the actors and carry forward to the camera. It all begins and ends with the performance: the performance of the actors and the camera working together to tell the story, with one giving reason for the other!

Choreography (Staging)

The staging of a scene, also known as blocking or choreography, is a key factor of the rehearsal process and one that is essential for actors, as the staging must motivate the actors toward a realistic performance. Staging should be pre-thought by the director during the planning stage and refined during the rehearsal stage. It should be natural and not forced for any reason. It is based on a set of realities of location, relationships, and the human condition—and of course the camera shots you wish to achieve. But it is never staged *just* for the camera. The camera can go anywhere, so the credibility must come from the actors first. One of the best exercises you can do to understand staging is to go to a public place, such as an airport or an amusement park, and observe people. What do they look like? How do they react to one another? Why do they move? How do they stand, sit, and eat? How do they relate physically to one another? In this way you will see naturalistic movement and physical relationships the way they are. You are in a profession of directing the human condition—what better way to know it than to watch it!

All staging *must* be motivated. Motivated staging will always help actors understand their inner truth, and it must be motivated by the concept and themes of the scenes and the relationship that one character plays toward another character. For example, the action of a simple kiss. Think of the different meanings if the guy kisses the girl or the girl kisses the guy. They are kissing each other, but what will the guy feel like when the girl introduces the kiss as being different than if it is vice versa?

Beginning directors often have a notion to allow actors to stage themselves and move whenever and wherever their instinct tells them. But working this way results in:

1. Actors never maintaining their continuity from shot to shot;
2. Camera shots for coverage[16] being inconsistent and difficult to achieve; and
3. Intuitive behavior to be one of the actor and not of the character.

Most important, when directors work entirely this way they will have a very difficult time in maintaining coverage. And it is *coverage* that gives the editor and director the ability to shift focus, develop dynamics, and accomplish the vision of the story in postproduction. However, if you give actors the freedom to move within a certain and specific space while keeping in mind where your camera is or can be, their instinct as the characters should help define their motivations. Coming at it with a definite idea, suggesting it to your actors, and then having them work within the defined space is best of all—especially when the staging may be limited by the type of camera equipment you are using.

When blocking, the closer you are able to keep the actors together, the easier it will be for them to maintain relationships through the single-camera narrative process. The farther apart they are, the more difficult it is for their creative energies to interconnect. That is to say that if you choreograph your actors with unlikely or atypical distances between them (as we often see on stage), the more difficult it will be for them to continue the nuances of their performances, as they will have to reach out to connect

---

[16] The series of shots that are planned and required to tell the story in the scene.

to their partner. Further, and more important, if they are staged this way, it will be difficult for them to maintain the nuances of their performances once camera placement invades and interrupts their acting space. So it is important that the staging and character relationships are moving in the right direction, with believable acting performances, before the camera is introduced into their space. This begins with natural staging with realistic spatial motivations, whether you are doing the master shot, the two-shot, or the close-up.

The equipment you use and the visual concept may also limit the staging. For example, certain types of dollies[17] have specific limitations that affect how they can be used. Hand-held shots that rely upon a certain visual style and steadicam[18] shots provide another way of staging. We will discuss these in a later chapter.

One of the problems inherent in directing for the screen involves the dynamics of the image as it relates to the staging. You are basically dealing with a flat image—the screen—so you must find ways to create depth and dynamics to bring the audience into the story. Cinematographers do this with light and shadow; directors do it with camera movement. But you can also do it with the staging. Once again, all staging *must* be motivated. Whenever possible, find motivated staging on the diagonal (diagonal as opposed to a lateral physical relationship of one character to the other). With the use of a foreground, middle ground, and background objects in the frame, you will be able to create dynamic shots for the camera.

Diagonal staging

---

[17] A platform on which the camera is mounted to permit it to move.

[18] A steadicam is a device that is worn by the camera operator on which the camera is mounted and through the use of a video assist the image from the camera appears to float in space and give a fluid camera movement. A steadicam is a staple in such shows as *West Wing* and *ER*.

Most important, though, is that the director must help the actor move in the right direction for the concept of the narrative through logical, motivated, natural choreography.

Motivating actors also means looking for those moments in the staging when physicality or physical action can be used to help actors get to where they need to be from moment to moment. It will draw out an inner truth in their performance, as physical action always elicits an internal response and permits the actor's psyche to get to a specific motivated moment during the camera coverage process. The movement can be as simple as an actor moving to another actor, a kiss, or a slap, or as detailed and specific as taking a drink or eating at a specific time in the scene. All physical action helps the instinct of the actor to remember the impulse each time that movement is performed, whether it is in conjunction with dialogue or other movement. It is one of the reasons why directors, during the process of camera coverage, look to physical movement as a starting and stopping point for a shot.

If the scene is choreographed well, it will create a realistic environment for actors, and the camera will find its own place to tell the story. *The staging and the actor must always motivate the camera, never the other way around!* And the camera should always be thought of as an additional actor and be included somehow in the staging. It too will need motivation, which we discuss in the next chapter.

CHAPTER THREE SUMMARY

➤ Intuition is your greatest tool in making artistic and directorial decisions.

➤ Initially, things begin with casting.

➤ Look for life in your casting session.

➤ The relationship between the actor and the director is unique.

➤ One of the first obligations for any actor is to play relationships.

➤ Directors watch for the actor's shortcomings, which lead to an implausible performance.

➤ An actor's psyche as the character needs constant reinforcement.

➤ The technique for rehearsal during production is plan, stage, set up, rehearse, and shoot.

➤ Directors must work toward maintaining an environmental truth for the actor.

➤ Staging must motivate the actor toward a realistic performance.

➤ Directors should create visual depth and dynamics in their staging.

➤ The staging and the actor must always motivate the camera, not vice versa.

"I wanted to talk about how easily we are able to point fingers at others. How we can make decisions based on fears and then find ways to justify those decisions . . . how we are all the villains and all the heroes."

— **Paul Haggis**, director, *Crash*

CHAPTER **4**

DIRECTING THE CAMERA

MOVEMENT—THE VISUAL LANGUAGE

Movement is the visual language for the movie director. In the previous chapter we spoke about one type of movement that a director works with: the movement of actors and the impact it has on the truthfulness of their performances. This is the basis for motivated movement of the camera and between images (editing). Directors recognize that there is a connection between these movements, and the connection is subliminally focused on theme and character. *Movement of the actors (performance) motivates the movement of the camera, and the results of the movements (or lack thereof) of the camera motivate and allow for the passage between the images (editing).*

Directors work from their imagination, both when they previsualize a project from the point of view of its theme, as well as on the set from instinct and actor staging to develop camera movements—which impacts the editing to finally realize the story and its visionary theme. In order to understand this more completely, we need to define some basics of image or camera movement. *First,* the camera can be used as an actor, a voyeur, a documentarian, or a combination of all three. No matter how the camera (shot) is used, it must always be motivated and be truthful to the story and the focus that the director wants to bring to the audience. There are only three basic rules in camera motivation:

1. *If it works, then it is right.*
2. *The closer the camera gets, the more truth it tells.*
3. *Shots are motivated by the performances.*

If you keep these precepts in mind as you decide on your camera shots, you will remain on track.

Movement of the camera is closely identified with movement of people and how they see images in life. This is why camera movement, when motivated, is and should be invisible to an audience. *Panning* is a movement of the camera to the right or to the left.[1] It is closely identified with the movement of the head or eyes to either the right or the left. A *tilting* movement is the movement of the camera up or down.[2] It is closely identified with the up-and-down motion of a person's head. A *dolly* movement is the movement of the camera when it is mounted securely on a movable platform called a camera dolly, which gives it mobility.[3] When the dolly moves, the camera moves. It is closely identified with the movement a person makes when they pass by, move toward, or move away from someone. A *pedestal* movement is the vertical movement the camera makes when mounted on a fixed pedestal tripod or pedestal camera dolly.[4] Both the camera and the pedestal move up or down. It is closely identified with the movement a person makes when they stand up or sit down. As you can see, all of these movements correspond to the natural view of how we look at life around us; therefore it translates invisibly as the foundation for the language of camera movement. When using other technical equipment, such as a *camera crane*,[5] a *jib arm*,[6] an underwater camera, an

---

[1] The command is "pan right" or "pan left."

[2] The command is "tilt up" or "tilt down."

[3] The command is "dolly in" or "dolly out."

[4] The command is "ped up" or "ped down."

[5] A camera crane is a device on which a camera is mounted that permits the image to make wide sweeping motions, such as the ten-minute crane shot that opens Robert Altman's *The Player*. When motivated, it is a cost-effective device that can provide the director with a visual look of a large scale project.

[6] A device similar to a crane that attaches to a dolly or tripod, allowing for a similar but smaller move as a crane.

Jib arm

Crane

Steadicam operated by cameraman Taj Teffaha and his assistant, Trish Soltsyn.

aerial camera or a steadicam, the basic language takes on other visual interpretations and enhances the basic language of motivated camera movement. It shows the audience different ways of looking at the world. Shots—and camera movement within those shots—make up other elements of a movie director's storytelling tools.[7]

A movement of the optics of the lens of the camera, rather than the camera itself, to make the existing image either wider or tighter while we are viewing the shot, is called a *zoom*. This movement, unlike the others previously mentioned, is an artificial movement and does not correspond naturally to a movement from everyday life. Although we can focus on a specific object with our eyes, during a zooming movement such as "zooming in," the image flattens out and, unlike a dolly shot, does not establish depth within the composed frame. Depth is needed for natural invisible dramatic motivation. Dolly moves are preferred as a natural movement, since dolly shots establish depth,[8] and depth is an important characteristic to establish in shots through either composition, camera movement, or staging.

---

[7] Passion for the material, the directing of actors, and the directing of the camera, combined with imagination, are the tools for the director.

[8] Although the zoom is artificial, the MTV generation has come to accept it as a natural movement. It really demonstrates its artificiality when used in context of other movements that the camera makes, and it is difficult to find a logical natural motivation for a zooming movement. It is generally used to shock the audience away from a natural view, or for effect. It was used extensively in episodic television in the 1970s.

ASPECT RATIO AND TYPES OF SHOTS

Directors must know in what form or forms their project will be screened. This could have an impact on the appropriate framing and size of the central subject within a shot. For example, a close-up in television shows less in its framing than a close-up for a theatrical release movie. Seeing an image on a thirty-foot screen has a different impact from seeing the image on a sixteen-inch television screen. What would be a medium close-up for television is a close-up for features, and what would be a close-up for television would be an extreme close-up for features. It all relates to the aesthetic relationship to the audience and an established industry standard.

Close-up television   (4-1a)

Extreme close-up theatrical   (4-1b)

As another example, an image composed for a specific aspect ratio[9], such as 2.35:1 is framed differently for 1.66:1, 1.33:1, 1.85:1 and 1.78:1 (HD), also called 16:9.

1:66   (4-2a) 1:78   (4-2b) 2:35   (4-2c)

Each has a slightly different aesthetic that could have a slightly different impact on the audience. Most important, directors must know how and where the project will be seen to determine which aspect ratio to use. The end use of the project must always be in the director's mind, as it could have a correlation to how the story is told.

---

[9] The aspect ratio of an image is its displayed width divided by its height.

Directors use different shots to plan, discuss, and describe specific images that are determined for the project. A brief review of some of them is appropriate. Several of them will be discussed in greater detail in another chapter.

- *Establishing shot (ES):* An image that sets the location or the action of a scene. Editorially it is usually the first image into the scene and the last to get out of the scene. It is sometimes used within the scene when the audience needs to be reminded as to where the scene is taking place. It establishes where we are.

- *Master shot (MS):* An image of where the action is played out through the entire scene, or a dramatic beat in which we see the physical relationships of all the characters at the same time. The master shot permits actors to set their relationships to one another in the scene or the beat, since the sequence is performed in its entirety without the camera invading the relationships. The invasiveness of the camera comes into play after the master shot and during camera coverage when the actors usually develop a deeper understanding for their moments of discovery. These moments are not easily affected by the invasive positioning of the camera because they have been introduced and set during the master shot. The master shot provides the map in detailing camera coverage in telling the story.[10] This will be discussed in detail in Chapters 5 and 6.

- *Two-shot (2S):* An image that shows two people on screen at the same time. It is referred to when the shot is a neutral shot outside of the physical relationship of the two people and it is often from the perspective of an audience watching actors on a proscenium stage.

Two-shot   (4-3a)

Two-shot camera position

---

[10] The master shot is not an establishing shot, although it can be.

- *Three-shot (3S):* An image that shows three people on screen at the same time.[11] It is generally (but not necessarily) referred to when the shot is a neutral shot outside of the physical relationship of the three people, and it is often from the perspective of an audience watching actors on a proscenium stage.

Three-shot   (4-3b)   Three-shot camera position

- *Over-the-shoulder shot (OS):* An image taken from over (or by) the shoulder of one character to another character(s). The shot does not have to be literally over the shoulder; it can be past the shoulder or past the body to the other character(s). This is determined by eye-line and motivated camera placement. The aesthetics of this shot are determined by not only the staging of the camera in relation to the actors, but also by the characteristics of the camera lens.

Over the shoulder   (4-3c)   Past the body   (4-3d)

- *Wide angle shot or long shot:* An image that shows a lot of information relating to the set or location and position of the characters in the set or location. It is generally an image

---

[11] Note: If there are four characters in the shot it is called a four-shot, five characters is a five-shot, etc.

that shows the characters from head to toe. It relates to the characteristics of the camera lens and is often, but not always, used as an establishing shot.

Wide angle   (4-4a)

- *Medium shot (MS):* An image that shows the character(s) from approximately the waist up. Depending on personal taste, the intended format of the project and thematic content of the story, the cinematographer or director may also frame the shot at just above the knees.

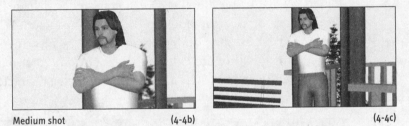

Medium shot   (4-4b)   (4-4c)

- *Medium close-up or medium single shot (MCU):* An image of a single character in which the frame line is cut at just below the shoulder. Depending on personal taste, the intended format of the project, and the thematic content of the story, it can also be framed at mid-chest level.

Medium close-up   (4-4d)   (4-4e)

- *Close-up or single shot (CU):* An image of a single character in which the frame line is cut at just above the shoulder,[12] depending on the intended format of the project.

Close-up   (4-4f)

The framing of the close-up is determined by the size of the medium close-up (if one is done). The strength or power of any close-up lies with the performance of the actor and the shot that is edited before or after it. A close-up has no power in storytelling if it is intercut with other close-ups. But if intercut with a two-shot or an over-the-shoulder shot it draws attention to the close-up.[13]

- *Dirty close-up or dirty single shot (DCU):* A close-up image that allows for a piece of another character in the frame.

Dirty close-up[14]   (4-4g)

The decision as to whether the shot is either a clean close-up or a dirty close-up should be determined by the physical relationship of one character to another in a scene. All types of shots must be motivated, and a close-up is often a character's point-of-view shot.

---

[12] It can also be framed at just below the shoulder depending if the framing of the medium shot of the subject is at mid-chest level.

[13] The tighter shot will always have the focus.

[14] The illustration is a 100mm lens with a narrow depth of field.

If you are not sure whether the close-up should be dirty or clean, the best way is to be the character looking *at* the other character who you want to have in a close-up. If what you see is an extreme close-up then the close-up should be dirty. But the extreme close-up (unless the characters are physically touching one another or in an embrace) will be clean.

- *Extreme close-up (ECU):* An image of a single character that is tighter than the close-up.

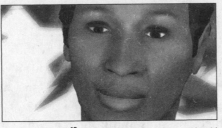

Extreme close-up[15]   (4-4h)

This is the shot that tells the most truth of the character. The strength of the extreme close-up lies in the performance of the actor and the shot that is edited before and after it.

Before shooting, the director and cinematographer should define clearly where the frame line is for the medium shot, the medium close-up, the close-up, and the extreme close-up. It is a subjective decision generally based on individual aesthetics and the emotional and dramatic concepts of the image toward the relationship of the story. For example, if the movie is

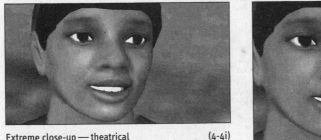

Extreme close-up — theatrical   (4-4i)

Close-up — television   (4-4j)

---

[15] Note the eye-line between illustration 4-4g and 4-4h. The ECU is the boy's point of view.

a comedy, close-ups tend to be cut at the shoulders rather than at the neck of the subject, as a tighter close-up may make the audience uncomfortable. It is also based on the end use of the project. For example, the frame line of a close-up for television is often the same frame line for an extreme close-up for theatrical release. Remember that a theater screen is thirty feet or more.

Subtle differences between shots can also impact the unconscious aesthetics for an audience. For example, if in a scene one close-up is framed slightly tighter than other close-ups, the audience may subtly and unconsciously give that character more importance. It is very important that the communication between the director and cinematographer be clear about these and other expressions.

- *Reveal shot:* An image that is designed to present a revelation to the audience. The revelation can be motivated by the intent of the creative moment or by the character in the sequence. A reveal shot is done through a movement of the camera, be it a dolly, a pan, a tilt or a crane movement. The shot generally motivates the reveal at the end of the movement, but not necessarily.

- *Dolly and crane shots:* The movement of the camera when it is placed on a movable platform or wagon that permits the camera to be mobile during the taking of the image. Dollies operate on a track or on a smooth, flat surface, depending on the type of dolly and the intended movement. Different dollies are designed to work in different space areas, depending on limitations. A dolly shot (as all shots) must be motivated and can be used as a master shot, an establishing shot, a reveal shot, or a traveling shot. They are often referred to as a *walk and talk* when used in association with characters walking (and talking) in a scene.

    The ending position of a dolly shot is the most important position of the shot, as it is the piece of the shot that links to the next shot in storytelling.[16] So once you have determined what the dolly shot is to be, the quickest way to set it is to mark the tail (the last position) of the dolly shot first and then back into the beginning or first position, making adjustments and setting marks for both the dolly and the actors along the way. This is done in congruence with the actor's (or a stand-in's) movements so the dolly has

---

[16] This is true with any moving shot: the last position of the move is the most important position, as it links to the next shot in the storytelling. It is good form to set the tail of the move first.

motivation throughout the move. In this regard, the director treats the movement of the dolly as another actor in the scene.

This same technique is used when setting a *crane shot*: set the tail of the shot first, as it is the most important part of the shot, then back into the beginning of the shot, marking the path the crane shot takes, including any stops it makes along the way. Again, crane shots, like dolly shots, must be motivated; they are often used to reveal something to an audience or to let an audience see life from a different perspective. Think of the last shot of the film *Pay It Forward*, when the camera cranes up and the image of cars coming from a great distance to the front gate of the boy's house causes every eye in the audience to tear up, or the magnificent ten-minute crane shot in a studio parking lot that opens Robert Altman's *The Player*.

- *Rack focus shot:* An image that also contains movement. But the movement is an optical movement within a fixed frame. It allows for one portion of the image to be in focus and, on a specific cue, immediately shifts the focus to another portion of the image. This is produced by an immediate adjustment to the depth of field of the lens. When this technique is used, it is motivated by the action or dialogue in the narrative when the director wants to shift the audience's attention in the shot.

Rack Focus   (4-5a)   (4-5b)

- *Zoom shot:* We have saved for last the discussion of a zooming move in an image and have included it in the discussion of shots for a specific reason. A zooming movement of the image is made when a camera is stationary or moving and is using a variable focal length lens.[17] The "zooming" movement of a zoom lens rarely has

[17] Commonly referred to as a zoom lens. When zooming in, the central image gets large in the frame and the variable focal length of the lens becomes longer (a long lens). When zooming out, the central image gets small and more information surrounding the image is revealed as the variable focal length of the lens becomes shorter (a short lens).

dramatic motivation other than a technical effect and is most suited to a specific narrative visual style. For example, in the *Austin Powers* movies, zoom moves are used quite extensively, since those movies mimick not only the style and culture of the 1970s but also the style of filmmaking prevalent in the 70s. It was common practice to use the zoom movement in episodic television in the 70s, as it was a quick way to do a move that closely approximated a dolly move without laying the track for the dolly or involving a lot of rehearsal time and personnel. The more it was used by different directors, the more it was accepted by television audiences and became a stylistic norm. A zoom movement does not look like a dolly movement. As previously mentioned, a dolly move is a natural camera movement that creates perspective with objects and people in the frame. A zooming movement is an unnatural move that flattens the perspective and therefore makes it more difficult to motivate it invisibly into a narrative.

There are, however, several in-camera visual techniques, some obvious and some invisible, that are motivated in narrative storytelling that incorporates the zoom, in a shot that we call a *zolly shot*. One visual technique allows for the central focus of the image to stay fixed while the background image appears to come forward or get larger.[18] Another allows for the central focus of the image to stay fixed while the background image appears to retreat or get smaller.[19] Both examples employ a dolly move and a change in the variable focal length of the lens at the same time. In the first example the camera is dollying *out* while zooming *in* to the central focus and in the second example the camera is dollying *in* to the central focus while zooming *out*. These two types of visual shots are often used to motivate or highlight dramatic revelations in the story or to the character. Although they are individual shots unto themselves, their use in context with other shots must be carefully planned out by the director as part of the coverage of a scene.

---

[18] This zolly shot can be seen in Paul McGuigan's film *The Reckoning* (2003), in the scene in which a troupe of fourteenth century actors perform a play in which they recreate a murder.

[19] There is a brief moment in Paul Haggis's *Crash* when the daughter of a locksmith ex-gang member jumps into his arms to protect her father from what she thinks is a bullet. The horror on the man's face and this effect in the shot has a dreadful and startling impact upon the viewer. And Spike Lee's *Inside Man* uses both types of zolly shots: one with actor Clive Owen and the other with actor Christopher Plummer.

When motivated they are effective to the story. The difficulty for the director is to work it into the coverage concept so it is not an effect done simply for the sake of the effect.

Two zooming techniques are virtually invisible to the audience but can be successfully employed by the director. They both involve dolly shots and are affected by circumstantial limitations. One is when you need a "dolly in" movement and do not have enough dolly track to successfully complete the type of shot you want at the end of the dolly move. *(Remember, we set the tail of the dolly first.)* When timed out carefully with the dolly move, a slight zooming movement during the end of the dolly movement will be imperceptible to the human eye if it is executed smoothly with the dolly movement. Using this technique, the lack of track will not prevent you from getting that most important last image of the dolly move. The other technique is when you are creating a dolly move that is parallel to the action and you have a relatively short amount of space in which to make the dolly move. When zooming while performing a parallel dolly, the perspective between the background and foreground will change, and although moving in just a short space (three to four feet), the shot will appear to be a longer and effective dolly movement.

SUBJECTIVE AND OBJECTIVE SHOTS

Every shot has a motivation. And every shot is either subjective or objective or can go from being subjective to objective or vice versa. An objective shot allows the audience to view the moment from an objective perspective, not being part of or one with the moment; a subjective perspective means being part of or seeing what is happening from within one character's viewpoint. The most critical and effective subjective shot rests with the close-up. Why? Because the close-up is a powerful shot unto itself and, when the performance is strong, can impact the audience powerfully when it is subjective. Eye-line in the close-up determines *how* subjective the shot is. The eye-line of the talent (determined by placement of the camera) is the determining criteria as to whether a shot is subjective or objective. Most shots that "look at" a scene are objective shots, unless they are intended to be either a character's point of view of what they are looking at or are intended to be the audience as a character.

By placing the camera in an objective position in relation to the subject of the shot, the shot will always provide the objective viewpoint. We define certain aspects of our being and communicating with other people in terms of our space; as in "our work space," or "our living space." We have all heard the expression "Don't get into my space!" or "Stay out of my face!" These expressions speak to the concept that we have an ownership of the space around us, whether it be a work space, a living space or an invisible space that our energy works within when we

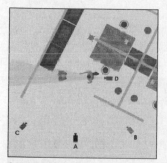

communicate with others. It also relates to ownership of our own subjective space that we occupy. To create a subjective shot (other than a point of view shot) you must first observe the physical relationship of the actors in the scene. Their physical relationship will be made up of their characters' space. This helps to understand where to put the camera for a subjective shot. It also defines the degree of subjectivity for the shot.

Camera positions

Camera A — objective   (4-6a)

Camera B — objective   (4-6b)

Camera C — objective   (4-6c)

Camera D — subjective   (4-6d)

As an example, we will look at a simple over the shoulder shot from Don the beachcomber to Jessica his friend. If we have Don hold up his arms in front of him at a 45-degree angle, we can begin to examine the working space that belongs to Don. It is all the space in front of him and behind him that is within those 45 degrees. The farther out we place the camera to one side of the 45 degrees, the less subjective the shot becomes. The closer we get to the apex of the 45 degrees or to Don's head, the more subjective the shot becomes. Jessica is on the left side of the frame (camera left) and Don is on the right side of the frame (camera right). In an over-the-shoulder shot you will see the shift in Jessica's eye-line change as the camera position gets closer to the apex. The eye-line refers to the bearing of where Jessica's eyes are looking toward the right side of the frame (set up as being Don's space) which establishes the physical relationship of *Don* to *Jessica* in the

Camera positions

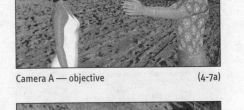
Camera A — objective   (4-7a)

Camera B — objective   (4-7b)

Camera C — objective   (4-7c)

Camera D — subjective   (4-7d)

Camera E — subjective   (4-7e)

scene. The closer the camera gets to the apex (or in Don's space), the more Jessica's eyes look toward the right center of the frame, and the more the audience feels they are one with Don. Of course, the camera cannot go past the apex, since if it did, the characters would switch positions on screen, with Jessica on the right side of the frame and Don on the left. This is called *crossing the line,* which we will discuss in Chapter 5.

SUBJECTIVE AND OBJECTIVE CLOSE-UP AND EYE-LINE

The concept is the same for a *subjective* close-up, although here it is more critical, since the close-up is a powerful shot and the placement of the eye-line is critical for its impact. If the camera position is outside of the 45-degree angle when doing the close-up, the close-up becomes *objective,* and the audience feels as if they are observing Jessica impartially. In this case, the eye-line will be such that the audience gets the visual feeling that Don is off camera. Jessica is talking to Don, and the audience is not within Don's understanding. If you want the audience to be more part of Don's character we position the camera to ensure that Jessica is looking more toward the center. Now the camera position for the close-up is going to be closer toward Don bringing the audience more into what Don is seeing,

Camera positions

Camera A — objective　　　　　　　　　(4-8a)

Camera B — subjective　　　　　(4-8b)

Camera C — more subjective　　　　(4-8c)

and perhaps feeling, depending on the dramatic action of the scene. Notice that Don's presence is still kept on camera right.

When deciding on the subjectivity of the close-up of Jessica, we look to the over-the-shoulder shot (Don's shoulder) to see where the eye-line should be. The over-the-shoulder shot is a subjective two-shot that establishes the physical relationships of one character to the other, and the close-up moves us further into the relationship.

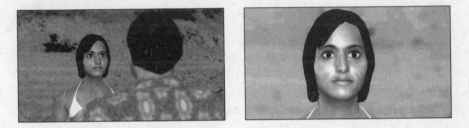

One more note for close-ups that, because of its importance, we will repeat in the section on coverage. The best close-ups for many reasons are shot with a long lens—a short or narrow depth of field. *First,* the long lens makes the subject look good. *Second,* the camera is positioned a fair distance away from the actors, not invading their space or affecting their concentration. *Third,* the cinematographer can light the shot better so that it can be free of boom or camera shadows. *Finally* (and most important), the focus of the shot draws attention to the subject, with the background (and foreground, if any) out of focus.

We have talked about eye-line. Eye-line establishes the physical relationships among characters in a scene. Eye-line is one of the most critical and tricky concepts for a director to understand and master. We will discuss it further in this book during the section on coverage. However, correct eye-line is important in establishing and maintaining the physical and spatial relationships among characters and between characters and the camera. And during production eye-line must be foremost in the mind of not only the director but also the cinematographer, the camera operator, and the continuity person, since incorrect eye-lines will affect the editorial magic of storytelling.

CHAPTER FOUR SUMMARY

➤ Movement is the visual language for the movie director.

➤ The camera is used as an actor, a voyeur, and a documentarian.

➤ Camera movement closely identifies with movement of people.

➤ The closer the camera gets, the more truth it tells.

➤ Shots are motivated by the performances.

➤ Individual aesthetics and the emotional and dramatic concepts affect the framing of a camera image.

➤ Every shot has motivation and is either subjective or objective.

➤ Eye-line establishes the physical and spatial relationships of characters in a scene.

CHAPTER **5**

CAMERA COVERAGE—PART 1

CUTTING IN YOUR HEAD

What is the decision-making process concerning what shots are needed to explore a scene? This is a question that faces directors from the very beginning of the directing process. Film school students are told that they must develop storyboards and shot lists and develop a shooting sequence of individual shots that comes from their imagination. They not only previsualize the shots but also when and how they want it to be edited. They go ahead and shoot the shots for the exact lines of dialogue they had imagined, thereby editing the movie before it is even shot—*cutting the movie in their head.* Forget that in the real world the director works with an editor and the editor knows the story only from the footage that he or she is given. Forget that the editor is only *as good* as the footage he or she is given. Forget that if it doesn't work, the producer is faced with pickup shots and reshoots. Forget that pickup shots and reshoots increase the budget of the movie. *Just remember that it is a mistake and incorrect directorial ideology ever to cut a scene or a movie in your head before or during your shoot. You must never cut in your head (or predetermine) but instead, as you shoot coverage, have a sense of the various ways it can be edited.* Performance must motivate the camera (shot). You must never force or motivate the performance because of the camera (shot). Cutting in your head before or during the production is bad directing, and you must learn not to do that. The coverage must come from and be motivated by the performances and through how the actors are staged to elicit the performance.

Director George Stevens (*Giant*) would cover a scene from every conceivable angle and make his thematic and aesthetic decisions in the edit room, where he would take days to finish a scene. Of course, this is going overboard. You must come to a balance between the amount of coverage you decide to do (which serves the story and its theme and provides story choices for you and your editor) and trust in your direction that the performances are being true to the story. It is true that narrative projects are "made" in preproduction and executed during production. But "making it" in preproduction does not include predetermining how you will be editing the movie.

COVERAGE AND THE THEME

In Chapter 1 we discussed in detail the theme of a project and its relationship to the vision. Directors, while keeping the development of that theme and vision in mind, must first be clear as to how they are to be interpreted overall by the camera.

Boxing is a large part of the movie *Annapolis*, directed by Justin Lin.[1] When Lin prepared this movie, he saw practically every boxing movie ever made so he could stage a fight that would present the personal journey of the protagonist, a working-class kid trying to find out who he is. Every time he stepped into the ring the audience was to get a sense of who he was as a person. Each boxing sequence had its own story carefully worked through between Lin and his cinematographer, using hand-held cameras for the close-up sequences. Lin took this visual style further by experimenting with shutter speeds and their thematic impact upon the audience.

Brad Silberling's *Moonlight Mile* is a movie about a young man who is trying to please everyone and is in a tug of war between his dead fiancée's

---

[1] Publisher's note: Justin Lin received his training as a director from the author while a student at UCLA. He also was his teaching assistant in advanced courses in directing.

parents and members of the community. In one scene, the character, played by Jake Gyllenhaal, goes to what is supposed to be a formal business dinner. Through the course of the scene it is revealed that it is a complete sham; the other people's real purpose is to hook their daughter up with Jake Gyllenhaal's character. There is a pretense to the premise of the scene: the scene itself is a lie, and Jake is part of that pretense and trapped in that lie and cannot get out.

There are many different ways to shoot a dinner scene, and it takes a skilled and focused director to find a visual way that supports the development of the theme. Silberling saw this dinner scene as being painfully formal, with Jake's character caught in the middle of this strange existence. He translates this early on with his coverage when, through the open back of an empty chair, he shows a shot of Jake apparently trapped and wondering why there is an empty chair at the dinner table. When the daughter arrives and sits in the chair, there is a shot in which her head obscures a portion of Jake. Jake's performance gives us that sense of "okay it's a setup, it's a trap, and I smell it, but I don't know what it is going to be!" His performance motivates the shot. Then Silberling proceeds to show Jake isolated at the table, the subject of the parents' hunt, yet separated from the social interaction. But if we examine the staging of the scene, another choice for coverage of Jake could have been a two-shot past actor Dabney Coleman, or any of the other characters for that matter. They were not used—and perhaps not even shot—because a two-shot would not show Jake alone as the subject of the hunt. Also, the hunt-and-hunter theme is subconsciously supported by the production design; there are paintings of animals that are caught in the hunt in the background of the shots of isolated Jake and those of his hunter, Dabney Coleman. To develop the visual to support the theme, Silberling designed all of his coverage on Jake from the daughter's perspective and on everyone else with no one else in the frame, and because of his performance, the audience sees Jake, the hunted, easily falling out of the trap. At the end of the scene, they realize (as does Jake) that the daughter has been trapped for a long time in the same existence in her family. How does Silberling do this? By covering her from Jake's perspective!

This scene demonstrates that directors should go to the basics: performance and staging to motivate the coverage for the scene. There are many different ways to cover a scene, and coverage should never happen in a vacuum. Directors must look to see what and how they can bring out in *pictures* what is happening emotionally to the characters and allow that to be the driving force for the coverage. And if you are lost in the question of which coverage shot to do next and the production crew is standing around waiting for you to make your camera decisions, it is time for you to be true to the story and go back to the characters for your bearing. You will find the path there.

THE MASTER SHOT

You must plan ahead and have an idea of how you will cover a scene. There are approaches that help you determine the camera shots needed to tell the story from a variety of angles once the scene has been staged. One successful method is to stage a master shot as a way to rehearse the scene so everyone on the set can see how the believability of the scene plays out. And then if push comes to shove and you really get into a time crunch and are unsuccessful in completing the coverage for the scene, you have the master to revert to. This also allows your actors to experience their environment and to liberate their instinct without having the camera invade their acting space, which can happen when you cover a scene. It permits them to anchor their approach or feelings about their relationships in the scene so they can either comfortably duplicate it or build on it during the various coverage shots. In addition, the *master shot* becomes the "chart" that shows you intuitively how and when to cover the scene. If staged correctly and looked at carefully it will also show you the most efficient and creative way of telling the story visually. Even though you have certain shots in mind but not a complete understanding as to how to achieve them, the creation and development of the *master* will be your compass and guide your creative thought process, since it lets you observe the actors' process and focus on their performances.

Creating the master shot may inspire changes to the ideas you brought to the set—inspiration is a wonderful creative ingredient for a director. The master shot, like all shots, should be motivated, as it is created by the story and what you do with the actors. It's founded in the characters and the story's theme and, in that sense, like all shots, should be looked at as another actor. One of the most common mistakes that new directors make is thinking that an establishing shot is a master shot when they decide on

Establishing shot   (5-1)

a wide-angle shot that establishes where the characters are (as opposed to who they are) and proceed to have the actors play out the scene in that wide angle. Establishing shots are not master shots, although master shots can be designed to start or end as an establishing shot.

Masters do not have to run throughout the entire scene. The scene can be broken up into dramatic beats.[2] For example, if the scene you are doing is more than a page and a half and the staging of the actors shifts drastically, and you find that it serves the production schedule to do more than one master shot, find a place within the scene to end one master, do its coverage, and then pick up the other master and its coverage later in the production day. The separation point between the two masters should be a moment in the scene when one or more characters make a logical emotional transition to a new dramatic beat and the staging changes to motivate the beat. This way your actors can focus easily on the discovery of the moment for each of the two masters during coverage without concerning themselves with the rest of the scene. You may find yourself working this way when you are confronted with limitations of equipment, locations, or other elements that are beyond your control. However, this decision should be made by how the actors are playing the scene and their need

---

[2] A dramatic beat is a section of dialogue in which the characters are relating to one another emotionally or on one subject and the dialogue takes a turn, indicating a change in the emotional beat. It can also be a section of a scene when one character exits or another character enters.

for emotional continuity in their performance. Again, the performance dictates how you use the camera!

Although preferred, it is not always necessary or possible to stage a master shot. In these circumstances developed coverage will change. For example, if the scene calls for a large courtroom with plaintiffs and defendants, their attorneys, the judge, and other officials as key characters in the story, along with members of the press and a gallery of people watching the proceedings from above, it may be difficult or impossible to do a master shot of the scene without the use of a crane. And even then it will be more of an establishing shot than a master shot that shows the dramatic and emotional action of the scene. This was the case with Oliver Stone's *JFK*. Again, the director goes to the basics: the characters in the story. In one courtroom scene, instead of a master, Stone shows shots of the various elements and characters that not only make up the courtroom but also relate to one another in the story while always coming back to the dramatic action with Kevin Costner, who speaks to the court and jury. In another example, the setup at the beginning of Peter Weir's *Witness* shows the audience a man murdered in a bathroom. After he is found, Harrison Ford shows up to investigate. The first image after the discovery of the body is an image of Amish woman, Kelly McGillis, with her Amish son (the witness) seated next to her. There is a wash of foreground wipes, and the camera tightens very slowly on her and the boy. With this simple opening shot there is a feeling of both characters being overwhelmed by what is going on. Weir didn't use a large master to develop the scene but for that brief moment went to emotional pictures showing the overwhelming nature of the situation, with people scurrying by and the counterpoint image of two calm people sitting in the storm of fury. That image said it all! It all comes down to the story, the theme, and its elements.

THE MASTER, THE MOVING MASTER, AND THE MASTER THAT MOVES

A master shot that is performed with minimal camera moves (or none at all) in which the audience *observes the action,* is referred to as a *master.* The viewpoint of the shot is as if the audience is fixed, watching the scene progress and actors move into the frame. In Tobe Hooper's *Poltergeist* there is a three-page scene which is done in one shot with no coverage. It is just before the clairvoyant and the mother go into another dimension to retrieve Carol Anne. The low angle shot starts out on a tennis ball on which a number is being written, and the camera tilts up and pulls back slightly revealing a five-shot with the actors staged carefully within the frame to establish the depth of the hallway in which the scene takes place. Zelda Rubinstein, who plays a clairvoyant, walks forward from the background of the shot to the foreground into a close-up as she "feels" the energy of the house. The other characters are soft focus as we see Zelda trying to get in tune with the house, while JoBeth Williams (as Diana), under Zelda's instructions, tries to contact her daughter. JoBeth is three-quarter body in the frame on one side of Zelda's close up, while Craig T. Nelson as Steve (Carol Anne's father) is full body on the other side of the close-up. To the side we see one of the paranormal technicians studying Zelda, and Beatrice Straight as (Dr. Lesh) is standing in the distance, hidden slightly by Zelda's close-up. When Zelda tells everyone that Carol Anne is unsafe where she is, the camera pedestals down slightly, leaving room for JoBeth and Craig to make a slight movement forward toward Zelda (still soft focus). In this single shot, Zelda, still in close-up, tells Craig that he needs to be cross with Carol Anne. Craig moves toward the camera and, because he is taller than Zelda Rubenstein, the camera pedestals up, and JoBeth moves into the frame right behind Craig as we see Zelda walk to the back of the shot (up camera) toward the door to Carol Anne's room in the background. The shot now becomes a four-shot (Beatrice Straight remains fixed where she is near the door). All the characters are soft focus except Craig, who is the largest person in the frame and facing the camera. As the scene shifts with Zelda now at the door, the camera dollys slightly past Craig to a three-shot with JoBeth in the foreground, Zelda right behind her, and Beatrice behind them as JoBeth, also facing camera, moves into a sharp focus medium close-up and talks to her daughter. When Zelda tells JoBeth to lie to her daughter to get her closer to the light, JoBeth turns her head toward Zelda, saying "I hate you." This motivates the camera to dolly past JoBeth while pedestaling down into a medium close-up of Zelda being shared with the door to Carol Anne's room. Zelda turns to the door and says, "Now let's open the door!" and the camera pushes in to the door. The eye-line to establish Carol Anne in the other dimension was kept above the top portion of the frame so whenever the characters were speaking to Carol Anne they looked up in the frame. This single, carefully constructed shot uses motivated movement of the actors, the depth of field of the lens, and motivated movement of the camera to develop the emotional nature of the characters. The ensemble performances of the actors and their motivated staging—and that of the camera—keep the viewer as a participant suspended in the fear of the moment and the characters' emotional roller coaster. Hooper chose to do the scene *in one*[3] and keep the audience watching from one perspective with the camera.

Another type of master is one in which the camera observes the action and moves along with it while observing the scene. This is called a *master that moves*. The most familiar is that of actors having a conversation while walking. In this master, commonly referred to as a *walk and talk*, actors are motivated to stop along the route specifically for coverage purposes. When the movement stops it gives directors the opportunity for coverage before the dolly moves again, as it is difficult (but not impossible) to match coverage on a moving dolly shot. This technique lets the editor edit the coverage in between the best moving moments of the dolly shot from multiple takes that the director may do. It also lets the editor re-pace the actor's performance, adjusting the rhythm of the scene. On one movie I directed we had a scene in which two characters were walking along a seedy street in Los Angeles, having a conversation. Cinematographer Tom Denove and I devised a *master that moves* dolly shot that would show the nature of the neighborhood, since it provided an important aspect of the relationships between the two characters. I staged the actors to stop at certain times as they walked, with the intention of covering the scene with over-the-shoulders and close-ups whenever they stopped. As it turned out we ran out of time because we were losing daylight and were able to get coverage at only one of the stops along the move. But this particular *walk and talk* master was conceived to have the actors move into a tight two-shot at the last stop along the walk, just in case we couldn't complete our coverage. So it turned out fine. Although we didn't have enough time to complete the coverage, we had the master to complete the story in that scene, which is what we used. The performance of the actors sustained the shot.

Another type of master is the *moving master*. This is when the camera is a participant, as opposed to a viewer, in the scene. In a moving master

---

[3] "In one" is a term referred to when a director makes a decision to do a single shot for a scene without any coverage. It is often used when you need a shot such as a person walking down the street. The choice for an "in one" shot is determined by the director and is usually done to save time in production on sequences that are not important moments to the story but move the story along.

the camera and the actors move to and from one another, engaging the audience as a participant in one way or another. A moving master usually involves the camera moving in the space of one or another character, employing close-ups, medium shots, and over-the-shoulder shots. Moving masters are always intensely motivated by the movement of the actors. This type of moving master uses primarily tight shots and angles combined with motivated changes in lens depth of field to direct the audience toward one statement in the shot or another. The moving master often has actors go in and out of the camera frame while disorienting the spatial relationship for the audience. Directors, when employing this technique, must carefully think through coverage to work with this kind of master shot. In the most daring instances, there is no coverage and directors must make sure that the performance is totally sustaining. Moving masters take a long time to stage and rehearse, and they run off a lot of film stock. So they must be planned carefully.

As discussed in the previous chapter, with all masters that have movement (and especially the moving master), the last position of the shot is the most important, as it links to the next sequence or scene in the movie. So the last position of the moving master is detailed first, and all other positions are coordinated backward, with adjustments made in motivation of staging, shots, and camera position. It is always a good idea to do more than one take of any moving master shot, even when you finally get the one you want. In all probability, the speed of the shot when projected runs slower than you perceived on the set. So after you have the master shot, you should do it again and ask your dolly grip to move faster and your actors to pick up their cues. Your continuity person will be able to give you the running times of both takes; you will find that, more than likely, the faster take is the one you finally use.

CROSSING THE LINE

Before we continue, we must first explain a concept that affects coverage deeply—*crossing the line!* Coverage preserves consistent screen direction through the simple logic of understanding the principles of crossing the line.

The line submits to the invisible line between the physical positioning of characters in a scene. It involves keeping the camera shots on one side of

Multiple axis eye lines   (5-2)

the line to safeguard consistent screen directions for all characters in a scene and makes it easier for the audience to understand the spatial relationships among the characters. This provides for the simple logic of the structure of the visual language. When this is understood, breaking that structure becomes easier. The invisible line is easy to see in a two-character scene, as each time the characters move their positions, the axis of the line shifts. But in complex scenes involving multiple characters who relate to one another and/or movement that creates physical regrouping and changes in eye-line, the scene may have more than one axis.

Coverage does not happen in a vacuum. There is logic to coverage, and not crossing the line is part of the logic of how the pieces need to work together. It refers to not only the way the actors' bodies are positioned but also to the placement of the camera. It affects the spatial relationship that offers a visual logic for the audience. If you end up crossing the line with your coverage, the characters talking to each other will be looking in the same direction and will appear to not be talking to each other. One character on one side of the line is speaking facing camera right, and by crossing the line with the camera the other character is also speaking camera right. Without having either of those characters looking camera left, the physics of the scene does not work. It makes for very bad editing and is not used.

Crossing the line—also called the 180-degree rule—has a direct correlation to film editing. It refers to the fact that two characters or elements in the same scene should always have the same left/right relationship to each other. Breaking the line or the line of action is crossing the line, and in effect, if it were a multiple-camera shoot and you were crossing the line, you would see the other camera in the shot. The line extends between shots as well as it relates to any action of a character. For example, if a person exits the right side of the frame in a shot, they should enter from the left side of the frame in the next shot if it is a continuous action. Leaving from the right and entering from the right will create a disorientation of the space in which they are moving. Although the concept of crossing the line is an essential element necessary for editing, the rule is not always adhered to as sometimes the director will purposefully break the line of action in order to create disorientation. But to purposefully cross the line, the director must know what it is *not* to cross the line and find a way to use the disorientation thematically.

This is not to imply that the coverage may *never* cross the line without disorientation, because it can—but only when it is motivated. In some cases the staging of actors will take you across the line.

```
Karen is in a park taking a picture of a statue.
From one side of the statue, Adrian approaches the
scene to surprise Karen. He stands next to Karen,
discussing the statue. They then move behind the
statue for a picnic that Karen has arranged in
the park.
```

When Adrian and Karen move to the blanket from their position of looking at the statue, this new angle and relatively new location can begin a new master, as it is a second beat to the scene. Although tied to the first part of the scene, the actors change their position when they move to the blanket, crossing the previous line and establishing a new line for coverage. Further, the visual cue of seeing some part of the statue from the first part of the scene ties the two locations together for the audience. In fact, if we could take the statue with us, we could shoot the second part of the scene on another shooting day in another grassy location, and the audience would think that the two locations are one, and the coverage then would maintain the line for that new master.[4]

---

[4] The audience knows only that which you show them through the lens of the camera, not how it got there! And if need be, the camera can create its own location.

The line can also be crossed by the nature of the location. For example, when Adrian stands next to Karen and they are both looking at the statue, the shot is from behind them to the statue. The reverse shot, from the statue's point of view, is motivated, since the statue is being treated like a character because it is the focus of attention of Karen and Adrian's conversation. In the first of those two shots, Adrian's back is on camera left and Karen's back is on camera right. In the second, Adrian is now camera right and Karen is camera left. When edited together, the two characters in the two shots would jump position on screen, but the physical relationship between the statue and the actors keeps the audience from being disoriented. We can also call this a *reverse master*, which is screen logical because of the location. But then, while looking at the statue, the coverage between the two characters would need to be from either behind them or in front of them in order to maintain logical coverage.

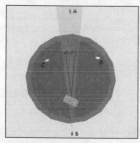

Camera positions

Many types of locations allow you logically to cross the line. For example: a jail cell with people on one side of the bars talking to someone in jail; a window with two or more people looking out of the window and shooting them from behind (inside the room) and from the front (outside the window); a local saloon where two people

Camera A — behind them   (5-3a)

Camera B — jump the line   (5-3b)

Camera C   (5-3c)

Camera D   (5-3d)

are sitting at the bar talking to the bartender and shooting from behind the patrons and from the bartender's perspective from behind the bar. In all of these cases the physical characteristic of the setting that motivates crossing the line logically helps the audience understand the physical relationships.

EYE-LINE

Eye-line is the logical continuity of the look or gaze from one character to another. Eye-line matching is based on the fact that when a character looks at someone in the off-screen space, the audience expects to see what they are looking at. Think of eye-line as the appropriate link to another character. The character is the object, the character looking is the view, and what they are seeing is the other character. Or to put it another way: the subject, the verb, and the object of a visual sentence are linked together by the trajectory of the eyes of the characters. The eye-line between characters is easily established in the wider angles. But as the coverage moves into the tighter angles, directors must maintain and adjust from shot to shot for the correct eye-line that was established in the wider angles. The adjustment for the correct eye-line is determined by the shot, the camera placement in relation to the distance and height of the subject, the depth of field of the lens, and the physical relationship of the actors to one another and to the camera. The difficulty in maintaining the appropriate eye-line comes into play when covering all sides and all angles of a scene. It becomes very difficult when there are multiple characters in the scene, as it is possible for an actor to have different eye-lines for different characters to whom they relate or with whom they have dialogue. Eye-lines are one of the most difficult concepts for new directors to master, because if not done correctly it may appear that while one character is looking into the eyes of the other character, that character is looking at the first character's forehead. Matching eye-line creates order and meaning in the spatial relationships of the characters.

Established eye-line   (5-4a)   Incorrect eye-line   (5-4b)   Correct eye-line   (5-4c)

UNDERSTANDING COVERAGE

One of the issues that affect directors (and others) during production is their perspective on the working physical space. The *reality of the production space* is not the reality of space that the camera creates when it is telling a story. Although the master shot generally allows for the creative environment for the actor to be played out in real time, that reality may not be seen in the shot, so the sense of the physical relationships among the actors established in the master needs to be maintained during camera coverage. But with coverage, the actual sense of space and real time shifts due to camera placement, choice of lens, and depth of field.[5] This juxtaposition of film space and time is intuitive to directors in their storytelling, although it is the stuff that critical film theorists talk and write about. The camera makes its own space. So when deciding coverage and camera placement and lens size, directors and cinematographers must continually adjust and match for the spatial relationships from one coverage shot to another in terms of what the camera is seeing and not to the physical reality of the production space. This often disorients actors (especially non–camera-trained ones), which is why directors must always be cognizant of performances and be sure they are true to the story from the master and the wider angles before further coverage begins. This is because as the camera begins to move in closer to the emotional content of the characters and invade the actor's acting space, the actor's physical reality begins to change. And because of this they rely heavily on the judgment of the director and their own acting tools to sustain and improve their performances as their physical reality shifts.

New directors too often get lost in the physical reality of the production space, thinking it is being duplicated in the camera. But the camera images that make up coverage create their own space, and directors must not be deceived by their own sense of the physical realities of space during production. *The camera image makes its own spatial associations.* If the spatial aspect of where one character is in relation to another character is different through the various coverage shots, then eye-line will shift. And

---

[5] Depth of field is the zone of sharp focus in front of, behind, and around the subject on which the lens is focused. Depth of field is governed by three factors: aperture, lens focal length, and shooting distance. The smaller the aperture, the greater the depth of field. The shorter the lens focal length, the greater the depth of field. The greater the shooting distance, the greater the depth of field. Depth of field is generally deeper in the background than in the foreground. And depth of field decreases with increasing focal length.

as we have already stated, if the eye-line shifts from shot to shot, it will be difficult for an audience to know where people are in a scene. If you decide on the wrong lens or put the camera in the wrong position as it affects the lens, you may again have one character looking at the forehead of another character and not at the other character's eyes. It is important for you—and even more important for your cinematographer—to know and understand the depth of field of fixed lenses and variable focal length lenses and to understand how and where the camera needs to be placed for coverage. It is not a matter of plopping the camera down a few feet from the actor to get a close-up or a medium shot, which is the practice in the "gun and run" or "shoot from the hip" style of directing. This way of working violates all aesthetics for good performances of both the actor and the camera. Although lenses are primarily the domain of the cinematographer, directors must have the knowledge to communicate with their cinematographer. *Lenses and camera position help the director tell the story, and the movie's cinematographer interprets it visually for and with the director.*

Coverage is essential in directing, as it offers the director and editor choices for dramatic and emotional nuances to the story. For example, it can allow for or create the expansion of an emotional or dramatic moment between characters that we may see only briefly in a master shot.

A scene takes place in a tunnel within a baseball stadium after a World Series game. Darren, the team hothead, is leaning on one side of the tunnel wall, bouncing a ball against the opposite wall of the tunnel. James, his teammate, comes walking down the tunnel to confront Darren about a fight in the dugout that happened during the game. As he approaches Darren, he stops for a moment and just looks at him. Darren stops bouncing the ball, looks at James, regretting the conversation to come, then moves to a bench sitting against the opposite wall. James walks over and sits next to him.

The shot is a wide-angle master two-shot shooting down the tunnel and showing the baseball field in the background. Darren is in profile in the foreground, bouncing the ball horizontally across the frame, and James is entering the tunnel toward camera. When Darren moves to sit on the

Diagonal two-shot   (5-5a)

Medium close-up James   (5-5b)

Medium shot Darren (POV)   (5-5c)

Darren looks up   (5-5c)

Medium close-up James   (5-5b)

Medium shot Darren crossing   (5-5c)

Medium close-up James crossing   (5-5b)

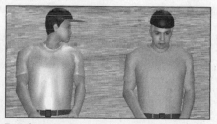

Two-shot   (5-5a)

bench and James moves to sit next to him, the camera dollies in to the two characters, making it a shared medium two-shot.

The action plays very quickly, but there is a brief moment of recognition between the two men at first meeting and a resolution in

Darren to move somewhere and sit to have the dreaded conversation with James. The shot plays as it is, and since it is the beginning of the scene may very well be the choice for the final edit of the scene. But if we shoot a medium shot of Darren from James's perspective as Darren bounces the ball, stops and looks at James, and then crosses to the bench, and shoot a tight shot of James as he stops in the tunnel and looks at Darren and then moves out of the shot and crosses to the bench, the editor will be able to expand that moment of emotional recognition and heighten Darren's trepidation. And since the shot of James is tighter than the shot of Darren, the emotional emphasis will be on James at that moment. The closer the camera gets to the subject, the more (inner) truth it tells. You need only to look to the Odessa Steps sequence in Eisenstein's *Battleship Potemkin* to see what having choices of images—which today we call coverage—can do to heighten a scene and expand an emotional moment.

STANDARD CAMERA COVERAGE

First of all, there is no "standard" camera coverage setup. The coverage of a dramatic scene is dictated by the theme, the emotional elements of the characters, the actors' performances, and the choreographic staging of the actors in relation to the camera. And since coverage does not happen in a vacuum, there is a logic to camera coverage with some basic rules to remember:

1. Do not cut (predetermine) in your head but have a sense of coverage or how a scene can be edited.
2. Do not cut (predetermine) in your head but have a sense of coverage or how a scene can be edited.
3. Do not cut (predetermine) in your head but have a sense of coverage or how a scene can be edited.

Now that *that* issue is clear, there are other concerns to remember:

- Avoid taking two or more shots of the same size from the same angle or approximate angle thinking they are different; the editor will use only one of them. Don't waste valuable time duplicating a shot. Coverage must be looked at very carefully, and no two shots should ever say the same thing. Each must say something different in terms of its relationship to the story, its emotional character content, or its theme.

- Establish depth within the composition of the shot for what is essentially a flat picture. Establishing depth is done not only through production design and lighting but also through diagonal staging; using foreground, middle ground, and background objects or characters in the frame; camera movement or camera positioning; and lens depth of field. Just as actors try to create dimensions to their characters, the camera image should also establish dimensions. Together they will impact the magnitude of your story, making you a superior storyteller.

- In creating coverage, *always* move the camera from one shot to another. Never merely adjust the lens to a different depth of field, as this will offer inaccurate eye-lines and most likely cause a *jump cut*,[6] editorially.

- Although individual shots have internal motivations—such as movement of the actors to encourage movement of the camera—all coverage shots (whether moving or not) are motivated by the story, the characters, or the theme and are either subjective or objective. It is by the use of objective and subjective shots that directors are able to manipulate the emotional connection with the audience. But most important, *do not cut in your head.*

DEGREES OF SHOT SUBJECTIVITY—TWO CHARACTERS

The previous chapter introduced subjective and objective shots. With coverage, directors consider the degrees of subjectivity and how they relate to the logical sequence of shots that cover a scene and tell the story. First, let's look at a simple scene in which two characters are facing and speaking to each other.

---

[6] A jump cut is a transition between two shots in which the image appears to jump, caused by frames that are quite similar. It sets the place above the action, which is contrary to the logic of narrative storytelling. By cutting out the part of the continuity as it relates to screen time, it shows the actor in a similar position in the same frame. Jump cuts can work into the style of the storytelling as in Wayne Kramer's *The Cooler.*

Medium two-shot 90 degrees   (A)

Medium two-shot 65 degrees   (B)

Medium two-shot 45 degrees   (C)

Medium OS shot 20 degrees   (D)

Dirty single 15 degrees   (E)

Close-up 5 degrees   (F)
(5-6 series)

Camera positions

On one side of the diagram you can see the space contiguous to Sandra and the 45-degree area that is considered Sandra's space. Note the camera's positions for the series of two-shots as it moves to look over Sandra's shoulder to her friend Eyan, with whom she is having a conversation. You will see that in each of the shots, as the camera moves closer to Sandra's head (the apex of the 45-degree triangle), the eye-line in the images from Eyan to Sandra move from being objective to subjective until in the final over-the-shoulder shot the audience is very much in Sandra's space. All the shots tell us that Sandra is on the right side of the frame, but with the most objective shot the audience is observing the conversation and with the most subjective shot the audience is participating in the conversation as if they were Sandra. Although the shot is over Sandra's shoulder to Eyan, his eye-line to Sandra leaves the audience in the psychological space of Sandra bringing them closer to the relationship of the two characters. The same would hold true if it were a close-up, with one exception. Having Eyan and Sandra in the frame at the same time in a two-shot and seeing the eye-line between them at the same time illustrates to the audience the physical relationship of one character to another. In the close-up it is only the eye-line that maintains the characters' physical relationship. Appropriate coverage from the over-the-shoulder to the close-up shot requires moving the close-up shot closer to the apex of the axis than the over-the-shoulder shot, with Eyan still looking camera right but more to the right side of the center of the frame. Sandra's close-up would be looking camera left, with the eye-line at the correct matching placement in the frame. The camera position and lens depth of field should match from both sides if possible to preserve the correct eye-line.

Other factors may affect coverage, such as the height of the actors. For example, if Eyan is shorter than Sandra, her over-the-shoulder shot might not be *over* her shoulder but *past* her shoulder, moving on the same 45-degree axis. Eyan's eye-line will be looking camera right, slightly toward the upper right side of the frame because of Sandra's height. But when his close-up is shot, the camera is raised up higher than the over-the-shoulder shot, past the shoulder, so that it approximates what Sandra is seeing from her height. Eyan would still be looking up in the frame, but not as far up as the past-the-shoulder shot. His eye line must establish his physical relationship to Sandra and the fact that she is taller than he is. The opposite would take place with the coverage to Sandra.

(5-7a) (5-7b)

The cinematographer and the director decide camera placement and therefore determine how objective or subjective the coverage shots will be. If the director wants the audience to "view" or "nearly view" the scene, the shot will be objective and the camera will be placed somewhere in the outside ranges of the 45-degree angle. As the coverage for the sequence goes further and further into the relationship of the two characters, the subjectivity increases and the camera positions adjust for that subjective increase. For example, if the director wants to begin the scene with the audience observing the action, the medium two-shot will be just outside the 45-degree angle; then, as the dynamics of the scene and the intensity of the conflict in the relationship increase, the over-the-shoulder shot would be further within the 45-degree angle; finally, to bring the audience into the intensity between the characters, the close-up moves closer to the apex within the 45-degree angle. This would be duplicated for the other character, though perhaps not repeating the objective medium two-shot since we

try to avoid shots from the same approximate angle. Besides, the dynamic coverage is in the subjective shots. This series of shots between two characters addresses to the theme of the scene and the director's interpretive vision, as it pulls the audience into the emotional context of the characters while at the same time providing for many editorial choices.

Camera positions

Can you find which camera in the floor plan above is shooting which shot? (Answer on CD-ROM) (5-8 series)

A word on camera placement for the close-up: as mentioned before, actors' performances must be securely in place once the camera position invades their acting space, since the camera shifts their sense of environmental reality. Camera position for the clean close-up is generally considered the most invasive moment of the actor's performance. Since eye-line is critical in this close-up, directors must find the right eye-line that sets the spatial relationships between characters. In so doing, they position the camera as if it is the character seeing the close-up, and the actor whom the camera is replacing is placed somewhere on the appropriate side of the camera so that the actor whose close-up is being shot has not only the correct eye-line but also their acting partner to play to in the scene. However, that actor placement can be awkward for achieving the correct eye-line, depending on the distance of the camera from the talent and the depth of field of the lens. The acting partner may need to be positioned directly behind the lens (but to the appropriate side of the camera), or the actor in the close-up may need to look at their acting partner's shoulder nearest the camera for the correct eye-line (or at a piece of colored tape placed on the outside perimeter of the camera lens). In these cases, the close-up is difficult for all but the most skilled actors. In the event you decide to shoot the close-up with a very long lens, moving the camera farther away from the actor, and should you be able to put the acting partner closer to the actor, the actor's movements in close-up will still be restricted due to the very narrow depth of field of the lens. The bottom line here is to recognize that in order to achieve the close-up shot you must alter the reality for your actors.[7]

As we have mentioned previously, coverage has logic. Its motivations come from the staging, the actors' performances, and the master shot (if one is used). For example, Edward Albee's play *The Zoo Story* is about a man (Jerry) who, consumed with loneliness, starts up a conversation with another man (Peter) on a bench in Central Park and eventually forces him to participate in an act of violence. At some point during the staging of this scene, Peter is trying to read his book while Jerry is carrying on

Camera positions

a conversation with him. In all probability, the actor playing Peter will be looking at Jerry sometimes and looking at his book other times. The fact that Peter's eye-line shifts in the scene from Jerry to the book provides a motivation to do *two head-on separate close-ups*,[8] a *subjective* one from Jerry's perspective and an *objective* one away from Jerry but subjective from the book's

Can you find which camera in the floor plan above is shooting which shot? (Answer on CD-ROM) (5-9 series)

---

[7] In *Flight Plan* with Jody Foster, the director does a 360-degree medium close-up dolly shot around Jody when she is looking for her missing daughter in the airport. This one shot totally breaks the actor's sense of reality, but her skill and imagination keep her in the moment of truth.

[8] The actor playing the role of Peter must do the moves from the book to Jerry in exactly the same spot on each take for matching and coverage purposes.

perspective. Each close-up means something different in relation to the scene; the first relates to Jerry, and the second does not. And in the editing phase of the project, the power of a close-up lies with the shots that come before it and after it, rather than in the close-up itself.[9]

Directors need to go to the basics to decide what the coverage will be. The theme of the movie or scene, the staging of the actors, the emotional characteristics of the performances, and the master shot (if any) will always provide the route for coverage. Coverage can be simple or complex depending on how the sequence is conceived. Often the scene itself will define the complexity of the coverage; preconceptualized shots can cause problems by forcing the actors into the preconceived camera frames. The director must see the scene staged to actualize how it will be covered. And with luck the preconceptualized idea will manifest itself.

Coverage of a scene changes as more characters are added, and eye-lines shift as the characters relate to one another. The first coverage shot of multiple-character scenes may define the remaining coverage in telling the story. Efficient creative directors understand how one coverage shot can be used (as opposed to "will be used") with another shot without cutting in their heads to tell the story. And it is the director's obligation *always* to tell the story.

THREE-CHARACTER COVERAGE

> From across the street, Robert sees Will and
> Maggie waiting for him so they can go off to
> dinner. He crosses the street to join them. Will
> is about to get into an argument with Robert
> about his relationship with Maggie, but Maggie
> stops him and suggests they go to a quiet café
> to discuss things. They all agree and continue
> down the street to the café where Will is the
> executive chef.

The director stages the scene with Robert walking across the street as he sees Will and Maggie on the street corner. The master shot begins on Robert in a wide angle to show him crossing the street; the camera stays with Robert

---

[9] The constant intercutting of close-ups in a scene may weaken the visual dramatic intent of the close-up, which is to convey the emotional expression of the characters.

as he becomes larger in the frame and then pans and dollies right to a reveal three-shot with Robert crossing to Will and Maggie. The eye-line for Robert to Maggie and Will is from camera right to left, and for Maggie and Will to Robert it is left to right. The scene has only a few lines of dialogue before the three characters move down the street to the café.

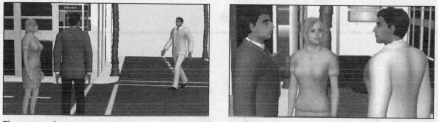

The master shot   (5-10a)   (5-10b)

    The first coverage shot the director decides to do is one that he previsualized and storyboarded before staging the actors because he liked the visual composition; it is a three-shot. The camera is placed behind and between Maggie and Will so that the image is an over-their-shoulder shot to Robert, with Robert in the center of the frame, Maggie's back on camera left, and Will's back on camera right.
Because we overlap action, the actor playing Robert steps into the shot and speaks to Maggie and Will, after which the three of them exit camera left. In this shot, Robert's eye-line is camera left for Maggie and camera right for Will.

(5-10c)

    The master tells us from which direction the coverage ought to go; the first coverage shot on a three- (or more) character scene may define the choices for the remaining coverage shots in telling the story. As mentioned before, efficient directors understand how one coverage shot can be used with another shot without cutting in their heads to tell the story. Keeping this in mind, we can see that this over-their-shoulder three-shot is problematic for any close-up coverage when used with the described master, since it changes the eye-lines that establish the physical relationships among the characters. Using the second three-shot will force the director to shoot coverage so that Robert is always looking camera left for Maggie and camera right for Will. The editor cannot go back invisibly to the master to establish the three characters' physical relationship. It also means that Maggie's close-up coverage will be camera right for Robert and camera left for Will. And Will's close-up coverage will be camera left for Robert and camera right for Maggie. The eye-lines between Maggie and Will in this coverage sequence also become critical in establishing where they are in relation to one another and to Robert, since the physical relationship in the master does not and cannot apply here. If this all looks very confusing, it can be!

Master   (5-10b)

Medium single — Robert   (5-10d)

Two-shot — Will and Maggie   (5-10e)

Three-shot   (5-10b)

This coverage could have been kept very simple if the *two-character over-the-shoulder shot to Robert* was eliminated from the coverage series, as it was an unnecessary (and confusing) medium shot of Robert. Why? Because the scene is a short scene and moves quickly. Instead, a medium shot of Robert looking camera left and a medium two-shot of Will and Maggie looking to Robert camera right would be simpler and more efficient. Closer coverage could then be contained to Robert always looking camera left and Will or Maggie always looking camera right, with the two different appropriate eye-lines in their close-ups to establish where Maggie is to Will and where they are to each other. The scene is a short scene and would not require much more than this. The emphasis toward character can be positioned by the amount of subjectivity in the shots.[10] The director needs to save that "special three-character over-their-shoulders shot" for another time.[11]

In the next scene in the movie, Maggie, Will and Robert are sitting at a café having dinner. The coverage for the scene will depend not only on what their relationship is to one another but also on where they are sitting. Are they in a booth? Are they sitting at a round, square, or rectangular table? Are they at a sushi bar? All of these things the director, and only the director, must take into consideration. For staging towards the thematic elements of the story motivates how the camerawork and coverage is designed. The technical issues of eye-line, crossing the line, and spatial relationships are also issues for a director to consider, but they come from the staging and are concerns of the cinematographer and the continuity person on the production set as well.

CHAPTER FIVE SUMMARY

➤ Directors must never cut in their head but instead must have a sense of montage.

➤ Coverage never happens in a vacuum.

➤ Actor performance and staging motivate the coverage for a scene.

➤ The master shot is the "chart" that directors use to cover a scene.

➤ Creating the master shot may inspire changes to the ideas you bring to the set.

➤ Masters do not have to run throughout the entire scene. They can be broken up in terms of beats.

continued on p. 110

---

[10] In *Closer*, Mike Nichols covers a three-character scene in which he develops two separate two-character over-the-shoulder shots: over Julia Roberts's shoulder to Jude Law and Natalie Portman. One is more subjective than the other. The most subjective two-shot is edited during moments of the scene that develop the secret relationship between Julia Roberts and Jude Law.

[11] In *Jarhead*, Sam Mendes uses this shot as his master shot several times in the movie. His coverage, however, consists of another three-shot with two of the characters on one side of the screen and one of the characters on the other. But the third character moves his head from one of the two characters to the other. No close-ups are done, and editing occurs on the third character's head move, thus making the sequence logical. The performances are strong so the audience is kept in the moment.

continued from p. 109

➤ A master shot that observes the action and moves along with it while observing is called a master that moves.

➤ The moving master image participates as a character rather than as an observer.

➤ Coverage preserves consistent screen direction through the simple logic of understanding the principles of crossing the line.

➤ Eye-line is the logical continuity of the look from one character to another.

➤ The adjustment for correct eye-line is decided by the camera position, the depth of field of the lens, and the physical placement of the actors and the camera.

➤ The camera makes its own space.

➤ Coverage must continually adjust for the spatial relationships from one shot to another in terms of what the camera sees and not the physical reality of the production space.

➤ Coverage can expand the emotional or dramatic moment between characters.

➤ Avoid two or more shots of the same size from the same or approximate angle.

➤ Establish depth within the composition of the shot.

➤ In creating coverage, always move the camera from one shot to another.

➤ All coverage shots are either subjective or objective and motivated by story, characters, or theme.

➤ There are various degrees of shot subjectivity and objectivity, and each has a different impact on the audience.

➤ Directors must see scenes staged to actualize how they will be covered.

➤ Coverage becomes more complex with more than two characters in a scene.

➤ With multiple-character scenes, the first coverage shot after the master sets the course for all coverage shots.

"I knew I needed forty-five days to shoot this film, but we got thirty-five. I had to cut all of my wonderful transitions with characters driving from this place to that because we didn't have the money to film driving scenes. I also knew my actors were really gifted, but we had very little rehearsal time. Also I gave everyone very little notes, almost no input at all. Somehow my actors took the words from the page and walked onto the set and gave them to me fully realized."

— **Paul Haggis**, director, *Crash*

CHAPTER **6**

CAMERA COVERAGE—PART 2

STAGING AROUND A TABLE

One of the biggest problems directors face are scenes with multiple characters around a table. Even when they consider the basics, they often get trapped. The first thing you must consider as director is the shape of the table. A square or rectangular table has corners and sides that help to define where people sit, whereas a round table does not; it is the same from every side of the table. And the size of the table needs consideration. But where people sit in relation to one another is the most important factor of all, and for that you need to look at the story and the relationships of the characters in the scene as this will affect the inner truth in their performances. Are boyfriend and girlfriend sitting next to each other because they are flirting with one another or did they have an argument and are sitting opposite one another with the table as a barrier? Is there someone who needs to be at the head of the table? If it is a family scene, where does each of the family members normally sit at the table? Where do the children sit? In the Thanksgiving dinner scene in *Brokeback Mountain,* Jake Gyllenhaal is sitting at the head and his wife at the foot of a rectangular table. His son is sitting on one side of the table and his in-laws on the other side. The scene involves his father-in-law getting up to carve the turkey as if he were the head of the family. Jake asserts his authority by doing the carving, which puts his father-in-law in his place. Director Ang Lee used this action to effect the theme and purpose of the scene and impact the character Jake played. The physical relationships at the table made it easier for the actors to maintain the environmental truth at an emotional moment in the scene.

Once you have determined the type of table and who sits where, then you need to examine the scene, its contribution toward the theme, and the dialogue and action that transpire at the table. Is the action important to motivate the characters? How do the characters relate to one another? Does the action at the table affect the characters, as it does in the poker game sequences in John Dahl's *Rounders*? How do you cover that action? What is the subtext of the characters in the scene? Which character is the focus of the scene? Answers to these questions and more are at the foundation of any table scene.

Before you decide the visual approach to take with the scene, first decide where your main character (the one who is affected in the scene) is to sit. That character's placement will set the master shot from which screen direction for all other characters at the table should flow. Intuitively or otherwise, the director will find the right place for the camera to cover the scene. What is important is the spatial relationship of one character to another and its preservation for the audience. Spatial relationship addresses screen direction and eye-line, and during a table scene these two elements must be the focus for the director and the continuity person assisting the production. One of the scenes in the movie *Syriana* involves many people sitting around a conference table in heated discussion. Although a master shot of the room, the table, and the many people around it was made, the coverage has no logic of focus and the screen direction of characters editorially is flip-flopped, disorienting the audience. The audience is confused as to who is where and who is talking to whom. In *The 40-Year-Old Virgin*, a scene is staged in a restaurant booth around an oval-shaped table. The central character in the scene is the Steve Carell character, who is sitting on one edge of the booth seat. The camera establishes the guys in the booth with a wide shot in the restaurant. In this shot, Carell is on camera left. The camera then establishes a shot from behind one of the characters sitting in the booth on the right side of the frame in the wide shot, with Carell on camera right. Because of these two shots, the eye-lines and spatial relationships in the coverage within the scene disorient the audience regarding who is where and who is speaking to whom. In the confusion the camera does not maintain the physical relationships of one character to another. The simple solution would have been to avoid the second establishing shot of the guys in the booth and allow the first shot to set the direction for the coverage. Or to put Steve Carell in the middle of the booth with the guys sitting on both sides of him. Since he is the subject of the scene, the coverage would have been simpler having those characters sitting to his right look at him camera right and those to his left look at him camera left. Carell would relate both right and left as needed. And by sitting in the middle, he would feel trapped, which would help his internal truth since it is the subtext of the character in the scene. All of this is insignificant because the scene is so funny nonetheless. But it would have made better visual storytelling.[1]

The first shot, which establishes the table and the people *at* the table, should be your map to maintain continuity and screen direction. It will show you which shots you will need to cover the scene. And always try to establish depth in the image if possible, such as shooting past one character to another or changing how someone sits in the scene. One visual trick is to show something on the table, such as a table centerpiece, that is

Master shot   (6-1a)

OS three-shot   (6-1b)

Medium shot   (6-1c)

Medium shot   (6-1d)

Dirty medium shot   (6-1e)

---

[1] Performances are always the bottom line!

constant in several coverage shots. It can help the depth of the image as a foreground object and ground the audience in knowing where the characters are sitting at the table.

MULTIPLE-CHARACTER SCENES

Every time a character is added to a scene, the coverage can change exponentially. The more complex the coverage, the more difficult it is to preconceive coverage and the more production time it takes to get the coverage to tell the story. Special shots or *beauty shots* should always be kept as additional shots unless they can be interwoven with the basic coverage needed to tell the story. Directors must first stage (choreograph) and motivate the actors in the scene, keeping in mind any of the shots they have preconceived with the hopeful intent of building those shots into the staging. If need be, the camera can be thought of as another actor and often is. If directors see only specific shots and cut in their heads only by shooting from a preconceived storyboard or shot list for scenes that have multiple characters, they will get into a lot of trouble telling the story visually. For the movie *Hunter's Blood,* the first-time feature director had a night scene to do with ten actors. It was an important scene, as it was the pivotal moment in the story when the bad guys discover the good guys and the suspense begins. In his planning for the scene, the director saw a detailed rack focus five-shot at a specific moment within the scene. This was the first shot he staged in the sequence. It was a nice shot, and the actors, although confused, said the lines convincingly, but after it was completed the director needed to stage the actors so the shot would be part of the coverage for the sequence. Staging a scene with ten actors is tough enough, but staging it so that it would make logical editorial sense with a coverage shot done before the staging of the scene, development of the emotional characteristics of the characters, or seeing how the logical choreography of the scene would and could motivate coverage, resulted in a badly directed scene. What coverage there was did not link together smoothly. The director was setting up shots and cutting in his head without overlapping action or seeing the nuances of the spatial relationships of one character to another or understanding how the scene needed to be played for the actors. Had he begun his direction from the standpoint of staging the scene first instead of a special shot, the dynamics and suspense needed for the scene would have been fully envisioned and realized. Instead, as the producer of the movie, I had to pick up at another time an important shot of the bad guys coming upon the campsite and manufacture the suspense in postproduction because the director did not achieve it with his coverage.

Staging a multiple-character scene does not have to be complicated. You just need to go back to the basics: the theme of the scene and coverage as dictated by the emotional elements of the characters, the actors' performances and their relationships to each other, and the choreographic staging of the actors in relation to the camera. The staging needs to have an authentic reality to it to reinforce the environmental truth for the actors. Once you have achieved that, then the camera often finds its own place in the scene, and the scene itself tells you how it needs to be covered. All the storyboarding and shot lists in the world cannot completely help you when you are working with many characters. In *The Godfather Part II*, Francis Ford Coppola was faced with a scene around a rectangular conference table that sits many people, including Michael Corleone (Al Pacino) and Hyman Roth (Lee Strasberg). Cuban President Fulgencio Batista at the head of the table is addressing the group and asking them to look at a solid gold telephone given to him as a gift. Coppola staged the scene by first taking a wide-angle fixed establishing shot and then a series of moving master shots using the telephone passed from one person to the next as a motivation for the move. He also included a fixed camera on the important characters in the scene. When the phone gets to Michael Corleone and Hyman Roth, we can tell by how they pass the phone to the next person what they are *really* thinking. And it isn't about their interest in the phone! This scene has many characters but very little coverage. Its coverage is effective storytelling motivated by the theme and the performances and the size of the table.

COVERAGE PROCESS

Directing coverage involves directors' thought processes and, if need be, their use of personal storyboards and shot lists. Although a storyboard and/or shot list is sometimes created for a specific moment in a scene and privately helps individual directors understand coverage, it must not become the manual for the sequence or for the process of coverage. Today the emphasis on storyboards is so prevalent that directors use them religiously. This is an error that directors should break away from. Doing a specific shot that may be in a shot list or storyboard *only* at a specific line of dialogue is an indication of a director cutting in his or her head. Further, it is not a creative way of eliciting a performance from actors, nor will it give the editor subtle choices with which to tell the story. *Do not cut in your head; rather, have a sense of editing.*

One director I know was covering a complicated scene. In his staging he would have his characters speak to one another, and in his sequence of shots he would do the over-the-shoulder shot of one character, then the over-the-shoulder shot of the other character, then go back to the over-the-shoulder shot of the first character, and so on as his sequence of storyboards directed him. He would then follow a similar process for the close-ups. He would also do the shots only in the sequence on the specific lines of dialogue that he had preconceived, erroneously thinking that this would help performance continuity for the actors. This process of coverage drove the director of photography crazy, as he was continually changing the lights and the camera from one side of the scene to the other and back again. It also disrupted the focus and concentration of the actors since their environmental reality was flip-flopping. If it was confusing to the cinematographer and disruptive to the actors, it was even more confusing to the crew. And more important, it unnecessarily and selfishly extended the amount of time it took to shoot the scene. Directors must always take into consideration an efficient use of time, even if it means putting the burden of maintaining and sustaining performances on their shoulders. Directors must remember that when making movies, the actors are acting for the director and the director is the actors' barometer for their performance.

The coverage process has logic. That logic is directed toward being creative and efficient and is developed through a firm grasp of the theme of the movie or the scene and of the characters' journey through the movie. It is further developed by the need to build on actors' performances within each scene and to maintain, as much as possible, the environmental truth for the actors.

There are some rules regarding the sequence of coverage:

First, after the master shot, always try to work all the coverage from one side of a scene or beat and then work from the other side or sides. This translates into efficient use of production time. It is critical when you have multiple characters in a scene. It may put the burden of sustaining the actors' level of performances on your shoulders, depending on the structure and staging of the scene, but the cost of lost production time working any other way is too great when actors and crew members are being paid.[2]

Second, always work from the wider shot to the tighter shots, playing out as much of the scene as possible in each shot. This will let actors gain confidence in their performances before the camera intrudes on their acting space.

Third, overlap the action of the actor at the start and end of each coverage shot. This not only gives more editorial choices but also provides a physical action for the actor at the beginning of the shot. A physical action, like sitting, standing, drinking, eating, pushing away from, or pulling to, and so forth, always helps an actor find the dramatic impulse needed for the coverage shot, especially if he or she has experienced the environmental truth in other shots.

Fourth, always move the camera from one coverage shot to another coverage shot. Never keep the camera in the same position, thinking that by changing the lens you are changing the shot. It is the angle of the camera to the subject that is more critical to the syntax of film language; even moving the camera a few inches to the left or the right provides for coverage logic and better editing capabilities. The camera can be moved higher and lower as well as left or right, but this is more problematic with coverage since the director and cinematographer must always be looking for a reason for the shot by asking themselves intuitively or logically, "What does the shot mean?"

Fifth, always keep in mind how one coverage shot can be (or will be) used with another coverage shot. This does not mean cutting in one's head. It means having a sense of the possibilities of how the shot can be used with others that are done. Also, when the sequential coverage of a scene is from the wider angles to the closer angles as mentioned above, the sequence will be easier to grasp, as the wider angle will be freshest in the director's mind. It will also help maintain the eye-line, since the approximation of the eye-line moves from shot to shot. It has focus in a multiple-person shot, but in a close-up you must approximate the eye-line to where the other characters are located outside camera range.

Sixth, always know how long the shot is to last by finding the correct stopping point. Generally (but not always) the correct stopping point is

---

[2] Directors have an obligation to finish a day's work within a sensible twelve-hour workday, including setup and strike.

when the action changes and the character moves out of the shot.[3] In some instances the stopping point can be a change in a character's eye-line. For example, a scene calls for Tito and Erica to be sitting at a table, and at the end of the scene Tito stands and moves to the side of Erica and continues the conversation from a standing position. When covering the scene and bringing the audience into the relationship of the two characters while they are sitting, the single on Erica is from Tito's sitting position. Once Erica's eye-line shifts to where Tito stands, the single on Erica is covered from Tito's standing position. However, if Tito stands *by his chair or pushes the chair back and stands where the chair was* when he gets up, the single of Erica when Tito is sitting can also be used for Tito when he is standing since Tito is physically in the same location as his chair. It will be Erica's eye-line that shifts to place Tito standing. But when we come around to the other side for the single on Tito, there will be two shots from Erica's perspective: one with Tito sitting and one with him standing. Thus the eye-lines will all match. *And it can be seen once again that staging may dictate how a scene is covered.*

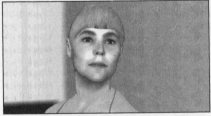

Erica sitting looking at sitting Tito   (6-2a)

Tito sitting looking at sitting Erica   (6-2c)

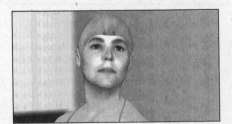

Erica sitting looking at standing Tito   (6-2b)

Tito standing looking at sitting Erica   (6-2d)

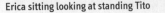

[3] The points when you start a shot and when you end a shot are not the points of dialogue that you have predetermined will be edited in the scene. This is cutting in your head. Directors look for physical action to start and stop the shot whenever possible.

Seventh, when developing the coverage for a scene, you must make each of the coverage shots as long as the shot will logically carry itself, even if your shot list or storyboard did not call for it. In other words, do not cut in your head by shooting the shot only for the duration of script that you *think* you want to use in the edited movie. Many directors end up going back to do pickups because they worked this way. Film stock is the cheapest commodity, and if you are shooting digitally, who cares how much stock you use? If you don't have the shot, you can't use it. So get it the first time.

Finally, keep the camera in front of the action. When the camera is behind the action it only increases the amount of coverage you need to do to tell the story, and more than likely your shots from behind the action will not be used. You will also be missing wonderful nuances of emotional character development from the actors. The action is determined by the movement and focus the characters in the scene undertake in staging.

BEST CAMERA POSITION

In interpreting a scene you are limited only by your imagination. *Creative directors try to set the location, theme, or mood of the narrative by the design of their shots whenever possible.* The shot does not have to begin necessarily on the principal action of the scene but might employ peripheral action as a motivation to arrive at principal action. For example, the director stages a medium shot of a waitress coming out of the kitchen with some food, and the camera dollies with her as she crosses to a table, where it settles on a two-shot of Tito and Erica deep in concentration, enjoying their meal.

When a shot is planned in a director's imagination, it can get them into trouble because the director may come to the set forcing the staging into the imaginary shot, and the angle of the shot may not necessarily be the best camera angle after the scene is staged. Often, directors are stuck in a visual mode and can't get beyond that. They place the camera either behind the central action (movement) of the scene or as if the camera is front row center in a theater with actors making entrances stage right (camera left) and stage left (camera right). You have to look carefully at the structure and choreography of the scene to find the best camera position. Best position refers to that camera position or shot that communicates the director's intent for the scene. Usually the scene itself will reveal it to you. Your cinematographer, whose major responsibility is to help interpret the movie visually, will be of great assistance in shaping your visual intuition of the sequence and will assist you in determining the best position for the camera. Your ability to be open and inspired may reveal it to you.

SPATIAL REALITIES OF COVERAGE AND DIRTY SHOTS

The composition of coverage shots has a major impact on storytelling. The spatial characteristic tells the audience what the physical relationship is between objects or actors in a scene and can address the theme or the psychological and emotional aspects of the characters. The physical reality of the staging is not always the spatial reality in the image, since depth of field and positioning of the camera in association with the subject creates its own space and will impact the composition.[4]

When directors storyboard a shot, they often don't think about how to stage that shot and set up the physical reality needed for the actors. Additionally, they fail to develop the spatial relationships necessary for the shot. This can be accomplished by developing naturalistic staging while maintaining any visual plans for the camera. The camera will find its own place in the scene as long as you are aware that the camera will be placed either as an observer, a voyeur, or a character in the scene and the motivations for each shot will fall within one of those parameters. It will be how they are used together that will allow for story dynamics.

When you are set on the staging and have determined how you will cover the scene, you need only to look at the physical spacing of the actors to see whether or not a shot is to be *dirty*. A *dirty shot* is a shot that focuses on a person or persons in the frame while at the same time showing a very small part of someone else in the foreground of the image. It is as if the camera is sitting on the shoulder or at the cheek of the foreground character as opposed to being behind the foreground character. There is not enough seen to call it anything else but *dirty*, so we refer to it as a *dirty shot*. Note: If we clearly see enough of the foreground person so that the camera placement is directly behind them, then it becomes a two-shot or an over-the-shoulder shot.

---

[4] The legendary director Alfred Hitchcock was a master of composition in telling a story. In *Dial M for Murder*, Hitchcock used an oversized telephone in the foreground of a shot that matched the real telephone in the master. The audience was not aware that it was oversized; they only saw the phone as representative of an ominous character that brought horror and fear to its owner.

Dirty medium shot   (6-3a)
Image tighter on Tito than OS

Over-the-shoulder — two-shot   (6-3b)
Image wider on Tito than dirty shot

The dirty shot can help set the spatial relationships between characters. For example, if the shot from one character to the subject of the image (the other character) is a dirty medium shot, then the close-up of the subject would be clean. Coverage can become disturbing when the spatial relationship is not logical. Again, you need only to look at the physical proximity of one actor to another to determine whether a close-up must be dirty. If the actors are two feet or less away from one another, then in all likelihood the dirty close-up is used. If you are not sure whether a close-up should be dirty, stand in the exact space of one of the actors and see what he or she sees of the other actor in the scene. If you don't see more than the face from forehead to chin, then the close-up (*head to shoulders*) is dirty. But the extreme close-up from forehead to chin is clean.

Dirty close-up   (6-4a)

Extreme close-up   (6-4b)

You should not be afraid to use dirty shots when appropriate, as dirty shots are dynamic and offer the audience a view of the physical and spatial realities of the characters.

REVERSE ANGLES, STAGING, AND EMOTIONAL MOMENTS

Being able to visualize all angles and shots from all sides of a scene and to make the choices for coverage is crucial to directing. But most directors see only opposite angles (as opposed to reverse angles) in relation to the context of the dialogue from one or two perspectives. This is especially true of new directors, as they are usually fixated on storyboards and shot lists and are blind to the scene that unfolds during staging and rehearsal.[5] Perhaps conditioned to look at drama as television narrative,[6] many beginning directors never see the myriad possibilities that coverage can offer them.

> Delphine comes out of the apartment and walks down her fire escape stairs with her suitcase. She pauses briefly on the landing at the top of the last flight as she sees her sister, Barbara, sitting on the stairs at the bottom of the flight. In the previous scene inside the apartment they had a hurtful argument concerning Delphine's departure. Delphine continues down the stairs and the scene continues at the bottom of the fire escape.

The director decides to do a master shot with Barbara in the foreground at the bottom of the flight and Delphine coming down the stairs behind her, over Barbara's shoulder. In the staging Delphine pauses briefly on the landing before continuing down the stairs, remembering the argument that she and her sister had a few moments earlier inside the apartment. The master shot ends in a two-shot with the sisters at the bottom of the stairs having a discussion. After the master, the director does the coverage at the bottom of the stairs, as indicated by his shot list, finding shots that are within the sisters' relationship—thus, in his mind, completing the scene. However, if the director had looked carefully at the staging instead of his shot pattern, he might have seen a low *reverse angle* from the top of the landing behind Delphine as she came into frame and paused with trepidation when she saw her sister. He might also have seen a medium shot

---

[5] Storyboards and shot lists condition directors to see coverage one way.

[6] Coverage in a television narrative single-camera show is limited because of the time it takes to do the show. An hour television show is shot in six or seven days, and the coverage is deliberately limited so that there are not a lot of choices available to the editor and the show can be completed quickly for airing.

of Delphine as she pauses at the top of the stairs, as well as Delphine's point of view of Barbara sitting at the bottom of the landing. These three shots might editorially have opened up an emotional moment for Delphine, and the audience, for the scene to come at the bottom of the stairs.[7]

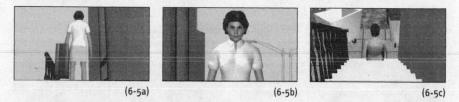

(6-5a)   (6-5b)   (6-5c)

If the director were truly watching the actress's performance, he would have noticed that her pause meant something emotionally to her relationship with her sister. Choices!

As a rule of thumb, if one character is watching something or someone in the scene, it is probably a good idea to get a shot of the character looking and a shot of what the character is looking at. It may not be part of the planned coverage, but it becomes coverage that is organic from the staging. Most of the time you will find that this coverage can be used to expand an emotional moment for the character and the story.

These shots are sometimes referred to as emotional *cutaways*. There is another form of a cutaway that is organic to the staging of the scene, called *inserts*. Inserts are images that may not have a direct correlation to the emotional intent of the scene but are part of the scene. They might be something as simple as hands that are held between two characters, which tell the audience about their tenderness for each other. In *The Zoo Story* example earlier, there could be an insert of the book that Peter is reading. You may not know how it can be used editorially in the scene, but your instinct tells you that it might be used somehow. This insert can be done from outside the relationship of the two characters or from either character's perspective. They each could mean something different to the story when it comes to an emotional moment. For example, we see Peter's book in *The Zoo Story* from the objective perspective, from Peter's perspective, and from Jerry's perspective. Each means something slightly different when edited in the sequence.

Emotional moments from actors inspire directors to see coverage differently. The planned medium close-up on an actor's speech might

---

[7] This is not cutting in one's head but seeing coverage that could allow for emotional options.

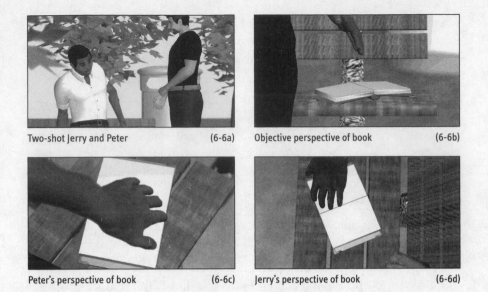

Two-shot Jerry and Peter   (6-6a)   Objective perspective of book   (6-6b)

Peter's perspective of book   (6-6c)   Jerry's perspective of book   (6-6d)

become a medium close-up that dollies into a close-up. Or the way the actor emotes during the dialogue may inspire the director to shoot an unplanned extreme close-up on the same emotional speech. Directors should always look for those moments and, through inspiration, be free enough to improvise so the coverage can become one with those moments.

COVERAGE AND CONTINUITY

As a rule, coverage shots should *overlap action* as much as possible. That is to say that each shot should start with some kind of physical action, whether it is the two-shot, the single, or the close-up. It not only gives more editorial choices but also provides a physical action for the actors to help them find the impulse that provides their motivation, since physical action will always cause an impulse (or physical reaction) in an actor. All action by an actor in a scene should be duplicated at the same place in the scene on each take of a shot and on all coverage shots that show the action. This will help match continuity for editing purposes. However, many directors like to give a certain degree of freedom to their actors and may not insist upon this. They are comfortable with the editor editing around the continuity issues. In the scene from the movie *The Score*, discussed in chapter 3, the drinking and hand motions of Marlon Brando were different in each take, but because Brando and Robert De Niro were in synchronicity with one another and playing new discoveries on each take, the scene always flowed smoothly. The edited scene in the movie uses moments from a couple of the takes.

Overlapping action is not always possible, especially when the shot is a close-up or an extreme close-up or is shot with a long lens that has a narrow depth of field. In those instances, a lift of the head or an eye movement may be all that is needed for the actors to establish their own reality to help them get into the beat of the moment. It also gives the editor the head or eye movement that might be used editorially in the scene. A wise director will always go back to basics to set the environmental reality for the actors and revert to the actors' greatest tool when the camera invades their acting space: their imagination.

Continuity of physical action is important not only for the actor but also for the visuals. There must be a visual continuity to the physical action, since it ultimately affects editorial choices and defines the spatial and physical movements of the actors. For example, if an actor exits a shot camera left in one physical space, then he needs to enter the next sequential shot in that space camera right. Entering camera left sequentially will disorient the audience. However, if a character exits a shot moving away from camera in the center of the frame, on the next sequential shot he can enter either camera right or camera left since the audience saw him leave the space from a neutral perspective. These issues of shot continuity are examined while they are being completed by the continuity person on the set, who functions as a check and balance for the director in this matter. Continuity also relates to such issues as dialogue, wardrobe, and props, and is looked for by the on-set continuity person and individual production department heads and should not be the concern of the director unless there is a problem. The continuity person should be on top of *all* continuity issues.[8] The continuity person is also the link to the editorial process and therefore must be on top of the elements when they are done on the set.

---

[8] Continuity is more than keeping track of the characteristics of each camera shot. It also involves the check and balance system of the single-camera narrative process for assurance of accurate matching (same) dialogue, action, and eye-line from shot to shot. Continuity people (as all other production positions) must only advise the director of the status of a situation and let the director make the decision as to what to do.

SELECTIVE COVERAGE AND MISCELLANEOUS COVERAGE ISSUES

Your knowledge of coverage, without editing the movie in your head, and with a sense of the possibilities for editorial choices, should be kept in your mind, giving you an idea of how you may want a scene to turn out. This thinking will prevent you from overdoing your coverage, which burns up not only production time but also your actors, who are trying to give you good performances on each take.[9] But be sure you have every possibility you may need to cover a scene, with the master shot first, followed by over-the-shoulders, or medium shots, then close-ups or extreme close-ups, for every beat of the scene. As directors are always working against time on the set, they may need to cut corners with their coverage plans or determine the *selective coverage* as it relates to a scene. Selective coverage comes from your analysis of the scene, its theme, its characters, and the elements of greatest importance. Focus your detailed coverage on that crucial segment, leaving the rest of the scene with minimum coverage.

Saving time on a set is always a director's dilemma. One way to save time is to be efficient with camera placement.

```
Tom and Trish are on backyard patio chairs, deep
in dialogue. Tom gets very upset with Trish and
stands glaring down at her. He towers over her
to demonstrate the authority he has in their
relationship.
```

The director planned on getting coverage of Trish from Tom's eye-line when he was seated and, by raising the camera, again when he was standing.

Tom's perspective seated   (6-7a)   Tom's perspective standing   (6-7b)

---

[9] On one project from my early days, I was working with the great star Bette Davis, and although she gave excellent performances on the master and all the coverage shots, she gave a brilliant performance on her close-up. When I asked her why she saved the brilliant performance for the close-up, she said matter-of-factly, "Because I want you to use it!"

The director wanted to show by the angle of the shot to Trish when Tom is standing that Tom thinks he has the power in the scene.

But the first assistant director tells the director that the actors have to be dismissed in fifteen minutes, and the director can get only one of the two coverage shots in that amount of time. The director is faced with the decision as to which one. The solution to the predicament is for the director and the cinematographer to determine the best camera height on Trish when Tom is sitting, the best camera height on Trish when Tom is standing, and to choose a camera height in between the two. It isn't the best for both needed positions, and it's not the ideal conceptual choice, but for this problem it is the obvious and effective solution.

Solution to time problem　　　　(6-7c/d)

Sometimes a director is faced with the possibility of doing coverage for one side of a scene on one day and the other side of the scene on another day, in different but similar locations. This can happen more times than one would like to admit. On these occasions, necessity can be the mother of invention, and with a little imagination and forethought a solution is not far off. In the previous scenario:

```
Tom towers over Trish who gets furious at him and
pulls a revolver from her purse and points it at
Tom.
```

The director has time to cover only the close-up and medium shot of Trish from the compromised camera position and chooses to do so with the barrel of the gun in the foreground pointing camera right at Tom. The next day the production is scheduled to move to another location, and another scene for Tom is scheduled but without Trish. But also on the next day the director does a reverse medium shot of Tom that was to have been shot the day before. The shot is done with the background behind Tom out of focus and the same prop gun in the foreground, but this time from the back of the gun as it is being held by a stand-in duplicating Trish's hand. Although covered at different times in different locations, the gun becomes the neutral object that blends both shots together. Of course, the director also does a close-up of Tom from this angle without the gun in the shot to ensure that the emotional dramatic moment can be edited in the scene.

The *rack focus* shot is a favorite shot of certain directors and film students, as it is a shot in which the focus is changed mid-shot, when the director wants to shift the attention from one object or character to another. A rack focus shot has two objects: one object is in the background, and one is in the foreground. The object in the background is in focus, while the object in the foreground is out of focus. Or vice versa. It is generally done with a long lens and must be carefully orchestrated and motivated by either the movement of the actor or a line of dialogue.[10] Rack focus shots, like all visually technical images, must be invisible. And they will be as long as they have motivation and are logical to the spatial and character relationships of the scene.

TWO-CAMERA NARRATIVE COVERAGE

Many producers of television movies and television series pilots who have limited budgets and are on limited production schedules require their directors to shoot coverage using a two-camera narrative technique. This technique uses two cameras simultaneously to shoot coverage. When employing it, directors must be inventive yet simple in staging, and cinematographers must be aware that they are lighting for two cameras for each setup, as opposed to just one camera. The cameras are used side by side in most cases, but never for the same size shot. Their placement relative to each other is critical, as it affects lens size, depth of field, and eye-lines. For example, in simple two-character coverage, the two cameras would be next to each other, with one set up to do an over-the-shoulder and the other to do a dirty close-up.

---

[10] *Rack focus* shots were used in the 2005 season of *The West Wing*, at the end of the show in which Alan Alda as the Republican candidate for president is about to go out and debate Jimmy Smits, the Democratic candidate. There is a tight profile shot of Alda as he looks camera left waiting in the wings to go to the stage, and he turns his head up to camera and the lens rack focuses on Smits, also waiting. The shot is duplicated in reverse from Smits to Alda.

Camera A   (6-8a)   Camera B   (6-8b)

2-camera coverage floor plan

Recognition of the subjective and objective relationship of one image to another becomes crucial in this situation. For example, if a close-up is to be a clean, subjective close-up in which the actor is looking directly into the frame, this close-up cannot be shot with the two camera technique but must be shot by itself, because the camera *becomes* the character seeing the close-up. Shooting two-camera narrative film style is a technique that should be used only when faced with time limitations that cannot be resolved any other way or on sequences where the director feels strongly that the actors cannot duplicate the emotion of their performances through many takes. In another chapter we will discuss using *multiple* cameras in various situations around single camera narrative film style directing.

THE "WHAT IF?"

Good directors think on their feet. Production is the most volatile phase of moviemaking, and many problems occur that are out of the director's control—problems that can affect the coverage. It takes directorial skill to think on the fly and solve coverage problems. Solutions come from inspiration, which happens when the director has firm control of the project. And directors find inspiration silently (or vocally) by asking themselves "what if?" This question keeps the internal creative process ever challenged. It is the search for the best results on the set. The production process is about coverage. And coverage is about the camera. And the camera is about the actor eliciting truth. And directors thinking "what if" is a method of finding that truth. *What if* the camera pushed in at this moment? *What if* you started the scene adjusting the model and then went over to the easel? *What if? What if? What if?* The "what if" comes from intuition—your intuition. And if you keep asking yourself, your actors, or your cinematographer "what if," you will nurture your own creative inspiration. If you lock yourself to preconceived ideas of shot lists and storyboards, you hinder your inspiration. From inspiration you find the layers of truth that you need in storytelling during the coverage process. So don't be afraid to ask the voice inside of you very loudly, *what if?*[11]

Coverage is one of the building blocks of storytelling. It is a building block that is handed off to the editor, who should be considered an amazing resource for the director. Editors must have a kinship with directors in terms of the story and their taste. They have an incredible objectivity as they look at your footage, since they know the movie only from what they see and not from how it got there. They are only as good as the footage you give them, and hopefully they will see in your coverage the layering of the story.

CHAPTER SIX SUMMARY

➤ Where people sit at a table in relation to one another is important. Decide on where the main character sits at a table scene in order to determine how to use the camera in the scene.

➤ Every time a character is added, the coverage can change exponentially.

➤ Special shots or beauty shots should always be kept as additional shots to coverage.

➤ Storyboard and shot lists must not be the manual for the sequence of coverage.

➤ Do not cut in your head but rather maintain a *sense* of editing.

➤ After the master, work coverage from one side of a scene first and then the other side.

[11] To implant one of your own ideas into the actor's mind, make a suggestion using the words "what if" so that the actor can think about it and eventually make your idea his/her own. Norman Jewison did exactly this when he suggested to Topol that he touch his hat during one scene in *Fiddler on the Roof:* "What if you touched your hat like this?"

- ➤ Always do coverage from wide to tight shots, remembering to overlap action at the beginning and end of each shot.
- ➤ Always move the camera from one coverage shot to another coverage shot.
- ➤ Always keep in mind how coverage shots can be used with one another.
- ➤ Always know how long the shot is to last by knowing the correct stopping point.
- ➤ Continue coverage shots for as long as each shot will logically carry itself out.
- ➤ Keep the camera in front of the action.
- ➤ The choreography of the scene will show you the best camera position.
- ➤ The physical reality of the staging is not always the spatial reality in the image.
- ➤ The placement of the camera will be either as an observer, a voyeur, or as a character in the scene.
- ➤ A dirty shot focuses on a person in the frame while at the same time showing a very small part of someone else in the foreground.
- ➤ The dirty shot can help set the spatial relationships between characters.
- ➤ Inspiration on emotional moments permits you to improvise coverage.
- ➤ Continuity of physical action is important for actors and the camera.
- ➤ Selective coverage and camera positions can save time.
- ➤ Asking *what if?* nurtures inspiration.
- ➤ Good directors think on their feet.

CHAPTER 7

MOVING SHOTS AND SEQUENCES

The last two chapters introduced you to the complexity and logic of camera coverage and its orientation toward the theme. I talked about the visual language of storytelling and how it fits into direction. This chapter includes further discussion of several of the moving shots that make up camera coverage, their difficulties, and different ways these shots can look into a scene.

DOLLY SHOTS

We have mentioned the dolly shot in several chapters in this book, since the dolly is the primary method of moving a camera smoothly through a scene. It allows the audience to move as either an observer or a participant and therefore is a critical component in the director's creative work. To reiterate, a dolly shot, often referred to as a trucking or tracking shot, occurs when the camera is placed on a moving platform and moves alongside the action, generally following a moving figure or an object. It is a very natural shot, as it invites the audience to see the action through the eyes of the camera as it *walks* or *runs with* or *follows* actors for a short distance. To best visualize what a dolly shot might look like you have only to look at something across a room and then walk, staying focused on that item, and notice that objects go by you as you move closer to the subject. Through a dolly move directors can follow action in a scene in a precise, natural way.

Dolly shots can be characterized in several ways:

- A *character dolly* is used to focus on one or more characters in a scene and is commonly known as a *push-in* movement. The camera may start on a full or medium shot and is slowly pushed forward to a close-up or an extreme close-up, the lens adjusted for the depth of field as it moves. Push-ins, when motivated, can magnify a character's emotion and heighten a dramatic moment in the story. If the push-in is fast, it could heighten a comedic moment as well, since the fast movement adds to the rhythm and timing that are necessary for comedy.

- A *pull-back reveal dolly* is used to reveal the full extent of a scene and is often the basis for a moving master or a master shot that moves. For example, the camera is focused on a child crying in a stroller in front of a grocery store on a New York street. The shot pulls back to reveal the child alone and the stroller unattended as the pedestrians move quickly along the street while paying no attention to the child. The audience gets a sense of the fear of the child and the cold-heartedness of the people passing by.

- A *depth dolly* is used when characters move toward or away from the camera. With this type of dolly shot, the camera can move past other characters or objects that may temporarily block the field of view, helping to establish depth in the scene. Or the narrative of the scene can be such that the shot starts on the actors in a wide medium shot and, as the actors move toward the camera, the dolly moves either away from or toward the actors. In the latter situation, the actors get larger in the frame, and the dolly shot ends on a tight shot of the actors at the most dramatic moment in the scene.

- A dolly that moves contrary to the flow of the action from the main actors is called a *counter dolly* and lets the audience participate in the action as if it were passing by and had stumbled on the scene.

- An *open-out dolly* follows the character who is moving away from the camera, and as the camera moves forward the actor walks away faster than the camera is moving. The audience becomes a character (participates) and immediately feels distanced from the character walking away. Directors use this type of dolly shot to end a scene or, conversely, might reverse this shot to introduce a character to a scene.

- A *tighten-in dolly* shot moves the camera forward as the character moves toward the camera. A form of a counter dolly, this type of shot makes a simple action more dramatic by combining two opposite actions. A variation of this dolly could have the character move toward the camera while the camera performs the dolly and pans up revealing the actor.

Dolly shots are the mainstay of most projects because of what they offer the director in terms of visual storytelling. The speed of the dolly, and thus of the movement, has intent since in most instances it tells the audience how to view the scene. A fast dolly movement means something different from a slow one. In that regard, the dolly grip, whose job it is to move the camera dolly, must be tuned in motivationally to the actors. In all situations, the dolly movement must be motivated, and the motivations come primarily from the theme, the staging of the actors, or the internal emotions of the characters.

To reiterate what was mentioned earlier, directors must stage the end of the dolly shot first and then, working backward, stage each movement of the dolly while adjusting actors and/or the dolly for the movement and shot. But wherever the dolly stops during its path and becomes a fixed camera is generally where coverage takes place, as it is very difficult (but not impossible) to match coverage on a continuously-moving dolly shot. Of course, the choice of coverage at these times is motivated by the performance of the actors and the theme of the scene. A smart director will find moments when the dolly movement can stop during the shot and then move again. This will allow the editor to use the better performances from the moving portions (from multiple takes of the shot) to enhance the sequence and the story while using the coverage to link the moving portions together.

Finally, the staging and rehearsal of dolly shots take a long time to set, rehearse and execute. Actors must be mindful that they are motivating the movement of the dolly and the camera. They must be attentive not only to the relationships they are playing with one another but to the mechanics of the shot, and they must make the latter invisible so that the former can result in a natural performance. Once you have approved (and printed) a take of a dolly shot, it is always a good idea to ask your continuity person what the length of time was to complete the shot from the time you said "action" to the time you said "cut." Then do a second take and this time ask everyone to move more quickly. The reason: dolly shots projected onscreen never play as quickly as you thought they did when they were performed on the set. Therefore, by doing another take of the dolly shot faster than the one approved, you will protect the editorial rhythm of the scene in postproduction.

HAND-HELD SHOTS

It was sometime in the middle 1960s that the synchronous motion picture camera became smaller and lighter and directors and cinematographers began to experiment with hand-held techniques in shooting narrative. But do not confuse a hand-held shot with doing a shot hand-held; the two are not the same. The *hand-held shot* gives a jerky, ragged effect that is totally at odds with the organized smoothness of a dolly shot and allows the audience to take part in the story in a much different way than they are generally used to. Doing a shot hand-held, on the other hand, is sometimes the choice of a director for the sake of expedience. This is especially likely when the camera and its operator need to work in tight areas where a tripod or another camera mount cannot fit. Today, the true hand-held technique (sometimes called a documentary style) is favored by directors who seek a gritty realism or a disjointed, documentary, reality feel to their projects. Like any other shot, the hand-held shot should be motivated by the story or theme, as in the case of *The Blair Witch Project* or sections of Steven Soderbergh's *Traffic*. The same theories of coverage, eye-line, spatial relationships, and crossing the line apply to the hand-held style, but continuity may be affected. And since many times the hand-held shot permits the audience to participate as a character, actors need to be more aware of the camera and what it is doing than they would be if the shot were fixed on a tripod. Finally, directors who mix the techniques of the fixed shot with the hand-held are faced with the additional problem of finding the motivation to go from one technique to the other smoothly and invisibly. It can be done, but again, it must be motivated by the theme, the story, and the emotional nature of the characters, as Soderbergh demonstrated so smoothly in *Traffic*.

STEADICAM SHOTS

In the late 1970s an Oscar-winning camera control device was invented that has profoundly influenced the look of both feature films and television. It is a device on which the camera is mounted that is worn by an operator and allows the director to create shots that have the ability to *float* through space without physical constraints. This is accomplished through the use of gyroscopic motion to counter any irregularities in a camera operator's movement. It is not just a mount worn by an operator but a motorized, multi-directional, DC-powered mechanical arm that links a padded vest in the camera operator's body with a sensitive *gimble* used for fingertip control of the camera head's pans and tilts. With a *steadicam,* a director can float the camera (and by extension, the audience) into a forest, through a crowd of people, or down into a cavern or turn the audience 180 degrees on its head. Used in television shows such as *ER* and *The West Wing*,[1] the steadicam puts the audience in the middle of the action as if it were another character in the show. Operating a steadicam is one of the most difficult jobs on a production and is done by an expert who has his or her own steadicam gear. For a typical steadicam shot, the camera operator must follow a predetermined path and simultaneously adjust the camera and avoid any obstacles while supporting more than sixty pounds of camera gear. The role of the operator not only requires great physical stamina but also calls for excellent abilities in shot composition. The director plans the shot with the steadicam operator and rehearses the actors, but the steadicam operator must execute the shot while the director watches on a hand-held-video monitor.

The best technique for steadicam operation depends entirely on the nature of the shot. To film a simple conversation between two actors, the operator may try to replicate the even feel of a dolly shot, keeping the camera perfectly level and moving slowly around or with the action. In this

---

[1] The productions of *ER* and *The West Wing* are designed around the use of a steadicam to give a certain look to the series. Sets are built to accommodate the space and hide lights, and actors are trained to motivate and work with the steadicam. Television shows use the same crews from episode to episode, and the cinematographer is helpful in the staging. The directors rotate in from show to show.

case the steadicam goes where a dolly and dolly track cannot. For a *flying sequence* over low ground, the director may want the operator to tilt the camera intentionally from side to side, creating a soaring effect. Steadicam shots, just like any other shots, need motivating. One of the most common uses of the steadicam is to track actors from the front as they move around obstacles or through complex, connecting locations. A shot such as this can be considered objective, as it views the narrative as it is taking place. For this sort of shot, the operator may walk backward through the scene with the careful help of other crew members. If the shot follows the actors, then the shot becomes subjective and is a participant in the scene. For this sort of shot the operator walks forward with the crew working together to make it happen. A complicated steadicam shot may do both. Steadicam shots should not be looked at as substitutes for dolly shots. They usually do not involve coverage when the shot is moving, but like a dolly shot, coverage can be developed when the shot stops moving. Coverage then follows the same principles as other shots.

There are some difficulties with steadicam shots that may hamper the creativity of the director. *First,* actors must be rehearsed in their staging corridor for the shot. They must perform it naturally, and their timing, rhythm, and pacing of dialogue and emotional intent must be realistic, as it is rare to be able to enhance their performance with editorial coverage. Developing an environmental atmosphere for the actors to work in will be extremely helpful. Background and foreground action of atmosphere characters (extras) must be carefully orchestrated as well. *Second,* actors must be aware of the shot and their physical limitations within the shot while they are moving. They must know their dialogue and pace themselves in relation to the steadicam, which may be difficult for some actors. *Third,* the steadicam mechanism and operator invade the actors' space, and actors must be comfortable with their environmental truth so they do not lose their focus while countless people are moving in front of them. *Fourth,* interior (and to some degree exterior) steadicam shots must be lit, and the lights must be placed carefully in specific locations for a steadicam shot.[2] This adds additional time to the production schedule. *Fifth,* steadicam shots take a lot of time and run off a lot of film. Although steadicams are the norm on big production shoots, they

---

[2] A certain amount of room in the frame must be given to the operator for the "floating" effect of the image, so the lighting has to be designed for that improvisational framing margin during the shot.

are used minimally on lower budget projects, and a director should decide when it will be a cost-effective, creative element in telling the story and then find a way to use it. *Steadicam shots should not be looked at as substitutes for dolly shots or hand-held shots.* It is true that steadicam shots have helped create some of the most memorable shots in film history, such as the steadicam shot Stanley Kubrick used in *The Shining* to zip down hallways of a haunted hotel or to follow Jack Nicholson through a snowy hedge maze. And of course, the memorable one that Martin Scorsese used to establish mood and setting in *GoodFellas,* which brings the audience into the bustling Copacabana restaurant in a single five-minute shot that begins on an exterior street at night and follows Ray Liotta through the back door of the club, through the kitchen, and into the club where he is given first-class treatment over bustling, waiting patrons as the club arranges a table for him ringside to a performing Henny Youngman. Absolutely one of the most mesmerizing sequences in the movie, and one that took a massive amount of set up time, crew personnel, orchestration, and rehearsal to accomplish.

CRANE AND JIB SHOTS

A *crane shot* is a shot with a change in framing rendered by having the camera above the ground and moving through the air in any direction. It is basically a dolly shot in the air that can move up, down, left, right, swoop in on dramatic action, or move diagonally out of it. Crane shots are accomplished by placing the camera on a large cantilevered arm or similar device, which is sometimes referred to as a *jib arm.* Most cranes accommodate both the camera and an operator, but some can be operated by remote control.[3] Cranes and jib arms move the camera into difficult-to-access places. For example, a scene may start high up in the trees and move down to focus on an action taking place on the ground. An obvious and common use of a crane shot is to view the actors from eye level and move above them and then away from them to show the actors in relation to where they are. This is a common way to end a scene as it gives a visual and sometimes emotional cap to the narrative while giving the viewer a feeling of omniscience over the characters. As *dolly shots in the air,* crane shots can also be used to achieve a flowing rhythm as they lend the camera

---

[3] *To Live and Die in L.A.* has some spectacular shots during the car chase that used remote cranes.

a sense of mobility for a long take, as in the opening sequence of Robert Altman's *The Player*. Mentioned previously, in this sequence Altman used the crane as one would use a dolly, but the mobility and flexibility that the crane provides—which the dolly does not—gave him the ability to develop a flowing rhythm that was motivated by the story and the characters and their movements. He also started the shot on an interior hallway with a clapstick, which adds to the overall theme of the movie. It is not uncommon to find the camera being kept through a production day on a boom or jib arm just to make it easier to move around ordinary camera setups.

Directors must be aware that crane shots take time to execute. Not only are you staging actors to motivate the shot, you are also designing the motivation for the crane movement and then rehearsing the crew personnel who must execute it. The camera is operated by one person, the focus is pulled by another, and the crane is operated by another; and they all must work in synchronous action. Since the ending of a crane shot is most important, as in a dolly shot, a director should set the end of the shot first and orchestrate backward to the beginning of the shot, making whatever adjustments need to be made between the movement of the camera, the crane, and the action of the talent. The speed of the crane movement needs motivation, so the crane operator (like a dolly operator) must be in tune with the emotional nature of the camera image and thus the crane movement. It should not be looked at as "just a crane shot." It must be looked at as a shot that assists in the visual narrative. A slow crane movement revealing a dramatic element of the story at exactly the right moment can be chilling, just as a fast crane movement toward and above treetops as a car is speeding away can be exciting. Finally, the action within the crane shot needs to be carefully timed with the movement of the crane, and the talent must execute it effortlessly.

A crane shot can be expensive,[4] difficult, and time-consuming and may be a hassle for the director and the production. For example, the director conceives an establishing shot that is high over city streets and elevated railroad tracks, moves down across the street as a car passes underneath, and ends up on a window of a fifth floor tenement apartment. Complicated and expensive? Yes! Difficult for the production crew to execute in the real

---

[4] An inexpensive way of achieving a "pseudo" crane shot (without the ability to create the sweeping movement that a crane can offer) is to use a scissors lift, which is commonly referred to as a *cherry picker*.

world? Yes! So the director looks in another direction to execute the shot which he or she must integrate seamlessly into the movie. For computer (CGI) animators, the shot comes without a hassle since they are not limited by mechanical cranes, cables, or traffic. Big projects and even some smaller projects look to 3-D computer animation to create a full scene and the shots within it, such as a cityscape, that match an actual location for a movie. Mike Nichols combined all of these techniques in the title sequence of his movie *The Birdcage.* The night sequence begins with an aerial shot flying over water as the image moves to the shore line of South Beach, Florida. As it moves closer to shore, the audience begins to barely make out images of people and crowded beach traffic moving back and forth along the coastal street, where the club, The Birdcage, is located. The shot then swoops to the beach and lowers to ground level and moves across the street, passing people and traffic and to the front doors of The Birdcage. One of the atmosphere extras opens the door to the club, and the camera walks in and moves through the crowded nightclub watching the stage show. It finally ends on the stage manager's booth stage left (camera right) where the club stage manager is complaining that the star of the show is locked in his apartment. A stunning sequence unto itself!

Nichols created this spectacular shot not only to serve the picture as a title sequence but also to establish the place, mood, theme, and characters. He combined several techniques to create the effect. A helicopter provided the image of the water, which was computer enhanced with a shoreline and CGI action of people and traffic that eventually matched the production shot taken by a steadicam on a crane. At a specific, imperceptible moment the image does a match dissolve from the CGI image to the steadicam shot on the crane. The crane was lowered to beachfront level. The steadicam operator stepped off the crane and walked across the street into the club, ending the shot on the stage manager.[5] The sequence was a complex one, storyboarded because it involved many elements, including coordinated extras and crew personnel, to achieve it successfully. And it was entirely motivated by the theme of the story.

---

[5] At the precise moment the steadicam operator stepped off the crane, someone else who weighed the same as the steadicam operator replaced him on the crane so that the crane, which was weighted for the steadicam operator, did not snap back and injure someone. Cranes are counterweighted to the weight of the people and camera equipment mounted on the boom arm.

VEHICLE SHOTS

Many movies include scenes that take place inside a car or other vehicle, and directors new to the experience of directing scenes in moving vehicles feel unattached to the scene because of the production and directing process of shooting in a moving vehicle. The process can be intimidating because it is highly technical and the actors' environmental truth is interrupted with lights and cameras in their faces, while the director, during shooting, cannot be seen by the actors. They can only hear his or her voice through a walkie-talkie.

The *picture car*, or vehicle that is used in the film, is towed by a *camera car*, or vehicle designed to tow another vehicle while supporting the production's technical and personnel elements. Because the camera car is towing the picture vehicle, the camera car driver controls the speed of the onscreen picture car. The driver of the camera car signals everyone when he begins moving by honking his horn twice; when the director tells him to stop, he honks twice again. This form of communication, along with walkie-talkies, saves valuable production time. Lights and cameras are usually mounted on the hood of the car or on the rear of the camera car, depending on the angle of the shot. The director and key crew personnel are in the bed of the tow vehicle, thus putting the director ten to fifteen feet away from the actors, with lights and camera between them. Support cars trail behind the towed picture vehicle to ensure picture continuity through the back window (or behind the car if it is a convertible). They also help prevent traffic from other lanes getting behind the picture vehicle and disrupting the shot. In many cases, the tow vehicle will have similar support vehicles on both sides of it for the same reasons. All of these support vehicles are generally driven by stunt drivers who know how to make the picture traffic look normal. Some camera cars have crane arms installed in the truck bed for more complicated shots motivated by the visuals and the story.

The shot from the front of the vehicle is considered objective, and subjective coverage is obtained by shooting from either side of the car through the driver's side and passenger windows. Cameras are mounted on a device called a *hostess tray*. Other subjective coverage shots may come from inside the car, with the camera replacing the driver or any of the passengers, thereby permitting the coverage to take the perspective of characters inside the car and/or allowing the audience to participate or view the scene from within the car.

More complicated shots from the side may require that the picture car be attached to the side of the camera car. A camera car can also push the picture car if the shot is to be from behind or if for some reason the shot requires looking out the front window. In all of these traveling sequences, the speed of the picture vehicle is controlled by the driver of the camera car.[6] Safety is a concern at all times, and it is the responsibility of first assistant directors, the safety officers on productions, to ensure that all safety measures are met. Appropriate permits and police officers are needed to support and escort the production for these sequences.

Directors must approach the direction of car sequences from a different perspective than those in a fixed-set environment for a variety of reasons. *First,* unless the director is using a video assist system[7] monitor, he or she is unable to get a clear sight of the actors to observe their performances. *Second,* the process is not conducive to a creative environment. And *third,* driving sequences take a very long time to complete. If the location for the sequence is endemic to the story and background needs to match from angle to angle, the camera car and rig must take the same route each time for each turn of the camera. If an actor flubs a line of dialogue or a technical problem occurs, it could mean going all the way back to the start of the route to do the shot again.

Taking these elements into account, you should do the following:

1. *Rehearse the actors in the vehicle while the technical aspect of the shot is being set up.* Try to develop actor business[8] that will help the actors maintain their environmental reality. Actor business will always bring the actor to where he or she needs to be for their sense of reality.

2. *Make sure that the actor driving the vehicle looks as if he is actually driving* and not just holding on to the steering wheel while looking entirely at the other actor in the scene. Nothing is more

---

[6] Camera cars can be expensive and are not always accessible. An inexpensive way of towing a picture car is to use an open-bay pickup truck with a hitch for a lowboy car haul. The picture car is put on the lowboy and towed carefully behind the pickup truck. Cameras and lights are mounted on the picture car using a car mount that is provided by the grip department. Since the angle of the lowboy trailer does not match the actual flat angle of a car on the road, this technique is best used at night when the difference in angles is less noticeable. Safety must be regarded at all times.

[7] A video assist is a piece of equipment mounted onto or inside a movie camera that allows (with the addition of a monitor) the director to see exactly what the camera operator is seeing and ensure that it is being shot and framed the way he or she wants.

[8] Character gestures or activities that define a specific character, such as drinking, eating, etc.

unconvincing than seeing an actor who is supposed to be driving a car looking at the actor in the passenger seat while driving; no one in the real world does that![9]

3. *Try to keep the actors close together in the seat unless it is motivated otherwise.* This will make for better camera composition and will make it easier for the actors to relate, since the closer you can stage the actors, the easier it is for them to relate to one another.

4. *Make sure you do coverage, if at all possible, since editing will help enhance performances if necessary.*

5. *Choose a location wisely.*[10] Using a location that has nondescript or matching geography will save production time.

6. *Make sure that all crew personnel are clear about the shot* and what you are expecting to accomplish with it. The camera positions selected for shooting car sequences should be carefully thought through, especially when the scene has more than two characters in the car. You don't want to find that you asked for a two-shot and the first assistant camera operator set a three-shot.

Unless the character relationship of driver to passenger is that of a chauffeur, one passenger is usually in the front seat next to the driver. When this is the case, the simplest and quickest camera placement for coverage is at the front of the car. This is to establish a two-shot from the center and objective singles or close-ups that are cross-positioned, as opposed to positioned directly in front of each of the front seat occupants.

By cross-positioning the cameras, you are creating the close-ups outside the relationship but from the direction of the person to whom the other character is speaking. This will ensure that the eye-line establishing the spatial relationship matches the two-shot. This can also be done with three cameras to save time. As mentioned above, you may decide to do the close-ups from the specific point of view of either the passenger or the driver; in that case the camera (and its operator) is replacing the actor

---

[9] In an episode of the TV series *Surface*, one of the characters is driving, and three times in the scene he unconsciously takes both hands off the steering wheel for gestures to accent his dialogue.

[10] In *The Sound of Music*, Robert Wise used a camera car for a portion of the "Do Re Me" song when he photographed Maria and the Von Trapp kids on bicycles. The location he selected was a long road with a lake on one side and a cliff on the other so that whenever they had a technical or choreographic problem with the shot they were able to continue on the road without having to return to the start of the route.

Floor plan using camera car

Center camera — two-shot   (7-1a)

Camera to right of center camera   (7-1c)

Camera to left of center camera   (7-1b)

for those shots. Of course, for driving sequences it is always a good idea to include with the coverage cutaways from inside the car of the passing scenery and/or exterior shots of the car traveling on the route, commonly referred to as *drive-bys*.

In learning to direct these sequences, it is important to remember what you should *never* do: for obvious reasons it is unsafe to have your actors *really* drive the picture vehicle with cameras and lights attached. There is no reason in the world to jeopardize someone's life for the sake of art.

Camera tow car

....

ACTION, STUNTS, AND FIGHTS

Directing action, stunts, or fights is collaborative. These sequences are often considered second unit[11] and are directed by a second unit director who has collaborated with the director of the project. However, the second unit generally does not involve the principal actors (although it can) and focuses only on the action of the stunt or fight and not on the characters' internalization or motivation during the action. That depends on the director, as primary directors of movies will often direct the action or stunts or fights themselves. But although the internalization as it pertains to the narrative is the director's realm, directors are not alone in the staging and placement of the camera to best demonstrate the excitement of the action. Staging for action is generally the domain of the stunt coordinator, who, after consulting with the director about character and story, will know best where to put the camera(s) to get the most exciting and dynamic angles for the action. Many stunt coordinators are also second unit directors for just that reason. These sequences can be costly and dangerous and are carefully planned down to the meticulous details of every second of the stunt; they take a lot of valuable production time to set, rehearse, and execute. Stunts or fights should be shot with multiple cameras. Stunt people get paid every time they perform a stunt or take a fall or do a fight, so it makes sense to do the stunt with multiple cameras rather than multiple times for one camera. Action can be combined with mechanical effects,[12] which complicates the direction of the sequence. And since some mechanical effects, such as exploding body squibs planted on actors, are difficult to time with the actor's reaction and/or dialogue, it is probably a good idea to use multiple cameras on those sequences as well.

You must make sure that no two shots on a multiple-camera shoot for action are the same but rather can be used with other shots to offer a dramatic narrative to the sequence. Also remember that it is not the action that should be important to the sequence but the focus on the characters

---

[11] "Some projects require a second unit director. The second unit is a second production crew that shoots selected sequences of the production (board) before, during or immediately after the main production unit shoots the majority of the project." *The Indie Producers Handbook, Creative Producing From A–Z*, Schreibman, p. 72.

[12] "A mechanical effect can be a bullet hit (on an actor) or an explosion; it can be effects such as steam, rain, snow, fog, fire or wind. Motivated by the story, any effect is planned and created mechanically during the process of principal or second unit production." Ibid., p. 136.

before, during, or as a result of the action. The action, fight, or stunt is only a means to an end in telling the story. It is not the story itself! This does not mean that the action should not be shot with excitement and exhilaration for the audience; it means that you have a responsibility to the emotional truths of the characters involved with the story, and your audience will be deprived if it does not see or experience that truth.

Stunts and fights should be storyboarded or previsualized through 3-D storyboards or animatics[13] during the previsualization phase of the project, especially when they will be combined with CGI backgrounds created later in postproduction. The storyboard should detail every shot, its angle, and the action so that the director can determine which shot would use actors or stunt doubles and what the production logistics are for each shot. A stunt double is a trained stunt person made up to look like the actor playing the role.[14] But, do not lock yourself entirely to the previsualized storyboards. Once your actors work with you and their roles, they might have some ideas about their characters and through your discussions and/or rehearsals you may find new and interesting story elements that can be integrated into the action sequences. This is where the "what if" factor can work successfully toward the integrity of the project; you will ultimately get a better performance, which must be any director's goal. Therefore, it is not unusual to revisualize the storyboards or animatics as a project gets closer to production.

There are two basic methods of directorial coverage when working on fight sequences. One method is to shoot the sequence objectively, using multiple cameras in medium to wide angles with trained stunt people dressed as doubles for your actors, and then use a hand-held camera to create tighter, subjective shots inside the fight with your actors duplicating sections of the movements.

Floor plan showing various camera positions for fight[15]　　　(7-2)

---

[13] Animated storyboards.

[14] Stunt players are members of the Screen Actors Guild.

[15] Shots can be seen in accompanying CD-ROM.

In relation to production time, this method is easy and quick, since skilled stunt people are trained to effortlessly make a fight look real. And when the subjective shots are taken, the double is there to help the actor duplicate the movement while you can focus on the dramatic intent of the character. This method of coverage requires many individual shots so that the dynamics of the fight can be created through editing. It may also require some rehearsal or training time for the actor before the day of the fight.

The second method is to shoot a fight with medium to tight angles both subjectively and objectively and to use the actors themselves for the fight sequence. It is possible to use multiple cameras with this method. This method will require your stunt or fight coordinator to spend time choreographing and rehearsing the fight with your actors, taking them away from doing other scenes in production or developing a rehearsal period for that purpose before production begins. It may also require your actors to spend time learning a special skill so they can perform the action realistically, as Hilary Swank did with boxing in Clint Eastwood's *Million Dollar Baby*. This method is more costly and time-consuming but is often preferred by the actors over the previous method. It also gives directors the greatest creative latitude for the story with little or no compromise. In some instances there might be a combination of the real actor and the stunt double as the shot and production requires. Many directors prefer this approach, as it does not set up as many visual limitations for the narrative and lets the actors develop for themselves a more believable environmental truth for the story.

One word of advice: Whenever you decide that you want to shoot a sequence using two or more cameras, you may be compromising the quality of the visual image: your cinematographer is not lighting for one camera but for multiple cameras, and therefore the lighting cannot be as exact. A wise director will make up for that with believability in performances, which rests not in the action but in the characters, their intent, and their reactions to the action taking place.

HIGH ANGLES, LOW ANGLES, AND POINT OF VIEW (POV)

In visual storytelling, directors and cinematographers are always concerned about camera angles. Certain camera positions in natural coverage allow the image to be subjective or objective. Camera angles can also demonstrate, by the relationship between the camera image and the subject, emotional information to an audience. This obviously helps directors communicate their vision about the characters and the theme of the project. The more extreme the angle (i.e., the further away from eye level), the more symbolic and heavily accented the shot. In general, low angle shots increase the importance or status of what is shown, whereas high angles diminish it. A very high angle is sometimes called a *bird's eye view*, because it can make a shot look as if it was seen from a bird overhead. It is a very unnatural and strange angle because it is one that the audience does not recognize for themselves as an everyday occurrence; familiar objects viewed from this angle might seem unrecognizable at first, such as a group of umbrellas in a crowd on a busy, rainy street. The shot does, however, put the viewer in a godlike posture, looking down on the action; people can appear to have antlike significance in the wider scheme of things. Alfred Hitchcock and Brian De Palma used this shot extensively in their movies, and it is a favorite of music video directors. The shot is often the tail or front end of a crane shot or a portion of a helicopter[16] shot.

Not so extreme an angle as the *bird's eye view* is the *high-angle shot*, which is taken mostly from a crane. It gives a general overview. High angles make the actor seem smaller and less significant, and depending on the height of the angle, the character can be swallowed up by the setting. When it is motivated by the story, the theme, or the characters it is very effective and connects well with the audience. In *Apollo 13*, director Ron Howard used the high angle camera shot effectively. Tom Hanks, portraying Jim Lovell, goes out in his back yard to look at the moon on the night of the Neil Armstrong moonwalk. Hanks looks up at the moon and, as if the moon is looking back at him, Howard uses a high-angle shot looking down on Hanks. Brilliant and well motivated, the shot sets up the next series of coverage shots, which concludes with a high-angle shot of Lovell and his wife in an embrace on a chaise lounge (as if being watched from the moon). When the scene cuts to the next scene, the shot is a bird's eye view of the mission control building at the Kennedy Space Center. Motivated by the theme of the movie, the composition and angle of the building unconsciously remind the audience of the Apollo 13 rocket. He used this shot again brilliantly in *Cinderella Man*, but this time as the neutral shot

---

[16] A remote-controlled model helicopter that contains a camera is called a *coptercam* and is used in some instances.

over the boxing ring, taking the audience away briefly from participating in the fight.

Low-angle shots increase the importance of what is seen in the shot. They tend to be the favorite of new directors when the theme they are working with is power and is used in conjunction with a high-angle shot. Low-angle shots can also increase the height of the subject and are therefore useful with short actors such as Tom Cruise. The perception of added height may give importance to the subject or inspire fear or insecurity in the audience, depending on the theme, the action, and the emotional traits of the character. These angles dominate the audience because of what they are seeing on the screen. When the low camera angle is used for a dolly or steadicam move, it can give a sense of speeded motion and can cause confusion or disorientation for the audience within the action of the scene. And since the background in a low angle shot is either sky or ceiling, the lack of detail in the setting adds to the audience's disorientation.[17] A low angle shot was used very successfully in the movie *The Clonus Horror,* when Richard, the clone, is running through hallways in the main building of the Clonus compound.

From time to time directors like to use a *dutch angle,* which is a tilted diagonal orientation of the camera and is often done hand-held. This is difficult to motivate and is generally used in certain thematic styles of projects as it reflects imbalance, transition, and instability, as in the movies *Titanic* and *The Clonus Horror.*

A logical motivation for such a shot might be a *point-of-view shot* (POV), in which the camera becomes the eyes of one particular character who may have fallen with his or her face sideways to the ground. Many different shots can be considered point-of-view shots. When two people are speaking to one another and the coverage includes subjective close-ups of each of those two people, each close-up is a POV shot. The technique of POV is one of the foundations of film editing. It is usually established by a shot being positioned between a shot of a character looking at something and a shot showing the character's reaction. It makes little sense to say that a shot is inherently POV, as it is the editing of the POV shot within a sequence of shots that determines POV. A POV shot need not be the strict point of view of an actual single character in a film. Sometimes the

---

[17] As opposed to an angle that is at eye level from which the audience sees the setting in the background.

point-of-view shot is taken over the shoulder of a character who remains visible on the screen. Sometimes a POV shot is shared and represents what two or more people are seeing. There is also a POV shot taken from a nonexistent character, which occurs when an actual POV shot is implied but the character is removed. The high-angle shot of the birds descending in Hitchcock's *The Birds* is a POV shot (from a deity's perspective). Acting performance, camera placement, editing, and sometimes special effects can all contribute to establishing and motivating a POV shot. In the movie *Hunter's Blood*, Sam Bottoms gets caught in a trap that springs him upside down hanging from a tree. From his point of view, the audience sees the character Washpot upside down approaching him and slamming a rifle butt into his face, knocking him unconscious. This is an *absolute subjective point of view* shot because it makes the audience the character, seeing and sometimes feeling exactly what the character is experiencing. In *Cinderella Man*, Ron Howard used this shot, along with other subjective and objective shots, as part of his coverage of the final fight scene between Jim Braddock and Max Baer, making the sequence a highly personal and effective experience for the audience.

CHAPTER SEVEN SUMMARY

➤ Dolly shots are the mainstay of most projects because of what they offer the director in terms of visual storytelling.

➤ There are various types of dolly shots, including the character dolly, the pullback reveal dolly, the depth and counter dollies, and the open-out and tighten-in dollies.

➤ Hand-held shots are different than doing shots hand-held.

➤ There are some difficulties with steadicam shots that may hamper the creativity of the director.

➤ Steadicam shots should not be looked at as substitutes for dolly shots or hand-held shots.

➤ A crane shot is rendered by having the camera above the ground and moving it through the air in any direction.

➤ Crane shots take time to execute well.

➤ The process of directing and covering car sequences can be intimidating.

➤ It is unsafe to have your actors really drive the picture vehicle with cameras and lights attached.

➤ Directing stunts or fights is collaborative.

➤ Stunts or fights (action) should be shot with multiple cameras and previsualized with storyboards.

➤ There are two basic methods of directorial coverage when working on fight sequences.

➤ Camera angles can demonstrate emotional information to an audience by the relationship between the camera image and the subject.

➤ A POV shot exists when the image becomes the eyes of one particular character and sees what that character sees.

"You must allow life to happen on the set. It is somewhere between knowing and unknowing that you get the best results."

— **Ang Lee** (on the need to prepare without over-rehearsing)

CHAPTER **8**

ON THE SET

This is where it happens! This is where the rubber hits the road. This is where everything you have planned for is executed. This is also where Murphy's Law can have a field day unless the production is well planned. The director is the sole person leading the production on the set, and with the cinematographer, sets the pace of each shooting day. Communication is mandatory, and directors must never be secretive about what and how they are working on a set. Everyone on the set is there to fulfill the director's needs. They are all creative in their own way. They want to express that creativity but need to know the approach that you, the artist, are taking.

Directors must be clear with their theme and vision, since it is on set that the micro elements of that vision are implemented. The director and only the director must be totally focused on the whole vision. Whether it be Ang Lee's vision of balancing the masculine elements of the Western with the romantic gay love story in *Brokeback Mountain* or Woody Allen's concept of a crime story that gives insight into the complexities of need and desire in *Match Point*, the director, with all the apparent confusion and innumerable people on set, is single-mindedly focused on the vision of the project. The director is the project's yardstick that everyone else must measure up to.

THE FIRST A.D. AND THE SCRIPT SUPERVISOR— THE RIGHT AND LEFT HANDS OF THE DIRECTOR

There can be—and often is—a lot of confusion on a set. The first assistant director (A.D.) is the right hand of the director, serving as the organization facilitator. The first A.D.'s job is to keep things organized, on schedule, on budget (if possible), and to move the day's work along from moment to moment as needed by the director. The interaction between the first A.D. and the director requires an essential bond, developed by the first A.D. getting into the director's rhythm and on the director's wavelength. But in order for first A.D.s to do their job well, directors must keep them informed of how each day's work will be shot, which has been scheduled with the producer for the production. This bond is critical because first A.D.s must know what directors are going to do *before* they do it, so they can make sure all is ready. Therefore, directors must do their homework and communicate the *how* of the day's work to their first A.D. before the day begins. A.D.s should prepare alongside their director a week or two (or more) before they get onto the set. In that way they will know exactly what must be done from the first second of the production period. A.D.s must motivate the crew and are unable to do that without information. They are at the director's side on the set: listening, watching, thinking, and anticipating any deviation from the plan of the day as motivated by the director's creative instinct when working with the actors and the camera.

First A.D.s never tie a director's hands but find ways to accommodate their director within the limitations the production is faced with each day. They must be ready for any improvising that their director wants to do and adjust the pace on the set accordingly. They orchestrate the director's vision, make sure all the resources are there to realize that vision, and they make sure that their director has the creative space and atmosphere in which to work. When nerves fray on a project, first A.D.s should be the ones who keep their cool and find logical solutions to whatever problems are causing everyone else to become irritated and angry. More important, their job is never to second guess their director or be a backseat driver on the project. They are planners, familiar with Murphy's Law, who assure directors by handling the logistics so directors never have to concern themselves with that aspect of the production.

Directors must stay focused on storytelling. If you are *constantly* trying to find ways to stay on schedule, you won't want to go that extra mile to be creative on the set. First A.D.s are there to think about the schedule so you don't have to. If you want to be creative, make sure that you are communicating with your first A.D., your right hand on the project, before you get to and during the time you spend on the set.

The left hand of the director is the continuity person, also called a script supervisor. Since continuity is responsible for logging and recording the coverage and the details of actors and camera during the coverage, continuity must work closely with the director as well. Directors usually meet with their continuity person and first A.D. on the set at the beginning of every production day. They go over the schedule for the day and provide any script or visual changes that may have been made since the previous day. Creativity is ever-evolving, and the first A.D. and continuity person must stay ahead of its evolution. This is especially true if the director decides to alter what is being shot that day. The right hand and the left hand need to know this information as they disseminate it to the production crew: continuity to the camera and sound departments, and the first A.D. to everyone else.

Finally, the major responsibility of the second assistant director, who reports to the first A.D., is the care and handling of the actors on set. Second A.D.s make sure that the actors are in and out of makeup and wardrobe at the right time for the director as determined through the first A.D. They also maintain certain Screen Actors Guild actor contracts and time sheets and relay any important information to the first A.D. regarding terms under which some of the actors are working. These terms may have an impact on how directors arrange work for the actors. For example, actors who are employed on a daily contract work eight hours before hitting overtime. Those eight hours include the time it takes them to get into and out of makeup and wardrobe but does not include the time they take to eat their lunch. Actors who are working on a weekly agreement work ten hours a day, with overtime starting at the tenth hour of the workday. They also get overtime if they work more than forty-four hours for the entire week. If overtime is a budget issue, directors must adjust their methods of working with their actors. This can have an impact on the creative outcome of the performances and the type of camera coverage that is designed.

ON-SET PREPARATION

Directors and their staff prepare for what awaits them on the set. That preparation is called preproduction, which we discussed in an earlier chapter. But as the project gets closer to the start of the scheduled production, directors and their staff discuss the production board for the project. The production board is an organizational tool that shows the logistics, cast, and personnel required for each day of the shoot. It is based on the shooting script and reflects the finalization of weeks of preproduction work. The scenes to be shot each day of the production are displayed on the board using quarter-inch strips with notations of critical information that stimulate the director's imagination and memory as to how each of the scenes are to be shot. Since single-camera narrative projects are not shot in story sequence, this practice is imperative to the success of the on-set process of production. Directors determine which scenes are important for each of the shoot days, and the production schedule is built around those scenes. That is not to say that each scene should not be important to the story. But it does address those scenes that are prioritized and will be the director's focus for the day. When determining this, directors must ask themselves which scenes they need to spend extra time on (both for coverage and for actors to get the performances that are needed for the story) and which scenes are so technically difficult to shoot that additional production time is needed. In general, movies schedule between two to three script pages a day and television production four to six (or more) pages a day.[1]

The discussion of daily schedules should take several factors into consideration:

1. In general, a production crew gets more work done before lunch than after lunch. So the more difficult directing scenes when possible should be scheduled before lunch.

2. A production can make only *one* full company move to a different location in a production day and expect the director to complete the day's scheduled work. So the work scheduled for a director on those days takes the move into account as part of the working day.

3. Directors must determine what time they want to execute their first shot of the day and the first shot after lunch. Directors use these

---

[1] Screenplays for television are written differently than for theatrical movies, which helps make this possible.

times as guideposts for their day's work. If they meet them they are on schedule. If they are ahead or behind them they are ahead of or behind schedule and adjust their creative work accordingly to complete the day. These times are agreed to by the first A.D., who must work out the logistics that will enable the director to stay on schedule.

4. Directors must determine which scenes they need to complete before the scheduled meal of the day, which is usually within six hours of the start time of the day. These factors are all logistical and are weighed by directors from a creative standpoint. Being responsible to schedules and budgets is a function of directing, and directors must adhere to those schedules and work creatively within that framework.[2] These are the only guideposts needed and used to make sure that the day's work will be completed.[3]

ON-SET POLICY

There must be only one director on a set.[4] Any crew member who makes directing suggestions should be released, as this is counterproductive to the entire creative process and undermines the director's authority. Directors must have the last word on the production set. No one should interfere with them or come between them and the actors. Although directors are hired by producers, the production set is the director's sanctum, and producers must not interfere with what goes on—at least not in front of everyone involved in the production, as this will undermine the director's influence. If producers have issues with directors, they should find the time away from the set to discuss and solve them. But conversely, directors must respect everyone and recognize that they all have a creative contribution to make with respect to their own responsibilities on the project. The entire company beams at any cast and crew screening of a movie. Even the teamster driver who drove the principal actor will swell up with pride knowing that he or she contributed by getting the actor to the set on time.

---

[2] The Directors Guild of America, the organization that represents professional directors and assistant directors in the motion picture and television industry, provides for their director members to give input to and approve schedules and budgets as developed by producers.

[3] Some film schools teach their students to decide the exact hour and amount of time to allow for each shot. This thinking does not reflect any reality of production.

[4] There are directors who direct in tandem, but that is a rarity and not the norm.

ON-SET WITH THE CREW

In an earlier chapter we discussed an on-set rehearsal, which is common in the industry and especially in narrative single-camera television. It lets directors create when all of the tools of production are on hand and requires directors to think on their feet. Time pressures and other limitations are on the director's shoulders. As problems occur and are solved, directors who are able to remain creative while focused on the story are those who know how to think on their feet. They will be the directors who succeed on all levels. The more prepared directors are and the more they trust people to do their jobs, the easier it is for them to think on their feet and be inspirational and creative. This trust and collaboration with the crew is very important to a successful on-set atmosphere. It is imperative that the cast and crew work together as one entity—one entity and one family all focused on one thing: telling the story. Your job as director is to keep that family together by respecting the contribution of each member of the crew, as all of them have their own egos that motivate them to contribute to the vision—your vision!

While actors are being rehearsed by the director, the first A.D. asks the crew to work quietly in getting things done so the director and actors are not disturbed. Crew members near the camera who do not have an assignment should be watching the rehearsal and visualizing how and what they need to do to make the shot happen.

Once the actors are staged in the scene and the shot is designed, readied, and rehearsed, the first A.D. requests the set to "settle down." This is done so the energy from everyone on the set calms and focuses on the action that will develop in front of the camera. The calmness and silence before the camera rolls are very important because it is during that moment of calm that not only the actors need to focus but also the camera operator, focus puller, dolly grip, or crane operator need to concentrate. Their contribution affects the visual movement, and it is movement that helps to tell the visual story. The first A.D. then asks for the camera and sound to roll. Once the set has heard the word "speed" from both departments, the second assistant camera holds the slate in front of the camera, announces the scene and take number, and claps the sticks on the top of the slate. Now all is ready for the director to speak.[5] Directors like to take a moment

---

[5] Some directors at this point say "Thank you" and then wait a few seconds for the set to settle from the technical sounds of starting the camera rolling. Crew members like to be appreciated, and this is a nice way for a director to often show appreciation during the shoot.

for the set to settle by waiting a second or two before saying *action*. It's a good practice to get into, since the word *action* is the last emotional bit of direction that a director gives to the actors and camera. And how the director says *action* will often provide further creative impetus to the shot. For example, if the sequence is high energy, *action* should be said with that energy. Or if the scene is very quiet, *action* might be said quietly in a gentle voice to help the actors with their mood in the scene. It is important for actors to hear the director and not someone else say the word *action*. On set, the director is the actor's audience, and hearing the director say *action* effectively lets actors know their director is watching them and cares. It is a good idea for directors to stand next to or near the camera when they are watching the shot. Actors want to know that their director (their audience) is right where the camera is and not off 200 feet from the set watching a video image of the shot in the video village.[6] Directors can be given palm-size monitors that will show them the video image if they want, but their physical presence by the camera is what gives comfort to the actors. The video assist system will record the shot, and the director can play it back if need be. Video assist systems usually record on VHS helical scan videotape for playback, although now there are digital video assist computer systems that are quicker and also offer nonlinear on-site editing capabilities.

It is also important for directors to wait a few seconds at the end of a shot before saying "cut," the command for the shot to end. Actors will hold the moment at the end of the scene, waiting to hear "cut" from their director, and in those few seconds they may impart usable reactions. When directors say "cut," they are making decisions as artists, since they must quickly decide whether the shot or any portion of the shot is to be redone for any reason. While quickly determining the quality of the actors' performances, they get a signal from the camera operator and the sound mixer as to the quality of their contributions to the shot. This is all done in an instant. Then they let everyone on the production crew know their decision by saying, "Let's do another"[7] or "Let's do a pickup"[8] or "Print

---

[6] It is common to use a video assist to see the shot while it is being done. This is seen on a monitor set up several feet away from the set so that several people can watch the monitor at the same time.

[7] In some instances, when a take of a shot is done and the director liked it but wants to do another, he or she might say to continuity "hold that one" and "let's do another," hoping to get a better take which can be used.

[8] A "pickup" is a portion of the shot that is redone. To do a pickup the director should go back to a moment in the shot in which physical action occurs in some form to help the actor re-experience the moment in the scene, since physical action will always elicit an internal response in an actor.

that," the acknowledgment of a good and usable shot.[9] While continuity is circling the printed takes in the continuity log, the director should make immediate contact and comment to the actors about their performance. Actors know that when the camera is rolling, all eyes are on them. When the camera stops rolling, their egos require that their director respond immediately to what they just did. Since the bottom line rests with the actors' performances, directors must remember to speak to them and acknowledge their performances very quickly after cutting (stopping) the camera. Inexperienced directors instead turn to the technical side of the shot, leaving the actors uncomfortably to fend for themselves. So what is always heard on the set after a shot is completed is something to the effect of *Cut, Good for sound, Good for picture*, comments to the actors, then, *Let's do another*, or *Cut, Good for sound, Good for picture, Print that, Great job, actors, The next shot is the over-the-shoulder*. The script supervisor logs the director's creative comments about the shot (*Great job, actors*) so that during editing the director will be reminded of his or her intuitive comments from that moment.

If the take is a *print*, directors must know the next shot in the coverage sequence and immediately announce it so the first A.D. can get the production crew moving to set up for it. Since the first A.D. needs to plan ahead of the director, First A.D.s try to know the next shot while another is being worked on. If directors stop after each shot to figure out what the next shot will be, they will lose both the confidence of the crew and valuable production time. And their actors may become creatively detached from their performances while waiting for shot decisions. When actors are in the moment and "on" with their performances, directors should push to keep that creative energy alive; a slowdown in the rhythm will squelch it. Trying to figure out on set where you will head with the camera will cause confusion and a breakdown of that creative energy. Directors must create an atmosphere and a rhythm on the set. Knowing what the next shot is *before* you get to it establishes that rhythm and develops an energizing atmosphere on set. This atmosphere is vital for actors, as they must never feel that directors have either lost control or do not know what they are doing. If they do, it might prevent their performances from being truthful. Performance is not an intellectual

---

[9] This command refers to the laboratory developing and printing the film of only "printed" takes. This is the norm when shooting 35mm or 70mm film. But when shooting 16mm or super 16mm film, laboratories print everything.

exercise; it is a physical sensation, and actors must work in a creative atmosphere to experience that sensation.

Working on the set and thinking on their feet can be insane for directors from time to time, but as long as they keep a fix on the theme, the story, and the vision and know what they are doing, creativity will flourish no matter how insane it gets. But most of all, directors must be in control and calm. You must remember that on the set you are not alone; everyone is there to serve your needs in getting the job done. Successful directors embrace and value that notion.

ON-SET WITH ACTORS

Directors' antennae must be up at all times. They must always be aware of what the actors are doing if they are preparing for the scene. You may be setting a shot with the cinematographer or discussing wardrobe with the costume designer while your actors are on the sidelines rehearsing their lines. Whatever it may be, you must always keep an eye on your actors, even from afar, as they are preparing on the set. That way you will have a sense of what to expect when you are ready for them. The practice for a director is to have the actors ready for performance when the camera is *ready* to roll and not before. Actors who have years of experience in front of the camera know this and are not likely to give a performance until the camera is ready and the director says "action." But since actors are not puppets and must be given the freedom to create, those actors who have little or no camera experience could present some difficulty for the sense of a balanced performance during rehearsal and when the camera rolls.

Inexperienced actors may have a tendency to be theatrical with their performance. And inexperienced directors have a tendency to stage actors as if they are performing on a proscenium stage, thereby signaling theatricality. But if you maintain truth and reality in the staging (choreography) of the scene and avoid, at all costs, any staging that would send signals of theatricality to the actors, you will be ahead of this problem whether they be experienced or inexperienced actors. Something as simple as an actor crossing to another actor with the body slightly open to the audience, as on stage, can cause the actor to be theatrical, but the actor crossing in a straight line, as in real life, may not. Staging should be somewhat natural as a result of the character's needs and conflict. The camera can go anywhere, so staging for authenticity will send signals for reality in the performance.

As mentioned before, choreograph the scene first so that the crew knows what it will be working toward. The crew needs to see only the basic physical choreography to decide where the camera, sound, and lights are to go in the scene. Actors are staged in their moves while a crew member marks their positions in the scene. Similar markings may be made for movement of the camera. Make fine adjustments to the performances just before the camera is ready to roll. Your actors will appreciate this approach and find it beneficial to their acting process and the creative rhythm on the set. When all is ready, make sure your actors understand the shot. This should be explained very quickly in a nontechnical, nonthreatening manner, as some actors are intimidated by the technical aspects of the narrative process. Never explain how or why you are doing the shot, just what the shot is—the less you say the better. When actors understand the shot, they should work toward making the shot successful with both their internal and physical performances. If actors' moves in a scene are intended to motivate the camera to dolly, the actors should pace themselves with the speed of the dolly move. If the shot is an over-the-shoulder shot, the actor whose shoulder is being shot over should understand that his shoulder can be seen on one side of the camera lens and remember to make sure not to change position, blocking his or her partner in the scene.

The actor in the foreground should take a step to his left

Notice that only the nose is in sharp focus when it is the eyes that should be sharp, as they are the windows to the soul

If the shot is a close-up on a long lens (narrow depth of field), the actor should be told how much room he or she has to move in the frame without moving out of focus.

Directors must realize that the actor's job is very difficult. "Actors have to master hitting their marks, not moving out of the frame, not casting a shadow on their partner's face, getting to the right place at the right time while moving at the required speed, and still give the best performance possible. Sometimes it's like patting your head and rubbing your stomach at the same time."[10]

Some actors have a love affair with the camera and come alive when the camera is on them. They are actors who think of the camera as another actor and engage in a relationship with that actor. All actors should think this way, but they don't. Allow actors the space to improvise if they are able. Some actors, such as Dustin Hoffman, "may want to improvise a scene or use the script as a foundation for interpreting the scene,"[11] whereas others may want to take off completely as a way of discovering what the scene is about. It is okay to let them do that on set, as long as you steer them back to where they need to be while being mindful of the camera and any technical limitations that face you. Eventually you will have to lock some of the movement in place to help the camera shots.

Many actors appear mechanical in front of the camera, and out of frustration you may want someone other than you to help the actors with their relationship to the camera while you go off and work with your cinematographer or speak to your producer. But directors are the only people who direct actors, although once in a while the cinematographer may provide a physical direction in terms of actor placement. But only directors direct actors on and off the set.

Your crew and your actors make up your shooting company. They work together to achieve the results you need. In some instances, for technical reasons or because of problems that happen behind the scenes, you may need to do multiple takes of a shot even when the actors feel as if they gave you their best performance on one of the takes that was technically flawed. They may get upset with the crew and not understand what happened, and it is important that you apologize if necessary and tell them that you are doing the shot again because of the technical problem. They must know it is not because of them! Share in their disappointment if need be, but encourage them that they can and will do better and that you know they have another take in them. And now you go to work! Help them. On the new take, give your actors slightly different motivations or objectives to work toward in the shot. Give them a fresh impulse to work with; a new but related emotional action to work toward. This will provide them with a fresh attitude toward the scene and give an alternative to the

---

[10] Salvi, p. 120.

[11] Brad Silberling Master Class, UCLA, March 4, 2005.

performance on the flawed take. You may use the flawed take after all in the final edited scene, but giving your actors minor adjustments from take to take—or shot to shot for that matter—keeps the performances fresh with possible new discoveries. This *adjustment technique* is most important as you develop your coverage, since at some point your actors will become aware that the shot is *their shot* or the camera may begin to intrude on their acting space. They may get a bit anxious and nervous knowing that all eyes, including the eyes of the camera, are on them for that moment and that they must deliver the right performance. Or they might get bored and stale from take to take. Giving them an adjustment for the shot will keep their minds focused on their internal characters and may forestall their conscious nervousness or cure their boredom and staleness and fine new moments of character discovery.

Inexperienced actors sometimes have a tendency to unknowingly raise their voices during a shot. Voice projection is a physical characteristic of a theater or inexperienced actor and is not something needed for the screen unless the emotions of the scene require it. If, during the take, you have a sense that actors are unnecessarily loud, more than likely their performance will be untruthful because the performance will be too big to be intimate. You may not see it when it is happening but it will be something you sense when you look into their eyes. The camera certainly will see it because the camera never lies. When that happens, you need only to remind them that the microphone is very near and they do not need to speak loudly. This should quickly bring their performance back to the level of truth for the camera and intimacy for the actor.

Acting in front of the camera is difficult, especially on a set when so many technical things are happening around the actors. Not only are the lights and camera on your actors, but perhaps the wiring of a squib is up a pant leg or the dolly track must be stepped over for the shot. Production days are spent mostly on the technical side of the art and craft until the moment when the actors are to deliver; that is when the crew and the actors must be as one. Your job on the set, as their director, is to create a safe environment in which your actors can be vulnerable—an atmosphere of creativity and focus so they can concentrate even when there seems to be chaos happening all around them (and you). You must be the quiet in the storm for them, for yourself, and for your crew. They will see you as the sturdy director, even if you feel otherwise. If your actors and crew see you tremble from the chaos, you could lose their trust and respect. You certainly will destroy the area of safety you have given your actors. Always maintain your focus of concentration and rely on your assistant directors and others to handle whatever chaos may arise. That's what they are there for. Some directors play music on the set while the crew is working to create an atmosphere, while others may try to keep discourse away from the main action. Tempers can flare, especially when long production hours are concerned. I try to keep some levity on set when I direct and have an arsenal of jokes at hand that I may recount to a group of actors and crew members from time to time. Humor is always a good tension reliever, but you must make sure that it does not offend anyone. Since your first assistant director is always concerned with the crew, protect your actors at all costs. Without them you have no picture. You must work to get that spontaneous spark from their acting, and to do that you must find a way to let the actors settle into the scene and work it until it is magic. Then, with your shot lists aside, bring the camera in to share in that magic. When the magic is happening, your crew gets excited, and when they get excited they deliver amazingly positive results no matter what the hardships.

Working with children on set can be more difficult than working with adults. Children do not have the patience or maturity needed to understand how things are done on set. In addition, children are restricted by law and the Screen Actors Guild regarding the number of hours they are allowed to work. Directors need to go back to the basics of the story to help offscreen what occurs onscreen and find methods to help child actors understand the characters they are portraying. With *Lemony Snicket's a Series of Unfortunate Events,* Brad Silberling wisely gave a video camera to Liam Aiken and Emily Browning, the two young actors who played the two oldest children in the movie. He asked them to interview one another as the characters they were playing. This "game" solidified their characters and established a rapport between them that they brought to the set. Some of the dialogue from the interviews also wound up in the movie.[12]

On stories where child actors are to play children of adult actors, arrange for all of them to have a lunch or some other kind of informal social activity before production begins and they walk onto the set. This will establish a rapport between the adults and kids, which will transfer to the story and make your directing job easier. Children need to be prepared for their roles

---

[12] Brad Silberling Master Class, UCLA, March 4, 2005.

before coming to the set, and directors should find ways to ensure that they are. The process is scary enough, and you should not be faced with a child who cannot deliver the relationships for the story. However, once children are working, do not treat them any differently from other actors. Do not pamper or talk down to them and understand that their bag of references are different than yours, so try to reach into *their* bag for communication and character suggestions rather than introduce them to a new one. It is all about encouraging them to find their voice and making them feel safe as they are discovering it. Sometimes a child's imagination can take them a long way.

A word about extras, often referred to as "atmosphere." They should be considered as important as your actors to the texture of the story. They are the wallpaper of a scene, and like wallpaper in a room, they can provide the nuances for defining the scene in the story. Can anyone doubt that the extras in the opening of *The Godfather* were friends and family of the bride and groom? Each had their own life, and the audience knew it by the way they were staged and directed. Many times, the staging and direction of extras is left in the hands of the first assistant director, after consultation with the director.

The process of single-camera narrative can be very boring for actors since they wait around for things to happen. And the technical aspects of the process with forty or fifty pair of (crew) eyes staring at them can be very intimidating. On the set, your job as director is to bring everyone together as one family. Production is strenuous, stressful, and challenging to say the least. You are all living together for whatever period of time is needed, so it is up to you to make sure that everyone, cast and crew, is together in a harmonious, creative, and enjoyable environment. If you do this, your job as director will be a good deal easier.

SOUNDSTAGES AND LOCATIONS— TIME MANAGEMENT AND COMPROMISE

Shooting on location is always more difficult than shooting on a soundstage. Sets on soundstages are more controlled and are pre-lit for production, whereas location shooting requires the production company to bring everything with them; in addition, unless the location has been secured for more than the day, the set is generally not pre-lit. Being able to record good sound is never a problem when working on a soundstage, since it is designed for sound recording. Recording good sound on location is always a problem, since there are unforeseen sound issues such as passing airplanes or distant jackhammers. Therefore, time management for directors working on location becomes a major issue.

Since soundstage work is controlled, directors are generally able to move more quickly with their coverage, depending on the complexity of the scene. Needed production equipment is ready on the stage, and actors' dressing rooms are within a stone's throw of the set. On a location, directors have an obligation to bring the location into the texture of the story, which may mean developing coverage differently than on a stage set. However, on location, equipment and dressing rooms are at a base camp, a distance from the set. Location work has more chances for volatility because of weather, cast and crew issues, and the geographic characteristics of the location. Producing for location shooting must be approached differently, and further problems can (and do) arise because of Murphy's Law. Therefore, directors may have to constantly rework their coverage because of their need to complete the scheduled work within the time allotted for each day. Distant location shooting has different problems from local location shooting, which again might cause directors to alter their planned coverage. As it relates to production, there is no substitute for preproduction. First-rate preproduction will reduce the chances that Murphy comes knocking on the door. It will also free directors from avoidable problems so they can focus on storytelling without having to continually fight time issues on the set.

However, it is foolish to think that directors are never confronted with time issues, whether on location or on a soundstage. Lack of time is the nature of the directing beast. It might be caused by problems in production, a location, or an actor who arrives late or is not permitted to work overtime because it will put him into a forced call.[13] Directors and their staff are forever finding solutions to issues such as these while juggling creativity. On a project I directed for the U.S. Department of Defense, we were shooting at Edwards Air Force Base in the high desert in Southern California. Tom Denove was the cinematographer. I asked the officials at the military base what the weather conditions would be like the week we were scheduled to be at the location. They told us that it is sunny 360 days a year and we would definitely have clear sun the entire time. Of course, our week turned out to be the five days they left out.

---

[13] A call to work for an actor less than the hours required after dismissal on the previous day.

During the week we shot, it rained, it snowed, and there was a sandstorm. Tom and I had to adjust the coverage and how and when we were able to shoot, since we had an obligation to finish in that location that week as we could not return.

On a feature project that Tom and I did together, we had a difficult production day on a busy main street on the east side of Los Angeles. The day was scheduled with the street exteriors first and then the interiors of a café that was to open later that day. When we showed up to work that morning, we found out that the production department had not arranged for a base camp near the location, and the trucks were circling the streets trying to find a logical place to set up. We were faced with delay for that day and the probability of not finishing the day's work and falling behind schedule. Our solution: download off the truck only that equipment that Tom needed for an interior. I saw a sushi bar on the portion of the street where we were to shoot the exterior. The people inside were prepping the fish so they could open at lunchtime. With the blessings of the producer, I asked the owner if we could use the location for the interior scene that we were scheduled to shoot later in the day. They agreed and, while the trucks were settling into a suitable base camp, we altered the scene from a café to a sushi bar and shot the interior at the beginning of the day. Did coverage change? Somewhat! The actors were not at a table as planned but at a sushi bar overlooking dead fish. Did it affect the story? Yes. It made it better. The words in the scene were the same, but they played somewhat differently because of the reality of the actors being in a sushi bar and staring at dead fish. Humor was added to the scene where none existed before. And we stayed on schedule and completed the production day.

The problems that may arise are many, and talented directors must think on their feet. When the problems arise, you go back to the basics: the story and its characters. The word *compromise* becomes part of the director's vocabulary. Your schedule may be such that you work on the end of a scene first and do the beginning of the scene after lunch. In that situation, it is best to stage and rehearse the scene in its entirety first so that the actors can experience the development of their relationships. But do not rehearse the scene anywhere close to a performance; hold some direction back, but be guided by the course that the scene is taking. Breaking the actors' continuity development is difficult at best, but if the schedule requires it, find a place to break the scene at a transition in the staging or an emotional transition in the dialogue; it will make your job easier when you are directing the scene topsy-turvy. The actors will trust you as their barometer, and although you are not cutting in your head, you must have a sense of the continuity of their performances when the end of the scene is shot first. Your direction must maintain the consistency of their energy and guide the believability of their performances. You may find yourself compromising your planned coverage by looking for that transition shot that will link the front end of the scene to the back end of the scene or to the next scene in the movie. But if you consistently help your actors to stay in the moment, the coverage transition shot will reveal itself. Keep it simple. When working this way, do not complicate your communication with your actors. Sometimes the less you say, the better; your job is to stimulate their creative intuition and keep them on track.

Your schedule and actors' contracts may necessitate actors finishing their day's work before the scene is completed. You may have to alter your sequence of coverage to accommodate that problem. Again, you may find yourself compromising and shifting coverage or asking actors to play their lines to the continuity person's offscreen voice. The burden falls on your shoulders to draw upon every ounce of creative directing talent to keep your actors at their performance best.

Sometimes you find yourself in a major time crunch. It may be because you have been shooting exterior night and the sun is about to come up. Or you are shooting exterior day, the sun is about to set, and you are at the mercy of the improvisation muse and must work within the confines of what your cinematographer can do quickly. In those situations, you compromise and adjust your staging and coverage for the limitations of lighting and camera. You will need to do all the wider angles first to take advantage of the night (or the day) and save all the close-ups for later, when you can add sunlight or match the night by shooting day for night.[14] You will have to compromise on performance since, depending on the number of characters, you will need to interrupt the continuity of actor concentration from the wider angles to the close-ups. But you never know; creativity flourishes with limitations and restrictions, and you may find a better outcome because of the problem.

---

[14] "Shooting day for night" involves photographic techniques using photographic filters by which exteriors in daylight are made to look like a night shoot under certain dramatic circumstances.

Magic hour can also be a director's nightmare. Magic hour is more like thirty minutes than an hour and is around sunset and sunrise on exterior locations. It concerns the dramatic shift in lighting conditions that occur in a short space of time when the color temperature of the light is approximately 3,100 K, producing a golden-orange color. It's what the cinematographer looks for when he or she is looking through a filter eyepiece at the light and saying "give it another five minutes!" The fact that it lasts only about thirty minutes means that directors must stage for the lighting condition and wait for it to be perfect. It also means that doing much coverage during any one magic hour is difficult, if not impossible, unless two or three cameras are used. And even then it is difficult. The prep time to get ready for the light to be absolutely right is critical. And if you decide you want to shoot at the ocean as the sun is rising or setting, it becomes even more difficult. As long as you shoot the coastline or the water you will see magic hour light, but doing reverse angles away from the sun rising or setting will be into the night and will not match the magic hour footage of the water. Again, a matter of time management and compromise. As mentioned earlier, can anyone ever forget the wonderful magic hour shot on the beach at sunset of the angels staring at the water in Brad Silberling's *City of Angels*? If the camera had turned and shown them head-on rather than in profile, it would have seen night behind them.

Maybe you find that you have two scenes to do on the same set or at the same location and those scenes are at two different places in the script. A time crunch has again set in, and you need to complete the scenes within the day they are scheduled. The logical solution is to use the same camera angles for both scenes and shoot each scene by the camera angle rather than completing one scene and its coverage before moving on to the other. Once the lights are set and focused for a camera angle, it is quicker to do all the shots from that angle before relighting and moving the camera. The responsibility of getting the best performances from your actors and keeping the continuity in place will be on your shoulders and those of the continuity person, as the actors will be performing both scenes, one after the other, using that angle. Maintaining camera eye-line and the spatial relationships from shot to shot also falls to you and the continuity person. This is difficult, to say the least, and not recommended because too much may be compromised that could affect the story, but it is done.

You must always remember that the audience knows only that which they see on the screen, not how it got there. The audience does not know what something could have been, but only what something is! So a compromise for you will not be a compromise for your audience. Paul Haggis had to compromise and drop some of the driving sequences in *Crash* because of time, yet the picture was applauded by audiences and critics alike. It even received the Oscar for Best Picture.

On a low-budget project that I directed, we kept moving a short visual shot that was to take place in a closet. The lead actor was supposed to go to the closet, find his old military chest, and remove his M16 rifle, while the audience saw family memorabilia in the closet to support the emotional content of the character at that moment. This one scene kept being moved on the production board until we found ourselves with it scheduled on the last day of the shoot: an exterior night. Tom Denove was again the cinematographer, and we found our solution in a dumpster with an old piece of carpet. Tom took the piece of carpet and placed it on the asphalt on the exterior location. We borrowed two muslin flats from a local community theater and put them on top of the carpet forming two walls that met in a corner of a closet. We then placed the military chest on the carpet near the corner. We put the camera on top of a ladder focused straight down on the military chest, and Tom dropped a light bulb into the frame. Voilà! The new shot was a birds-eye view from the ceiling of a closet. I staged the actor to walk into the frame, open the chest (now dressed with the family memorabilia), load and lock the M16, and look up at the light as he turned it off so the audience could, for a brief moment, see his emotion in deciding what he needed to do. When the audience sees the image, it never knows that it was shot in an alley at night in downtown Los Angeles.

Compromise on a set is something that directors learn very quickly, whether it be on location or on a soundstage. However, as long as you go back to basics and keep your focus on story, theme, and character, *any* compromise could turn out to be a moment of brilliance.

CHAPTER EIGHT SUMMARY

➤ The director is the sole person leading the production on the set.

➤ Everyone on set is there to fulfill the director's needs.

➤ The first assistant director is the right hand of the director, serving as the organization facilitator.

➤ The left hand of the director is the continuity person, also called the script supervisor.

➤ Directors determine which scenes are important for each of the shoot days.

➤ A production crew gets more work done before lunch than after lunch.

➤ Directors use times during a production day as guideposts for their day's work.

➤ Directors must have the last word on the production set.

➤ Staging for authenticity will send signals for reality of performance.

➤ Directors must create an atmosphere and a rhythm on the set led by the energy of the actors.

➤ Actors must relate to the camera.

➤ Direction must maintain consistency.

➤ Shooting on location can be more problematic than shooting on a soundstage.

➤ As it relates to production, there is no substitute for preproduction.

➤ Compromise is part of the director's vocabulary.

"I didn't know what was going to happen when Arab and Israeli actors re-created the Olympic athletes' murders at the airport. When the first take was done, the actors began sobbing and the Israeli and Palestinian actors rushed in and all began hugging each other. We were unglued and I said 'Peace is just around the corner waiting to happen.'"

— **Steven Spielberg**, director, *Munich*

CHAPTER **9**

THE DIRECTOR AND . . .

Directors should be seducers, not dictators. They should be able to guide their vision through sly manipulation and respect for other's creativity rather than by direct force of will and intellect. Directors must keep in mind that at the end of the day they (and everyone else involved) are telling a story, which might be intense and genuinely emotional, sometimes rooted in the subconscious, and therefore surprising and shocking in its revelations. Direction is not a matter of coaching actors toward this end but instead a matter of "turning psychological events into behavior and inner events into visible (and visual) external patterns of life (onscreen)."[1] Directors need to be collaborators and must know the language of collaboration. It is best to make sure that your producer surrounds you with the best possible people who share your vision of the story. This will guarantee a terrific, respectful cohesion and communication among departments with you at the helm. A young director once asked an older and wiser director the question, "How do I put my vision on the screen?" And the older and wiser director said, "You don't put your vision on the screen. You talk to other people who put the vision on the screen, except they don't know how to talk."

---

[1] Elia Kazan's definition of directing. *Elia Kazan*, by Richard Schickel 2005, p. 21.

Directing for the screen cannot be done in a vacuum and certainly cannot be done without teamwork. Never speak about the project as "mine" but always as "ours" to cement the team's attachment to it. This brings everyone in and massages their contributing egos. When you are clear with your communication, you will hear and hopefully see the team own the project because they feel confident in your respect for them and they for your vision.

PRODUCERS

The relationship between directors and producers is unique. Above everything else, they should be a team, each having trust in the other. Producers think like producers, and directors think like directors. They have two very distinct thought processes. A creative producer is one who has or shares in the vision of the project and has the courage to work with a director to interpret and carry that vision forward. Producers must know how directors affect their art and provide the latitude for them to work creatively. And for directors, vice versa! The creative producer thinks inventively and ingeniously, whether in telling the story, working with a writer, casting collaboratively on the project, raising the finances, or, in some cases, marketing the picture. A producer's role can have many manifestations, depending on the relationship with the director. Roles the producer does *not* take on are those of production manager, location manager, line producer, production coordinator, director's assistant, or fundraiser for the whims of the director.[2]

Producers are problem solvers and should have the unique ability of foreseeing the possibility of a problem and presenting a solution so the problem doesn't happen. Their job is to make the production process as creative as possible for directors to do their job, while keeping an eye on the fiscal possibilities and the vision of the project and doing whatever is needed to keep the camera rolling. A creative producer at any moment in the life of a project plays many different roles: the mother, the father, the lover, the romancer, the persuader, the psychologist, the comic, the best friend, the teacher, the warrior, the negotiator, the arbitrator, the dreamer. Producers play these roles so directors can direct. Directors look to their producers as redeemers. As their consciences. As their confidants. As the

---

[2] Many directing students in film schools believe this to be the task of a producer.

coach of the project. Directors recognize that without a producer their voice may not be heard; they should look to producers as their other half in the visionary process. It is precisely the reason why producers receive the Oscar for Best Picture every year and directors receive their own Oscar for their contribution to the totality called a movie.

BUDGETS

Directors must understand a production budget. They must know what *negative cost*,[3] *above the line*,[4] *below the line*,[5] and *deferments*[6] mean. They must understand how the specific numbers in certain cost centers relate to the ability to realize the vision and the story. They must understand the fiscal restraints on their project and give input in areas of the budget that do not hinder their creativity. They must understand the concept of making the "shoe fit the foot"[7] as it relates to budgets and be able to make adjustments in the story, the schedule, or their direction to best solve the problems. They may need to adjust their coverage or suggest monies from other areas of the budgets to help their needs without hampering those other areas. Directors need to know where the money during the production phase should be spent and where it can and must be saved. Directors have a fiscal obligation to a production and to working with whatever fiscal (and/or production) limitations may exist. Never fear limitations, however, since creativity flourishes with limitations and restrictions. Your creativity will rise to the top to always find solutions to those problems.

Budgets are created by producers, with input from production managers, line producers, and postproduction supervisors. Producers will clearly know the budgetary numbers for above the line (cast, director, writers, etc.), and postproduction supervisors will know the numbers for the postproduction phase of a project. But production managers and line producers develop budgetary numbers for a production within a creative

---

[3] The total cost of a project including deferments.

[4] Those positions and elements of a budget that could be part of a recognized guild in the entertainment industry.

[5] Everything else in a budget other than above the line.

[6] Part of a budget that provides for a promise to pay a fee at a later time.

[7] The foot is the budget and the parameters of production and the shoe is the process of production, *The Indie Producers Handbook, Creative Producing From A–Z*, Chapter 2.

Production Budget Top Sheet

Acct. #	Classification	Page #	Budget Notations	Totals
100	Story & Other Rights			150,000
200	Continuity and Treatment			350,000
300	Direction and Supervision			650,000
400	Cast, Day Players, Stunts			1,250,000
500	Travel and Living			425,000
600	Extras			62,075
800	Fringe Benefits			438,926
	TOTAL ABOVE THE LINE			3,326,001
2000	Production Staff			327,895
2100	Visual Preparation			248,000
2200	Set Dressing,			875,000
2300	Set Construction			1,345,000
2400	Properties Department			62500
2500	Special Effects			98000
2600	Camera Department			389,000
2700	Electrical Department			176,935
2800	Set Operations/Grip Department			145,792
2900	Wardrobe Department			567,378
3000	Makeup and Hair Departments			32,819
3100	Sound Department			43,889
3200	Transportation Department			231,079
3300	Location			680,075
3400	Stage & Process – Production Effects			25,000
3500	2nd Unit, Miniatures, Prod. Effects			156,780
3600	Production Film and Laboratory			187,935
3700	Tests			7800
3800	Fringe Benefits			834,012
	Total Production Period			6,434,889
4000	Editing – Picture and Sound			286,392
4100	Music			750,000
4200	Postproduction Sound Laboratory			330,657
4300	Postproduction Film/Digital and Lab			298,546
4400	Fringe Benefits			73,498
	Total Postproduction Period			1,739,093
5000	Publicity			52,000
5100	Insurance			67000
5200	Miscellaneous			43,598
5300	Fees and Other Charges			125,000
	Total Administrative Charges			287,598
	TOTAL BELOW THE LINE			8,455,580
	ABOVE THE LINE		3,326,001	
+	**BELOW THE LINE**		8,455,580	
=	**DIRECT COSTS**		11,781,581	
+	**CONTINGENCY FEE**		1,178,158	
+	**COMPLETION BOND FEE**		388,792	
+	**OTHER FEES**			
=	**TOTAL**			
+	**Deferments (if any)**			
=	**TOTAL NEGATIVE COST**		13,348,531	

vacuum, not entirely recognizing what the director needs in terms of time and on-set preparation for cast and crew until it is too late. So for that reason alone, directors must provide their input on the budget before principal photography begins—not to get more money for the project but to indicate a plan for how they will fiscally impact the production phase of the project so that the producer can provide the funds to support it. One of the main rules in the industry states that what you don't do in preproduction affects production and what you don't do in production affects postproduction; in this case, directors must give their input and recognize the importance of the budget as a guideline for the project. The Directors Guild of America, the organizing body for directors, production managers, and assistant directors, understands this importance and by signatory agreement with producers ensures that their director members give input on a project's budget. It is one of the ways to protect the creative vision under the care of the director. However, directors should not abuse that privilege by being unreasonable. They have as much responsibility for bringing the project in or under budget as the producer and are accountable for their actions if they go over budget. Many a director who did not pay attention to this accountability has been the cause of a project being shut down because of money running out, or has been fired and the project finished by a completion bond company.[8] Several completion bond companies require the director to sign their adherence to certain budgetary guidelines before they agree to bond a project. This is sobering to a first-time director.

PRODUCTION DESIGNERS

Producers and directors work with the production designer on the creative plan and the coordination of all of the visual elements of a project, which are sometimes referred to as the visual character or texture of the project. Production designers work closely with the director of photography and the director in creating the "look" of the film. Production designers guide the creative muses of the wardrobe designer, the art director, the set decorator, the property master, the makeup and hair designers, and the minute details involved in the visual layering of the image. If the project is to employ

---

[8] A completion bond company is provided a fee for guarantees to the studio or investment that a project can be completed in a first-class, distributable manner for the money stated in the budget.

CGI and blue screen and there is a visual effects supervisor, the production designer works in close collaboration with him or her on the planning and execution of each element required for the visual effects. Although the collaboration of the production designer and the cinematographer involves discussions of light, color, visual texture, and cinematic feel, it is the director who, during preproduction, plans with the production designer the visual subtleties needed for character and story. The production design must be a priority for directors as, among other things, its result provides elements for an environmental truth for actors. Although actors may use their imagination during rehearsal, they can easily maintain their sense of believability when they see others in makeup, hair, and wardrobe and experience the location and set with all of its design realities.

Although budgets may dictate the amount of production design for a project, the shooting format and end use of the project will also have its effect. A project shot for the wide screen will show more production elements than one shot with 1.33:1 or 1.66:1 aspect ratios. A project shot for television will generally show less overall production design than those for feature distribution.[9] Design begins in some fashion in the imagination of directors (and producers) when they first read the script. The reading may conjure up images that may or may not be in the writing but are in some vague manner in the director's mind. These images may take some sort of shape as you do research on the theme, story, and characters or drive to work and see someone wearing a hat that you might think would be perfect for one of the characters. Maybe you drive by a location that "clicks" for a scene or you see a truckload of railroad wheels that, if they got loose, could be a good component within an exciting action sequence. But these are all ideas, and it is not until you have the right production designer that the ideas and the images can take the shape needed to tell the story.

Hiring the right production designer is a task for the director and the producer. Although many directors and producers prefer to work with the same production designer on each project, you have to start sometime in finding one that you are comfortable with. This should be done in an informal atmosphere after the candidates have read the script. Once you have selected the designer, discuss the project in terms of the characters and not just the sets, locations, effects, and constructions. This will put you on equal footing with the designer and right away he or she will begin to

---

[9] See Chapter 10.

translate your discussions visually; you will not have to wait until the fifth
or sixth meeting to get your ideas across.

Production design as it relates to locales can take on different forms
depending on the size, scope, and theme of the project. Production design
takes into account the production needs as well. While location shoots
such as those in Alexander Payne's *Sideways* rest with practical locations
and set dressing, John Singleton's production designer, Keith Brian Burns,
needed to match practical exterior locations with a reconstruction of
a neighborhood residential street exterior on a soundstage for the film
Four Brothers. The shootout needed the control that only a soundstage
could provide. As if that wasn't difficult enough, the story takes place in
Detroit and the exteriors were shot in Canada. Brad Silberling's *Lemony
Snicket's A Series of Unfortunate Events* depended on a combination of
practical location, CGI and blue screen, and design and construction of
sets. The production design must be organic to the story and therefore to
your direction. Sometimes production design works with previsualization
storyboards and sketches to get everyone on the same visual page. The
elements of the production design must share in the telling of the story and
not be simply background for the actors. It is the inexperienced director
who does not recognize this and prevents audiences
from experiencing the production design as
another element in the story. The clone room in
Robert Fiveson's low-budget movie *The Clonus
Horror* stands out in an audience's mind. And is

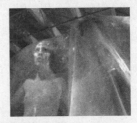

The Clonus Horror

Land of Plenty

Don't Come Knocking

there any doubt that the small-town locations and geographic beauty of the mountains in Ang Lee's *Brokeback Mountain* or the scenic details of a post-9/11 society in Wim Wenders's *Land of Plenty* affect the interpretation of the characters in the stories? What about Nathan Amondson's production design in Wenders's *Don't Come Knocking*, which evokes a tone and texture that impacted audience and critics alike? Production design is very much a part of these stories.

CINEMATOGRAPHERS

The marriage of the director to the cinematographer, or director of photography, is crucial to the visual interpretation of a project. All creative people that directors work with are a little bit like actors in a sense because they are all artists. Cinematographers express their art in their own terms. A cinematographer is motivated by the story, its characters and theme, and the director's vision for the project. In some situations, the cinematographer is looked at as a lighting director or someone who creates the mood, texture, and feeling of the image with light. In other arenas, the cinematographer also works with the dramatics of the shot and in the interpretive use of the camera in telling the story. It all depends on the working rapport between director and cinematographer. A director will have ideas about shots and coverage, and the cinematographer will build on those ideas, refine them, and enhance them. Cinematographers look at scenes in terms of what is to be achieved visually in tone and emotion, and directors should build on their suggestions and ideas. The final decision should be with the director, but a wise director trusts and nurtures the creative storytelling ability of the cinematographer and makes him or her a cohort in the vision.

Tom Denove has been the cinematographer on several projects that I have directed and has also operated the camera on most of them. At the end of a shot, I would look at him as he took his eye away from the eyepiece of the camera. His look often told me whether the camera captured the best possible performance of the actors. If the scene moved him, I could see it on his face and I could rely upon his sensitivity to give me the right indication.

The marriage is perfect when both the director and the cinematographer are on the same wavelength and enjoy a shorthand communication with each other. A shorthand communication is very important since it can save time on the set. The director and cinematographer's relationship begins in preproduction; you might call this their courtship. Directors have many meetings with their cinematographers, during which they discuss the project with reference to paintings or other art or even other movies. They discuss and decide on camera philosophy and the use of lenses to tell the story, all the while keeping in focus the theme and the journey the characters take. These decisions are not always decisions of intellect but sometimes of instinct. The director doesn't know why the two of them see the image a certain way, but just knows it is right for the story, as it usually comes from the emotional focus of the characters. For example, a project titled *Coming of Age* is a story of an eighteen-year-old boy during a crucial year in his life when he is confronted with the emotion of his mother dying while trying to maintain some kind of stability away at college. In lengthy thematic discussions on the script, the director and cinematographer have decided to shoot the college sequences using a fixed camera, while the troubling portion of the boy's life dealing with his mother's death will be grittier and shot with a hand-held camera in moving masters. The two different camera approaches are intended to heighten the emotional journey the central character takes. Another example can be seen in Steven Soderbergh's *Traffic*, in which he uses the documentary, hand-held approach for the gritty aspects of the story while using long lenses and fixed cameras for the controlled backstory that is woven throughout the picture.

In discussion with a cinematographer, a jumping-off point must be the emotion of the story. It is easier to work through and break down the emotional steps if you and your cinematographer look at the story backward. By examining it from the end to the beginning, you should clearly see the emotional context of the characters without the hindrance of a direct, linear plotline. Ideally, the conversation will include composition, staging, points of view, visual transitions and shots between scenes, philosophies, use of light, production design, lenses, and, if need be, color saturation of the image and the color journey the cinematography might take in developing the emotion of the situation, the locale, or the characters. Janusz Kaminski and Stephen Spielberg do this brilliantly in *Munich* as the emotional subtleties of the story shift paralleling the paranoia of Avner, Spielberg's lead character. Spielberg and Kaminski use the cinematic grammar of rack focus shots and images quite frequently. This is an inspired choice; it warns the audience that the elements in the center of the frame may not hold all of the information it needs, and it leaves the viewer with uneasiness and uncertainty.

If working digitally, your discussions may go so far as to include the technical processes. Should it be shot in 24P video, finished to hi-definition and filmed out to 35mm, or shot in 24P video and finished in DV cam? Or shot in hi-definition and film out to 35mm? Or shot in hi-definition and recorded tapeless (with a back-up on DVD) and downloaded directly to a laptop computer? Or shot in super 16mm and finished to hi-definition or scanned to the digital intermediate process and filmed out to 35mm? It involves you and the cinematographer firing off ideas to each other, examining the pros and cons as they affect the project.

A cinematographer should not only be someone who is creative and knowledgeable but also someone who knows how to help the director by balancing the crucial relationship of time management with production issues—after all, the grip, electrical, and camera departments work directly for the cinematographer on a production. Other departments also interact with the cinematographer, such as wardrobe, makeup, props, and special effects. No matter how well prepared the director is, if the cinematographer is slow with decisions and execution, or unsure of what to do with the camera, it can cost the production time and cause the director to eliminate coverage. Scheduled scenes for each day of production may not be completed. But if the cinematographer and the director use a shorthand communication with one another and are in sync, things will go quickly, artistically, and smoothly. Their preparation before coming to the set is vital.

Creative producers will require cinematographers and directors to provide *beauty shots*. They need these images for marketing the project. And producers often make sure that a first-time director works with an experienced cinematographer to shelter the cinematic side of the project with experience.[10] Cinematographers have their own quirkiness. Some like to mix film stocks, some like to test, some like to use less light while others like to use more. It should make no difference to you what their preferences are as long as they are telling the story the way you and they have discussed. They have their own creative muse they must answer to, and

---

[10] The look of an episodic television show is developed and maintained by a consistent cinematographer throughout the series. Directors rotate in to direct individual episodes.

directors should give them the freedom to exercise that expression. Above everything else, whatever the quirkiness, the marriage between the director and cinematographer must be one that is founded in passion for the work.

BAGEL AND LOX MEETINGS

Directors need to meet with their cinematographer, production designer, wardrobe designer, and all other production personnel early on in the project at one session. All of them have done their own creative preparation and come to the meeting with ideas and suggestions ready to collaborate. At this meeting, every scene in the script is discussed, from page one to the end. This meeting is referred to as a *bagel and lox meeting*. Organized by the producer, the meeting usually lasts six to eight hours, during which refreshments are available for all to partake. This usually consists of bagels, cold cuts, lox, juices, fruit, coffee, pastries, soda, and other such tasty foods that provide sustenance to all in attendance. It is led by the director and designed to get everyone on the same creative page as the director's vision and unveil the visual style of the project. Characters are discussed in terms of what they look like; sets and locations are discussed in terms of the story. Perhaps the creative team has brought pictures or photographs to the meeting to assist the discussion. The creative interplay should be alert, and excitement builds as certain ideas are discussed. Francis Coppola held such a meeting when he started *The Godfather*, out of which came the ideas for the use of light and dark and the nonmoving camera for the movie. *The camera was always (on a dolly or tripod) four and half feet off the ground and always had a forty millimeter lens.*[11]

One more bagels and lox meeting is needed as well. But this one is held closer to the start of principal photography and is led by the producer. At this meeting, the production board and shooting schedule are discussed. All creative logistics are talked through, making sure that the cinematographer's and director's creative needs will be met for their work on set. Prospective problems are solved and compromises are made so that all potentially goes well. This gives directors the security of knowing that everyone will be ready. Narrative projects are "made" in preproduction, and this one last meeting gives directors the opportunity to assure everyone that they are ready too.

---

[11] Francis Coppola Master Class, UCLA, October 24, 2004.

EDITORS

Editing is the movement and manipulation of frames of images. It is the rhythmic, instinctual, emotional, psychological, artful, and theoretical consideration of the effect of one shot on another. It draws on the total talent of one person, the picture editor, who collaborates with the director to create a cumulative sensory event. Editors organize details, strengthen subtleties, heighten emotions, and blend limitless elements of image and sound in *their* storytelling.

Editors are only as good as the footage they receive from directors. They know the project only from what they see in the coverage and will often have a different viewpoint than what the director may have originally conceived. The magic of editorial storytelling is a different kind of magic, as the editor may see character and story moments that the director may not have noticed during production. It may be the tilt of an actor's head, the movement of the camera, or one of those moments at the end of a scene when the camera lingers on the actor before the director says "cut." Creative editors know how to expand and enhance a moment or shorten the spatial connection in a scene. Directors should always respect their editors, since their creative contribution to storytelling is invaluable. Many times, their perspective on the artistic nuances will be just as valid, if not more so, than that of the directors. A director's degree of involvement in the editing may vary greatly depending on the director and the project. In certain television projects, directors merely turn their work over to the producer to work with the editor. On other projects, directors who are members of the Directors Guild of America are entitled to put forward to the producer a *director's cut* as a condition of their employment. Some directors negotiate beyond that for the *final cut*. Directors must direct with a sense of montage, without cutting in their head or predetermining how a project will be edited; yet, because of this, directors and editors should have an affinity for one another.

When directors and editors have worked together on successive projects, they develop a collaborative arrangement in which the editor understands the director's vision and adds to it. These editors work with their directors from the beginning of a project and are involved in the preproduction phase so they can get on the same creative wavelength with their director early on. Editor Michael Kahn has been collaborating with Stephen Spielberg for years[12] as well as editing other films such as *Lemony Snicket's A Series of*

Unfortunate Events and *The Haunting*. And Thelma Schoonmaker has been Martin Scorsese's editor since *Raging Bull* in 1980. The history between Schoonmaker and Scorsese is famous and is an example of how a deep-seated relationship between editor and director can be developed. One of the innovative techniques that Schoonmaker employs when working with Scorsese relates to the screening of rough cuts of his movies that she has edited before screening it for him. After screening the rough cut for six or eight people, she then gets them together to gather their impressions and debriefs each of them. She starts off by saying, "I will never tell Marty (Scorsese) anything that will hurt him, so you can tell me everything." Her emotional attachment to Scorsese and his film projects is so durable that she wants to be sure that comments about the cut are valid.

Barry Zetlin,[13] an editor I worked with on several projects, used another innovative technique. When the picture was locked and before it went to the sound designer for the next phase of postproduction, he would go through every cut of the movie and take one or two frames off of the head or tail of every shot. When I asked him about this practice, his comment was that "we have been working on the editing of the picture for many weeks, and we are so used to the image that our brain is adjusting for the rhythm as we want to think it is, and more than likely it is playing just a bit slower than we think. So the imperceptible technique of trimming each shot will assure that the rhythm is what we want." Because of the concept of *persistence of vision*, this made sense to me and of course it works.

Although the working experiences are different with different editors and directors, there is a similarity in how they work together. First, your editor must be a good storyteller and have a great sense of editorial rhythm. Second, your editor should be on the same wavelength as you so that he or she watches your dailies[14] with some knowledge to see by your coverage where you are headed with the scene. Third, your editor should have an affinity with your vision in terms of your taste. Fourth, your editor should bring objectivity to the footage they see; your perception may be slanted by what happened during production. A talented, objective editor may make

---

[12] Michael Kahn/Stephen Spielberg movies: *Munich, Indiana Jones, War of the Worlds, Peter Pan, Minority Report, Saving Private Ryan.*

[13] Barry Zetlin edited such movies and TV shows as *Hunter's Blood, Friday the 13th, Into the Sun, Starting Over, Celebrity Mole, The Shadow Men,* and sixty other projects.

[14] The footage shot each day of production.

discoveries in editing that you may not have thought of. And there are a million ways to cover a scene. Hopefully your editor will maneuver your footage to adjust for the storyteller's point of view.

Some directors want their editor to wait with all the dailies[15] before beginning to assemble the picture, as they want to construct the film along with the editor. It is not a good practice, as directors need to keep some mental distance between the production process and the editorial process. Having an editor assemble the picture as the project is shooting is not only creatively sound but fiscally prudent. And working this way, your editor will let you know if you have missed a shot with your coverage of a scene, such as a close-up of a character. You are then able to do the shot during the production's work schedule with your actor without having to do a pickup shot weeks, if not months, later after you have completed production.[16] Pickup shots are costly and difficult to arrange, so it is a practice that the industry frowns upon. Fortunately this practice happens less and less today because of competitive release dates of projects being sooner than in the past.

The time to speak up in terms of which performance takes from your coverage you like is during the process of watching your dailies with your editor.[17] This can be a time-saver, as it will help your editor find the course you want to take with the performances. Although some directors choose to let the editor know which takes of each shot to use, others tend not to say anything at all, giving the editor freedom to exercise his or her objectivity in selecting the performance for the story. (The continuity log notes also provide your editor with the comments you made to the actors on the set.) However, one word of warning when viewing your dailies: *do not be fooled in deciding which is the best take of a shot!* During dailies you will always have an emotional reaction to the first take because you are seeing it for the first time. And you become numbed in viewing subsequent takes of

---

[15] As a creative practice, directors must see dailies within twenty-four hours of when they are shot. This practice will ensure the quality of the project and avoid a host of problems that could arise if there is a problem with the shot footage.

[16] This is one of the problems for film students who edit their own projects. They wait until they finish shooting, then develop the film and move into postproduction. Months later, they find out they need to do pickup shots.

[17] Dailies must be seen every day and not wait to be seen at the end of a weeks shooting or at the end of production.

the same shot. So look carefully at performances of both the actor and the camera when checking for the best take while viewing your dailies.

If your editor is doing an assembly while you are in production, you will finish shooting before the assembly is completed. This should give you an opportunity to get your mind off the project and clear your head for a week or two so you can approach working with your editor with a fresh eye when you view the assembly.

The assembly will be your first opportunity to see what was disjointed now joined in some narrative fashion.[18] It will be a shock! Although there may be pieces missing (especially if the project includes CGI or visual effects) the story will be defined and laid out for you to see.

Once you have viewed the assembly, it is time for you to work with the editor scene by scene. As director Alexander Payne once said about letting go of scenes you may love, "When you trim a steak, you've got to cut into the meat." It is recommended that you start at the beginning of the project and work in continuity with the story. That way you can see what your editor had in mind and work off it, its rhythm, and your own ideas. Editing at this level is also collaborating, but now you are collaborating with an editorial maestro who is attuned to the editorial rhythms of the story. Although some directors will instruct an editor to take two frames off from this end or three frames from this shot, it is best when first working with your editor to approach the work from the story perspective. You should not give your editor specifics about how and where to edit but rather talk to him or her in a manner such as, *It would be great if at this point we could enhance the fact that she is deeply in love with him but is avoiding the moment of truth because she was hurt by him in the previous scene. How can we build that into the scene?* Then let your editor try to shape it in that direction. He or she will know how to do this much more easily than you, and appealing to the editor's creative ego as a storyteller is a positive approach to the director-editor relationship. Of course, with nonlinear digital editing systems this is done quickly and efficiently. To bring things full circle, the director becomes aware of one draft of the script during rehearsal, another when shooting, and the final draft in the edit room.

---

[18] "When I look at a film for the first time, I tell the editor, 'Don't take a thing away from my silence when we're done. Don't take a thing away from the fact that I'm going to probably walk out the door and not come back for the rest of the day. But I will come back in the morning and we will get started.' And that's what I do. Seeing the assembly is always a shock to the system, but the great thing is you may wind up finding some great discoveries." Brad Silberling Master Class, UCLA, March 4, 2005.

Once you have worked your way through to the end of the project, you and your editor should take a breather. The two of you will have a tendency to be tired of the project, and taking a break will recharge your creative batteries. Give yourselves time to clear the editorial cobwebs and then run the project on a large screen (as opposed to a computer monitor). Editorial rhythms change when seen on a large screen, and you may find, for example, that you went to a close-up too soon. It looked fine on the small monitor but gives away too much too soon when projected as a larger image. Once you have made any new adjustments with your editor, screen the project again on a large screen, but this time with people who are close to you and whom you trust to give you honest feedback before you turn in and screen your director's cut for your producer. However, honor your own integrity to the work. Honest feedback is good, but you must evaluate and filter the feedback. Most of all, it is important that you remain true to your own taste and feelings about the work. If you bring the passion, admiration, and trust of your editor into play and if you are true to your own passion for the story, by the time you screen the movie for your producer, very little of your vision will be changed, and your director's edit will become a locked cut picture.[19]

THEN WHAT?

Once the edited picture is locked, the creative aspect of sound is applied to the project. The director's job now is to nurture the creative talents of the sound designers, sound editors, composers, and postproduction sound mixers toward the final result of the vision. That is, of course, if the director is vested in following the project to its conclusion along with the producer. The layering of the sound will be dependent on the project, its budget, and its end use.

Sound is half of any project. Relatively speaking, while the visuals are expensive, sound is not. In postproduction, sound is turned over to a sound designer, an artist who is working with all the possibilities that sound can bring to a project.

Postproduction sound should be the spouse of the picture. It needs to create its own tapestry that blends, motivates, enhances, and moves an

---

[19] The final edited picture before moving the project over to postproduction sound.

audience in a certain direction. During this period, the director may be needed to listen for background sound or for music cues and direct any automatic dialogue replacement (looping) with the actors. But certainly the director should be at the final sound mix of the project to make suggestions for fine-tuning the emotional impact that sound and music make with the image.

The very last element that a director contributes rests with the color texture of the *answer print* of the project. To this end, and in collaboration with the cinematographer, the director should work with the laboratory manufacturing the final project. The color timing of the answer print is the last area where creativity can be applied. Color timing the negative involves color correcting the print from the negative scene by scene for tone, mood, texture, and dramatic feeling. It relates directly to the visual arc of the project. Directors should be discussing the timing in terms of descriptive emotion, which the color timer will translate technically to achieve the apt effect. If the project is in video and is to be transferred to film, the same process is followed, only this time it is done shot by shot through a video process suitably called the *da Vinci process*. There is another process with film that is costly and is being used more and more, called the *digital intermediate process*. Just as you master digitally, the DI process assumes that you shoot the film digital master/color correct digitally and then output back to film for distribution. This gives you lots of creative control and freedom in the final phases of your work in post. Working in the digital environment, a colorist has the ability to create almost any look imaginable and control the color within the image of a frame. In addition to the advanced color control advantages of the digital intermediate, the process also avoids many of the conventional optical printing steps in the film answer print delivery process. Because the original camera negative is scanned and all subsequent processing is done digitally, it is possible to eliminate the inter-positive to inter-negative process all together. Once the digital answer print has been approved, it will be filmed out to meet the requirements for film distribution. If this sounds expensive—it is! This is why it is not a common practice yet. But if it is important to the project and planned for by the director and the producer from the beginning, the budget should allow for it. It does provide the greatest and widest latitude for the most effective color timing affecting the visual arc of the project.

CHAPTER NINE SUMMARY

➤ Directors need to be collaborators.

➤ Directing for the screen is never done without the teamwork of others.

➤ The relationship between directors and producers is unique.

➤ Directors must understand a production budget.

➤ What you don't do in preproduction affects production, and what you don't do in production affects postproduction.

➤ Directors are responsible for bringing in a project on or under budget.

➤ Production designers work closely with directors in creating the "look" of a project.

➤ Production design must be indigenous to the story and therefore to direction.

➤ The marriage of the director to the cinematographer is crucial to the visual interpretation of a project.

➤ In discussion with a cinematographer, a jumping-off point must be the emotion of the story.

➤ Directors and cinematographers should be able to use a shorthand communication.

➤ Directors meet with the creative team early on in the preproduction phase.

➤ Editors are only as good as the footage they receive from directors.

➤ Editorial rhythms change when a film is seen on a large screen.

➤ The director's job is to nurture the creative talents of sound designers toward the final result of the vision.

➤ The very last creative element is color timing.

"All great love stories have to have severe obstacles or else it's not a love story—it's just love."

— **James Mangold,** director, *Walk the Line*

CHAPTER 10

DIRECTING TELEVISION, PART 1: SCRIPTED FORMATS

What do Steven Spielberg, Clint Eastwood, Norman Jewison, Sydney Pollack, Edward Zwick, Brad Silberling, Martha Coolidge, Greg Hoblit, Neema Barnette, Gyula Gazdag, Ron Howard, Garry Marshall, Gil Cates, Rob Reiner, Penny Marshall, Robert Altman, Peter Weir, and I all have in common? We all started our film directing careers in television. Some of us started directing in the theater. But television is one arena in which many directors first find employment, in spite of the unfortunate fact that the training in most film and cinema schools focuses on directing the original feature project.

Television is a writer/producer's medium, whereas features and short narratives are a director's medium. Features deliver projects on film; television delivers projects on video. Directing features is a different process in most instances from directing television, but the results are the same: *an entertaining and/or thought-provoking project that inspires or moves an audience.* And the common denominator that does not change from medium to medium is that, in most cases, directors direct the actors and talent in front of the camera.

Television is a good training ground for directors because it is economically more dangerous than features in terms of how quickly things have to happen and the risks you are required to take. This teaches you how to think on your feet. Directors *are* needed in television, and the writer/producers who employ them (with studio and network approval) look for directors who understand the mechanics, the collaborative processes, the politics, and the dynamics of the separate formats and mediums and, most important, the voices and vernacular of their characters and the audience they appeal to.

With the exception of movies for television, directors must alter their thinking toward the various narrative modes that television offers. Only with movies for television is the director and not the producer assigned the leadership on the project, at least through the production phase.

MOVIES FOR TELEVISION

Planned and executed as low-budget theatrical features, movies for television require directors to work with a shortened production schedule and complete more pages in a day's work than on a feature made for theatrical release. Because of this, a television movie may be shot digitally and/or use two cameras to save time, and directors must learn to compromise more than they would for a theatrical release. The development of the vision and the story is exactly the same, but the time frame is shortened. It takes a director such as Emmy and DGA award–winning Joe Sargent, who is experienced not only in guiding the script and directing actors but also in knowing how to tell a story with the camera and develop the story within the limitations of time and budget that television requires. Since the end product is television, skilled directors know that the audience must see only the important information, which is usually the internalization of the characters. For that reason and those mentioned in the following discussion of episodic narrative television, movies for television incorporate more close-ups and extreme close-ups than features. Directors of movies for television also recognize that the framing of shots is slightly different and the audience does not have to see the establishing shot to know that there is a storm or a blizzard, for example. Directors of movies for television are economical with their choices, knowing that the delivery of a television movie does not have the same distribution requirements of a feature film and may be televised relatively quickly in a network's schedule. Directors and producers of movies for television will attempt to get production values that go beyond those of any other narrative television format. But wide-angle lenses that show the depth of production design are more frequent in features because they show better on the large screen. Restricted by budget and time, production elements are planned out carefully to get the maximum production value in the shortest amount of time. This is all done under the guidance of the director, who knows exactly what is needed to tell the story. And since the delivery of movies for television is on video, these movies, although shot on film, are rarely edited using the original picture negative but instead completed in postproduction through the digital medium. The original picture negative is never touched.

EPISODIC NARRATIVE TELEVISION

Framing for episodic television is also different from framing for movies for television because in many (but not all) cases episodic television is still shot in a TV format, whereas most movies for television are shot in the widescreen format.[1] Most episodic television series, though shot using the single camera narrative technique, have a *house style* that is set by the writer-producer and the director of the pilot episode. So unless you are hired to direct the pilot, you will need to study the style of the show before you tackle it. In most cases, you will prepare for a week or two and then find yourself on set for six or seven days, expected to complete six to eight pages of script a day, with the editing decided and completed totally by the show's editor and producer. You learn very quickly the concept of selective coverage and how and where you can cut corners to save time and still deliver options for editing. The unvarying elements from episode to episode are the cinematographer, the production crew (including the first and second assistant directors), and the principal cast. They know the routine, the shortcuts, and are already working as a well-oiled piece of machinery. Episodic, hour-long narrative television is written to be shot in

---

[1] As widescreen televisions in homes become more prevalent, more and more TV programs will move into the widescreen format. Eventually, it will entirely mimic the widescreen format of theatrically released movies.

six or seven days, mostly on stages, using principal sets. One or two days may be scheduled for exterior locations, but writers and directors try to keep the episodes working around the permanent sets. Although the focus is still with character, there has been a move with such shows as *Las Vegas*, *NCIS*, *CSI*, and *Studio 60 on the Sunset Strip* to offer the perception of enhanced production elements, in order to compete for audience with cable television projects, features, and other entertainment mediums. This is the result of excellent writer-producers and prudent directors collaborating within the time restrictions that television imposes.

When directing episodic narrative television like *Law and Order*, *Crossing Jordan*, *24*, or *CSI*, the first thing you realize is that you must deliver the episode in the style and manner the audience expects while at the same time hoping to do your own storytelling. Episodic directors are often called traffic cops because they have the task of keeping actors out of each others' way when they stage. But the balancing act between what is expected of you as a director and your own creative integrity is the internal dilemma that you will face. The secret is to recognize that you will not be able to put your visual signature on the project but instead have the chance to work positively and creatively with the actors on the show. This can be looked at as an advantage: they know their characters better than you ever will, and you can learn about the characters from them. For example, there is nothing you can tell Mariska Hargitay of *Law and Order: Special Victims Unit* or Kiefer Sutherland of *24* about their characters. They know them inside and out and have probably, with their executive producers and writers of the show, developed some of the character traits throughout the seasons those shows have been on the air. So what would be important (if you were directing an episode) would be for you to establish a trust with them and the other regulars on the show before you get to the set. You are their substitute teacher for the week. Of course, you will be able to work on the performances of any guest actors who have been cast for the episode. Here your challenge will be to make them real people and not just the functional characters of drug dealers, attorneys, detectives, military personnel, or spies that are called for in the script.

One way to establish trust is to discuss with the actors the characters' journey in the episode sometime during your prep week. If they are working during your prep week, visit them on the set and introduce yourself and schmooze with them until they get a break and you can chat about their characters. More than likely they haven't yet had the opportunity to read the script you are directing. In fact, in some cases there may not be a script because the writers may only have a story outline when you are preparing. The script often arrives a few days before you start to shoot the episode. And rewritten colored pages from the producer may arrive even while you are shooting. The entire reason for meeting the actors is to establish a trust with them so that on your first day of work on the set you are already part of the *team*.

Directing narrative dramatic episodic television still requires you to know the story, the theme, the complexities and arc of the characters, and how and when the plot twists and turns. You must consider the episodes as one-hour mini-movies with a fixed set of characters presented in a set style. And you must be able to adapt to that style. When blocking your actors on the set, you will find they know more than you about how they should interact with one another and where they should move. Your job will be to keep the actors out of each other's way while taking the advice of your cinematographer about where to place the camera. Camera shots and coverage for episodic television are different from those for features in the following ways:

First, in episodic television, directors avoid shooting establishing shots unless they are needed to frame the episode in some way.

Second, since television is intended for a small screen, the important information must be near or in the center of the frame.

Third, the close-ups and extreme close-ups are usually tighter than you will find for features. Seeing a face thirty feet high on a movie screen is aesthetically different from seeing it on a twenty-seven inch television set. Although the same theory of *the closer the camera gets the more truth it tells* still applies, the delivery size of the image has an impact on your audience, and directors adjust the aesthetics accordingly.

Fourth, if it is within the style of the show, shots like rack focus, steadicam, and hand-held are more the norm than the exception. Of course, since the cinematographer you are working with has done many episodes of the show, all you need to say is the type of shot you want, such as "let's do an extreme close-up," and the camera crew will frame and shoot it accordingly.

Your ability not only to know story, theme, and characters and adapt to the visual style of the show but also to direct guest performers, work as a *team member* with the regular cast and crew, and your knowledge of coverage for editorial choices will send the word to producers and network executives that you can direct episodic narrative television. This, by the way, is an excellent foundation for directing features.

SITCOMS

Some television situation comedies, such as *My Name Is Earl* and *Arrested Development*, are shot in the single camera narrative style. But television situation comedies such as *Everybody Loves Raymond*, *Will & Grace*, *Reba*, and *Two and a Half Men* are directed half-hour plays that are shot with multiple film or tape cameras. Situation comedies are stories that put a series of set, individual characters in a variety of situations that are reflective of the personalities and sensibilities of the show. Whether shot in front of an audience or not, multiple camera sitcoms are all approached basically the same way from a director's standpoint:

- The sets are designed as stage sets for a proscenium theater, with entrances and exits stage left (camera right), stage right (camera left), or upstage center.[2] The sets are usually the same for each episode and are familiar to the audience as being endemic to the show and its characters.
- Each weekly episode is a half-hour play.
- Actors are staged and directed exactly as they would be for a play. The staging is usually around a central set piece, such as a sofa or a kitchen table. Actors are not concerned about camera language, shot, or playing to a camera as actors would be in the single-camera approach. They are more attuned to acting within the ensemble, executing their actions, and timing the delivery of their dialogue.
- Three or four cameras mounted on movable pedestals or dollies move around the front of the set area in coordination with the actor's movements while documenting the action and characters of the play. They function in a cross-shooting pattern, thereby creating coverage as the scene unfolds.

---

[2] Directors working in sitcoms use theater terms such as "stage right" and "stage left," as opposed to the camera terminology of "camera right" and "camera left."

(10-1a)

(10-1b)

(10-1c)

Sitcom floor plan

Multiple-camera sitcoms are developed, rehearsed, and completed through a five-day weekly process. The first day of rehearsal is a table read with actors, writers, producers, and the director, during which they work out the dialogue and jokes of the weekly story. On the second and third days, directors block and rehearse the actors on the set, working through each scene of the script. Each scene is then polished and the dialogue refined, with the writers present during these rehearsals. Also on day three and on all of day four, the director blocks the cameras to the action, using the timing and rhythm of the actors to make sure that every nuance of comedy from each character is being caught in some way by the camera. For example, four cameras on a scene with Raymond, Marie, Deborah, and Frank in *Everybody Loves Raymond* might have a four-shot of everyone, a two-shot of Raymond and Deborah, another two-shot of Frank and Marie, and a medium shot of Raymond if he is the focus of the joke at that moment. As the scene progresses, the cameras will shift to different shots through repositioning or centering on different characters, or both. All cameras at all times are shooting some aspect of the scene as determined by the director.

During camera blocking, some directors work first from the set, methodically blocking the cameras through each of their shots while walking the actors through the staging and fine-tuning the placement of the actors or the cameras, and then work from the control booth (if recorded in video), where they see the shots from all the cameras simultaneously.[3] Camera and dolly operators prepare shot lists and must learn their staging to make sure they don't bump into one another; and, as for actors, marks are put on the stage noting the various movements of the cameras. During

---

[3] If a sitcom is shot on film, the three or four film cameras record the images continuously, and all editing is done in postproduction. Video assist may be employed.

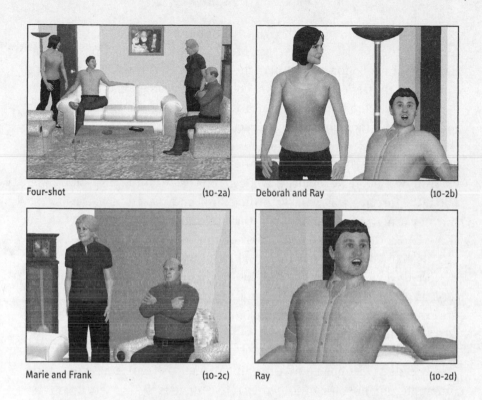

Four-shot (10-2a)   Deborah and Ray (10-2b)

Marie and Frank (10-2c)   Ray (10-2d)

rehearsal the camera people get in sync with the actors so they will be on top of their game throughout the performance.

The fifth day of the week is *production day*. A dress rehearsal is scheduled in the morning, cleaning up any last-minute problems before the *final performance*, which is done later in the day and which might be scheduled in front of an audience. The performances must go like clockwork, with cameras doing the *dance* they did during rehearsal and both actors and cameras stopping at the end of each scene. If there is a flub or a set problem, the recording stops, things are reset, and they begin again. Multiple runs of the scenes are scheduled; this protects the project, and allows for writers to rewrite jokes that did not work for the audience, and directors to change some of the camera shots to give the editor a variety of reactions from different characters for editing.

If the show is taped (as opposed to shot on film), the cameras will be cabled to a control booth, and the director will *call the show*, laying down

---

[4] A line cut is the director's choice of shots electronically inserted in sequence as the project is being acted or performed. In certain styles of narrative television it is used as the first cut and is polished with other shots inserted by the director working with the editor.

a *line cut*[4] of the scene. In the control booth, the assistant director and technical director use a marked script to indicate the sequence of shots that has been designed for each camera for each scene. The assistant director's job during the performance is to make sure each camera has the shot that was rehearsed; the technical director (also known as the switcher) listens for the precise moment that the director says "take" and motions to click the appropriate prearranged and rehearsed camera image into the line cut. The director watches the camera monitors, listens to the actors, feels the rhythm of their performances, and calls for each shot at a specific time. Later, the director will work with the editor and make corrections to the line cut using performances from the multiple takes of the scene. If the show is recorded on film, then each of the cameras for the process will use film cameras, and the episode will be edited entirely afterward. This is preferred when the producer and director want the show to have a "film" look as opposed to a "videotape" look. *Seinfeld, Friends,* and *Will & Grace* are examples of sitcoms originating on film, while *Two and a Half Men* and *Reba* are sitcoms that originate on videotape. In both cases, however, the delivery of the final project is on tape.[5]

The shots designed for a multiple-camera sitcom are significantly different from those for any other narrative form. *First,* there are no reverse angles or insert shots. *Second,* the camera is an observer (of the characters), as if the viewers are in a theater watching from the right, the center, or the left side of the audience seating. *Third,* the shots are rarely tighter than medium shots. *Fourth,* sitcoms never use dolly movements but instead use a zooming movement when needing to widen or tighten a shot on camera. *Fifth,* actors allow the camera to view what they are doing rather than embrace the camera as part of the scene.

The focus in multiple-camera sitcom direction rests squarely on the rhythm of the ensemble acting, timing of the dialogue, and delivery of the actors' action. When there is a live, in-studio audience, the actors play for the reaction of the audience. The visual rhythm in sitcoms comes not just from the rhythm of the editing, as it does in single-camera narrative, but primarily from the rhythm of the actors in their playing of the scene. In some cases, directors will mix styles: multiple-camera and single-camera techniques. However, these cases are rare and are usually used when the

---

[5] There have been "special event" broadcasts of episodes of *Will & Grace* and *Friends* that were recorded live (on tape). This was also done with *ER* in the 2003–2004 season and *The West Wing* in 2006.

stories are taken to exterior locations, when it becomes easier to use the single-camera approach.

Comedy is difficult and needs to be directed and played honestly and sincerely in order to be funny. This can be done only by excellent writers, a skilled director with a sense of humor, and an ensemble of actors who are theater-savvy. There is a theatrical and friendly appeal in the half-hour sitcom format. The actors portraying the characters are often thought of not as who they are but as the characters they play. And when a sitcom is successful, the television viewers invite these characters into their homes as welcome guests whom they know and love.

SOAP OPERAS

Soap operas, or "soaps," are ongoing episodic works of fiction and a genre of television that has existed for decades. What differentiates soap operas from single-camera episodic television or sitcoms is the open-ended nature of the storylines. Plots run concurrently and lead to further developments. They are generally programmed Monday through Friday in daytime broadcast slots. An individual installment of a soap will generally switch between several concurrent story lines that may at times affect one another or may run entirely independent of one another. Some of the installments will refer back to other moments in the lives of the characters.

Daytime soaps are usually one hour long. They are structured so there is some rotation of both storylines and characters, so that any given storyline or actor will appear in some but usually not all of a week's worth of installments. Soaps rarely "wrap things up" and avoid bringing all the current storylines to conclusion at the same time. When one storyline ends, there are always others still going at different stages of development. Episodes invariably seem not to finish, as they always involve a cliff-hanger of one sort or another. The audience needs to return to see what happens.[6]

Although most soap operas are seen in the daytime, some nighttime television shows, such as *Desperate Housewives*, *Lost*, and *The OC* incorporate elements of the soap opera. But because of the way they are produced and directed, they fall into the category of single-camera episodic television. They differ from the general format of soap operas both in practice and in approach, and they generally, but not always, feature an entire cast in

---

[6] Portions courtesy of Wikipedia, September 2006.

each installment. Each week, they refresh the audience's memory in the opening teaser. Also, unlike daytime soaps, they generally are broadcast one night a week and run for only a part of the year. They therefore tend to bring the stories to a dramatic end-of-season cliff-hanger.[7]

Directors of daytime soaps such as *Days of Our Lives, General Hospital,* and *All My Children* are faced with the problems and issues of directing a full hour episode (forty-eight actual minutes of story, allowing for commercials) in as efficient and creative a method as possible. Direction still involves actors and visual storytelling, but in a fashion that pulls audiences into the story at each installment. There are some basic elements that are inherent to all (daytime) soap operas:

- They are shot with multiple videotape cameras on sets at studios. All cameras are cabled to a control room.
- As in sitcoms, cameras are placed in front of the set and actors are staged near the cameras. Lighting for soap operas is for multiple cameras and primarily for the actors.
- There are multiple sets for the multiple storylines that run in the soap, for the multiple scenes for each episode.
- There are always sets intended to give a sumptuous and luxurious look that reflect the wealth of the characters.
- Soap operas rarely feature a practical exterior location, so they recreate the outdoor locale in the studio. On the few occasions when scenes have been taken out of the studio, single-camera narrative direction technique has been employed.
- The close-up is the most important shot in a soap. Therefore, soap operas will use more close-ups and extreme close-ups than audiences see in any other form of narrative television. Soap opera audiences want to be inside the characters they love and with whom they identify.
- Audiences are used to and expect a zooming camera movement. Although avoided in single-camera narrative as an unnatural way to visualize a scene, the large videotape cameras are difficult to dolly or truck during taping, so the zoom has become an accepted norm for soap audiences.

---

[7] Shows like *Las Vegas* and *Desperate Housewives* are redefining the television narrative format. Although not dealing with the same story content as a soap, they both have a cast of characters with weekly stories that complete themselves while also developing storylines that carry over from episode to episode with a cliff-hanger at the end of the season.

- Actors are staged in classic soap opera staging for camera. This staging includes shots such as a *stacked two-shot*,[8] in which one character is looking at the camera while the other is behind that actor's shoulder looking at the character facing camera.

(10-3)

- Cameras are employed in cross-shooting a scene to benefit coverage.
- There are no in-studio audiences.

As in sitcoms, all cameras are recording at all times, and actors play out the scenes as if it were a play. But the camera shots in soaps are different. Whereas in sitcoms the camera *views* the story, in soap operas the camera (and audience) is *part of* the story and feeling what the characters are feeling. And in that sense, directors of soaps must tell the story with pictures.

Television soaps are headed up by producer/writers, although the director is very important to the success of each installment. Because of the number of shows that must be delivered, all soap operas have more than one director working on separate episodes. Each episode is linked to the others, so the process of directing a soap opera allows for that linkage. The director eventually winds up in a control booth assigning a shot at specific points in each of the scenes. So in the planning stage, directors must know the choreography of the cameras in connection to the blocking of the characters.

When directors of soaps prepare, they first read the script and, if need be, study the outline of the stories of each episode. They then review segments of other installments that feed into the stories of the episode they are directing. This review shows them the staging launching-off point of their segment from the story of the previous episode. Pickups occur 20 percent of the time and are revised replays of scenes.

Next, the producer sends the director the floor plan of the sets in which the stories for their episode take place. Most of the sets are permanent *standing sets* reflecting the living rooms, bedrooms, kitchens, and so on, of

---

[8] A form of an over-the-shoulder shot.

the characters. Working alone, the director lays out on paper the staging and camera shots of the entire episode, recognizing that in most cases the cameras are downstage of the set. Conceptualizing the *hook* of the episode is extremely important. The hook is a great shot at the beginning of the story that immediately grabs the audience. Skilled soap directors search for that shot while at the same time working on finding transition shots that are needed between scenes for each of the seven acts of an hour-long soap opera.[9] When this preparation is completed, the director has gone through the entire show on paper: preparing the shooting script, designing and numbering each shot, and assigning a camera for each shot. The script is given to the technical director, who makes a second set of floor plans marked with every camera angle and the positions of the actors in each scene for the seven acts.

On day two, the director holds a production meeting with the lighting director, the prop master, the costume designer, the special effects person, the set dressers for each set, and the technical director, who provides copies of the new floor plan, which is used for discussion at the meeting. A shooting schedule is also prepared at the meeting. It is designed around the accessibility of the sets, actor availability, and other logistics inherent to the production process. After the meeting, the technical director, using the director's script, records a shot list for each camera called a *shot card*.

On day three, the director arrives around 6:00 A.M. to walk quickly through each set with the production set dressers, fine-tuning the positions of all furniture and props and laying down lighting marks on the floor. Kept very simple, these marks indicate not only where the actors will stand for the shot but also the placement of key furniture so that the lighting can be fine-tuned for the taping. Actors are called into makeup from 6:00–8:00 A.M. At about 7:00 A.M. the stage managers, set dressers, special effects, and additional prop people who work the show meet with the director and talk through the entire show in shooting order, in terms of what actions the actors will perform and when they will execute those actions. This would include such things as: when does the actor light the cigarette, drink the coffee, get the bottle from the bar, and so forth. At 8:00 A.M. the actors arrive on the set, and *dry blocking* of the first half of the show begins. Dry blocking is the staging of only the actors in the scene. Directors of soap

---

[9] An *act* comprises the scenes that take place between the commercials. Some acts have three scenes, while others may have four.

operas rarely work the actors in terms of their characters since, as in series television, the actors know their characters best. However, because of the respect and trust established between actor and director, directors may often help the actor find new values in their character that they had not realized. When a new character is introduced to the story, the actor playing the role has already discussed the character with the producer/writer and is up to speed regarding who he or she is in the story. The director will further help to assimilate the new actor into the show's ensemble.

Camera blocking with the actors immediately follows the dry blocking, with the director working from the floor and the assistant director and technical director working from the control booth. Although the number of cameras can go to six or seven, the director usually works with three cameras in one set. Actor blocking is usually horizontal on the set, moving actors downstage (toward the cameras), although when necessary, the cameras can shoot through open doors and windows to get a specific angle and make the audience feel part of the scene. Camera blocking is the time when the director makes physical adjustments to the actor blocking, prop placement, or a camera position to fine-tune for the camera shots that were conceived days earlier on paper. At the same time, the camera people, using their shot cards, work through the technicalities of what they need to do and where their cameras need to be from shot to shot so they do not get in the way of other cameras' shots.

After camera blocking a scene, the director goes into the control booth to direct first a dress rehearsal without stopping and then, after actor touch-up for makeup and hair, a final taping of the scene without stopping. During the taping, each camera's image is independently recorded[10] and also fed to a switcher operated by the technical director, who is cutting the scene into a rehearsed line cut on the director's command. The shots that the director desires are aimed in the line cut, but the timing of them may be off by a second or two, and one or two of the shots may have been missed. During the taping, the director may give notes to the assistant director so that the tape can be corrected or tweaked in editing. During the taping, the producer is in the booth also making notes on the scene that may be used to fine-tune the edit.

Most soap directors do not see the finished show. However, the editor uses the director's notes and compares them to the line cut before showing it

---

[10] These are commonly known as ISOs (isolated recorded images).

to the producer, who may adjust the edit before the show airs on television. Unless a portion of the episode is shot in single-camera narrative style, the director is not involved in the editing process. DGA Award-winning daytime soap director Herb Stein has final approval of all of the shows he directs on *Days of Our Lives*, but that is rare in the industry.

The director's creativity with multiple-camera direction of soap operas rests with translating the script into a visual story about the characters and their relationships. Directors work toward reaching their audience by taking them on the emotional journey of the story, episode after episode. They cause the audience to empathize with the character they love and with whom they identify day after day. Their skill underlies, in part, the success of this powerful genre.

....

Award-winning director Herb Stein contributed information concerning directing for daytime soap operas in this chapter. His credits include *Days of Our Lives*, director of *Escape to Love*, and writer of the TV movie *American Eyes*.

....

CHAPTER TEN SUMMARY

➤ Television is a writer/producer's medium.

➤ Television is a good training ground for directors.

➤ Directors in television work with a shortened production schedule and complete more pages in a day's work than feature directors.

➤ Episodic narrative television is written to be directed in six or seven days in a controlled situation.

➤ Episodic directors are often substitute teachers for the week.

➤ Episodic directors must deliver the episode in the style and manner the audience expects.

➤ Camera shots and single-camera coverage for episodic television are different from those for features.

➤ Directors of episodic television should gain trust from their actors before they begin working on the set.

➤ Multiple-camera television sitcoms are directed half-hour plays.

➤ Multiple-camera sitcoms employ a format in which the audience observes the characters.

➤ Soap operas employ a multiple-camera format in which the audience becomes more intimately involved with the characters.

➤ Sitcom direction focuses on the rhythm of the ensemble acting, the timing of the dialogue, and the delivery of the actors' action.

➤ Soap operas are ongoing works of fiction with an open-ended nature to the stories.

➤ Directors of hour-long daytime soaps are faced with the problems of directing forty-eight minutes of story in as efficient and creative a method as possible.

> *"I want to do things I think I can really bring something special to and not do anything for the sake of just being out there."*
>
> — **Clint Eastwood**

CHAPTER **11**

DIRECTING TELEVISION, PART 2: NONSCRIPTED

Television not only tenders narrative programming but also forms of programming such as variety-event, documentary, and reality formats that in their own unique ways require direction. These formats are considered nonscripted and function primarily as types of multiple-camera formats, although they may also use a single camera for various aspects of the project.

VARIETY EVENT TELEVISION

Variety or event television is produced in front of an audience. There are two styles to this format: one whose primary purpose is for a ticket-paying theater audience, such as *The Eagles: Hell Freezes Over* or *Queen on Fire: Live at the Bowl*; the second, whose primary purpose is for a television audience, such as The Academy Awards, The Grammy Awards, *Inside The Actors Studio, The Tonight Show, The Late Show with David Letterman, Oprah,* and

Saturday Night Live, for which the audience does not pay admission but is part of the viewing event.

These shows:

- Are scripted, loosely scripted, or not scripted at all.
- Are talent-driven; that is, focused around the skills or personality of the talent.
- Are produced on location using remote television facilities that are set up the day of the event or days ahead of the event or are produced at studios where audiences are brought in.
- Use upward of six to eight cameras and can use as many as twenty or thirty cameras depending on the complexity of the event.
- Are rehearsed according to the schedules and logistics of the talent.
- Rely on spontaneity and other elements of the event to add excitement for the television audience.
- Have individual elements that are endemic to the project.
- Have massive organizational logistics that require skillful producing.
- Must work for both the audience in the theater or studio and the audience at home.
- Have a central theme, host, or concept that is the focus of the show.

The structure and logistics of these shows require directors to work differently from the way they would work on scripted narrative projects. Directors must first determine their cast of characters and production elements. For an award ceremony it would be the host, the presenters, the nominees, the winners, the entertainers, the audience, prerecorded segments and clips, and perhaps things that go on behind the scenes. For a musical concert it would be the artist, the musicians, the on-stage spectacle, and the audience. For a late-night variety show or daytime talk show it would be the audience, the host, and the guests. Each of these events has its own cast of characters and prerecorded segments; directors (and producers and writers) determine the best presentation for the television audience.

Like narrative television, variety event shows begin with a concept, and directors look for the concept when meeting or working with the talent. I directed a variety event show seen on HBO. It was a concert by the musical group Chicago when they were on tour. It was taped at one of their performance venues in Pine Knob, Michigan. In meeting with the group, I noticed how close and warmhearted they were with one another offstage and felt that was an important part of who they were in their music. I wanted the television audience who had heard and known them for years to see that part of them. Because it was at the height of their musical touring career, I knew the venue audience would be excited to see them when they finally arrived on stage. So in the opening of the television program, we intercut the pre-concert anticipation of the audience with the pre-concert anticipation of the group backstage. The musicians were all together with their families, and from the footage we shot you could see the love they had for one another blended with their nervous energy as they prepared to go on stage. As it got closer to showtime and the offstage announcer raised the crowd to a fever pitch, the guys began their walk from the dressing room to the stage—this aspect of the show was recorded single-camera, reality style—and in postproduction we continued to intercut these images with images of the fervent audience. The stage was dark except for the backlit platforms, musical instruments, and silhouettes of the group as they walked to their microphones. The theater audience was frantic. This was all part of the visual opening for the television audience. The chords of the first musical number began. The lights on stage came up. And the audience screamed as the concert audience saw Robert Lamm, James Pankow, Peter Cetera, and the rest of Chicago. The television audience was watching this when we instantly cut to a medium shot of Robert Lamm at the keyboards starting the vocal of the first song, and we were on our way. The concert ran two hours, and we recorded the event with eight cameras from a remote truck behind the scenes. We focused on the show theatrics that the venue audience saw while bringing the warmth and personality of each of the artists through close-ups and other shots that brought them closer to their music. This opening of the television show appeared to be duplicated by many others for years to come.

Another project I directed (and co-produced) for Columbia Television was a pilot of *The Mickey Finn Show*, a syndicated weekly variety show. Mickey Finn was a piano player whose group consisted of zany musicians, each with their own comedic personality that contributed to the musical craziness of the act. They were a popular show that at that time headlined in Vegas showrooms. The program was conceived as an hour of madcap music performances interspersed with written comedy sketches performed by members of the group and guest stars McLean Stephenson, Debbie Reynolds, and Rip Taylor. It was a fast-paced variety program chock full of sketch blackouts, surprises, and insane comedic musical circumstances. Produced at the Six Flags Magic Mountain amusement park in Valencia, California, the sketches were shot all over the park, single-camera style, and the musical performances were shot using multiple cameras in one of the park's outdoor theaters. The audience was brought in specifically for the taping of the musical performances. There was a two-day shooting schedule, and the logistics of the project were very complex, especially since we decided to open the show with a shot of the empty amusement park and the distant strains of a marching band making their approach led by our cast of characters, before all of a sudden the park magically filled with people. Using the University of Southern California marching band, eight remote cameras, and our cast, we shot the beginning of the parade before the park opened and then, with locked-off cameras in position, did a portion of it again when people were in the park. We created an opening sequence designed to grab the television audience and set the ambience for what was to come.

There is an immediate pressure in directing variety events since directors are always fighting time and sometimes the talent can be unpredictable.[1] During the taping of the musical segments of *The Mickey Finn Show*, Debbie Reynolds decided she did not want to stay to do the single-camera sketches she was scheduled to do and announced to the stage manager that she was going to leave right after the musical numbers. I was already behind schedule, and the pressure was on when this was relayed to me in the control booth. I quietly took my headset off and walked out of the booth to the stage, where I met Ms. Reynolds. I asked her what was wrong and she told me what I already knew, which was that she had to get back to Reno, Nevada, for a show she was appearing in that night. I assured her that we would be finished with her work in plenty of time. But she still insisted. I paused and remembered that she worked for the great producer Louis B. Mayer, and in my Louis B. Mayer voice and attitude and with a twinkle in my eye, I said, "Debbie, get into your #$%&#@ wardrobe for the sketches, and we will do it right next to your #@%^&# dressing room

---

[1] In live broadcasts like the Oscar, Grammy, or Emmy telecasts, audiences at home love those unpredictable moments.

so you are ready to leave after you complete the #$@%^& work we are paying you for!" There was a pause of at least ten seconds as she stared at me and then let out a raucous laugh and said: "I like you!" And she gave me a kiss on my cheek as she passed by me to her dressing room to change for the sketches. From that moment on we were friends, and many years later when I attended one of her charity events she told me that story, which of course is one that I will never forget.

When directing a multiple-camera variety event show, directors lay out the camera positions that provide them with a shot pattern they can follow logically in calling the show. The first camera position that is determined is the camera that tells the viewing audience *whom* they

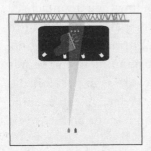

are seeing. This is the primary camera and the one that is usually focused on center stage or wherever the main talent is to be speaking to the theater audience. The second camera position to be set is the camera that tells the viewing audience *where* that person is. These two cameras are usually set side by side, with one camera wider than the other. Or they are set in the same line toward the stage.

Floor plan establishes first two camera positions

(11-1a)

(11-1b)

After those two cameras are set, directors consider the other elements that make up the unpredictable spontaneity and visual presentation of the show and set the cameras accordingly. They can be fixed, hand-held, or on a remote-controlled boom, which allows for greater mobility. Cameras can be positioned onstage, backstage, or at various places in the audience: wherever they need to be to tell instantly what is happening and advance the visual theme of the event as it develops.

Once the cameras have been set, the images from each camera are fed to a control booth and to a digital switcher so directors can call for shots as they see fit. Directors try to maintain a shot pattern motivated by the movement of the show and its talent, allowing for an escape camera for those moments when the unexpected happens. The *where* camera is often considered the escape camera. It is the safety shot that keeps the audience centered on the spatial relationship of where things and people are when the shot pattern needs to get back on track. It functions as an establishing shot would in the single-camera narrative and is always there if and when the director needs it.

Directors who direct this type of programming, such as Emmy and DGA Award-winning Louis J. Horvitz,[2] are attuned to what the talent is saying as well as anticipating what they will be doing so they can make sure they call for the right shot at the right time. Their minds are always anticipating, listening, and looking for the next shot and thinking ahead while a shot is *on the air*. Directing from the control booth, the director calls the shots as he sees them on the monitors. In this situation the director is visually, for a nanosecond, *cutting in his head*, but the cutting is based upon what is being seen and heard from the talent. For every shot, the director in a split second is looking for the motivation for the cut. And the motivation is usually the basic motivation for all edits, showing the audience what they need or want to see when they need or want to see it.

Variety-event direction depends greatly on the skill of the camera people. They must have an eye for finding the right moments and framing the shots—whether subjective or objective—that will develop the theme. Some shots are called for by the director, and some are not. Directors must convey concept and theme to their camera people and key personnel before rehearsal or taping, giving them some indication of what to expect. Rehearsal for camera is always preferred, but some of these shows have rehearsals for camera and some do not, as talent spontaneity is part of the show. Those that are rehearsed for camera are never rehearsed thoroughly but rather for their logistics. Those that do not rehearse for the camera are the most difficult, and if the director can watch a rehearsal of the talent to get an idea of what and how they do what they do, all the better! The

---

[2] Credits include *The Annual Academy Award Shows* since 1997, *The Kennedy Center Honors, AFI Tributes, People's Choice Awards, Emmy Awards,* and many more (and being my old college roommate and friend for over thirty years).

more familiar they are with the elements of the event, the easier it is for the director to succeed.

Keeping this in mind, on one award show the producer scheduled a rehearsal with stand-in talent who substituted for the nominees. At the rehearsal, the *sitters* were in the seats they were assigned. Without knowing the winners, the show was rehearsed so that everyone was ready for whoever won in their respective categories. When the first winner was called during the actual show, the cameraman went to the seat where he thought the winner sat. Lo and behold someone else was sitting in the seat. It was discovered that none of the nominees were sitting in their assigned seats because during the pre-show party all of the guests enjoyed themselves at an open bar. When called to go into the theater for the event they sat wherever they wanted and not where they were assigned. Panic set in! But because the director was ready with an escape camera and the other seven cameras were positioned appropriately, the shot pattern changed immediately. When the winner was announced from the stage, the director cut to the escape camera (a high angle shot of the audience) and slowly zoomed in to the first person who rose out of his or her seat, then cut to the camera closest to the person, which followed the winner to the stage. Once the winner got to the stage, the cameras that told *who* and *where* took over. Directing on the fly and solving such emergencies helps you think quickly on your feet—something that translates well into directing single-camera narrative.

NONFICTION—DOCUMENTARY AND REALISM

Documentary film is a broad category of cinematic expression united by the intent to remain factual or nonfictional. It is a genre unto itself, and documentary features are a large part of the commercial world, although documentary has found a particular home in cable television. There is a logical format for nonfiction on specialized cable stations such as the Science Channel, the Discovery Channel, the History Channel, and the National Geographic Channel. Although we refer to it as nonfiction, there are some schools of thought that say that there is no such thing as nonfiction. There are only scripted and unscripted programs and films. Even a documentary, though often referred to as nonfiction, begins with a script or an outline, both of which motivate the coverage as the director directs for the spontaneous. For example, say you have a scene of a man wrestling a bear. The bear is not going to stop and do it again, so how do you as director plan to get the coverage needed? There are various choices. *One*, it can be shot with multiple cameras. *Two*, it can be documented and analyzed as it is being shot, with inserts shot for coverage to strengthen the drama through editing. Or *three*, work with a camera operator who knows how to use one camera to create coverage through a simple, fluid move of the camera and a change of the focal length of the lens, which can create another angle to cut to later.

The nonfiction documentary director who operates the camera can be passive when framing the action and let it run or active when letting the action run but capturing it in such a way that once inserts are applied and shot angles maneuvered, the result is an internally manipulated *vérité*.[3]

So how do nonfiction directors control or direct a sequence if they are not really in control? By the choices they make visually, on the spot in production or in the editing of images in postproduction or both. Documentary directors find the drama in reality in the postproduction phase of the project. They look for the thread that links the story together, and usually it comes out of nowhere. Nonfiction directors are only as good as their footage. For example, it will be impossible to go back to Uganda and recapture the reality once the material has been shot there, so directors of nonfiction generally shoot a lot more film or tape than directors of fiction. But reality can be measured in degrees. And the documentary director decides that measurement, since it is determined not only by the event being covered and its limitations but also by the extent to which the director prepares and gets the footage needed for postproduction.

There is another nonfiction "reality" available to the documentary director. This is the one that is *practically* staged. It is of actual people and events doing what they would normally do in the place they would do it, but now for the benefit of camera. For example, a director flies to Africa, picks a village to shoot, assembles the village, and selects the most pitiful looking people there to make up a family for the camera. He then removes the animals from the corral, strews some bones in the foreground, and shoots it in such a way that with the right narration in postproduction a reality is created that is manipulated for effect, may be false as staged, and yet is intended to reflect the reality of the region. The practically staged reality!

---

[3] Events occurring naturally in candid realism.

In nonfiction/documentary, the director is often the producer. But there are instances in which there is a separate producer, who is usually referred to as an executive producer, or EP. In those situations, directors outline the visual objectives and style in service to the story and tone of the work. They then execute it and accommodate not only the project's objective but also the needs of the editor and ultimately the audience. They work under the guidance of the EP.

However, the best documentary directors know the nuances of the technical side: when the lighting is good, when the shot will work, what they have obtained vs. what is still needed to make a sequence work, what the needs of every member of the production team are, and so on. From the outside looking in, this would appear easy. But understanding the inner rhythm of a sequence that can never be repeated and has to organically connect to what preceded, what will come next, or what will be reinvented on the spot calls for an understanding of the gestalt of the process. Then in postproduction, reinvent and reveal as close as possible the planned sequence. This is the nature of the documentary director. It is a medium unto itself, and it takes a director who thinks a specific way and investigates the thread of a story through the material *after* it is in the can.[4]

REALITY TELEVISION

Reality television is a genre that commonly is unscripted. It is not fiction but documents actual events. It features ordinary people rather than professional actors. Exploding onto the scene in 2000, reality shows can actually be traced back to the 1950s with Alan Funt's *Candid Camera*. The genre was then fully realized in 1973 with *An American Family*. The visual directorial style of reality shows began to define itself in 1989 with the show *Cops*, which showed police officers on duty and introduced the gritty hand-held feel that is the norm for many reality shows today.

In 1992, MTV's *The Real World* created the concept of putting strangers together in a selected environment for an extended period of time and recording the drama that ensues among them with cameras placed throughout their living quarters. (Cameras also tagged along when cast members left their residence.) This has led to *Survivor*, *Big Brother*, *The Bachelor*, and a slew of other shows using the same formula. The first

---

[4] A term referring to footage after it is shot.

self-improvement or *makeover theme* reality show appeared in 1996 with British TV's *Changing Rooms*, in which couples redecorated each others' houses. It was copied in the United States with the show *Trading Spaces*. Makeover shows such as *Supernanny, Queer Eye for the Straight Guy, Extreme Makeover*, and *The Biggest Loser* are variations of this type. At first, reality shows appealed to the audience's voyeuristic side. However, as the popularity of reality programming increased, the entertainment factor became important. When reality shows moved into the prime-time television hours, they adjusted themselves with an element of fantasy or adventure by putting their participants in exotic locations or in unusual situations. Producers determined the reality and created rules that were defined by the concept of the show. The behavior of the participants operating outside their own reality became the dramatic basis of the show, heightened the voyeuristic element for the audience, and offered a degree of entertainment. When the *Survivor* series began, it added the additional element of competition. Its carefully selected participants, who lived together in an alien location, also became contestants battling each other to complete striking and improbable tasks. The twist: they were removed from the show until only one winner remained. *Survivor* initiated shows such as *The Amazing Race* and *Fear Factor*, which operate with similar premises, promising rewards along the way, and a big monetary reward at the end to the winner or winners. The Emmy Award–winning *The Amazing Race* does it in serial fashion, whereas *Fear Factor* does it anew every week.

In reality shows, the viewers are passive observers or voyeurs as the camera follows people going through their daily personal or professional activities, whether they are ordinary people (*Big Brother*) or celebrities (*Celebrity Mole*) and the audience feels like a "fly on the wall," witnessing what is happening. The plots are constructed either through editing or through planned situations and have an almost soap opera appeal. On-camera hosts interacting with the participants make statements or ask questions in the hope of the camera catching an emotional response that might be edited into the show. This concept continues with people competing for jobs or stardom that will be life-changing on such shows as *American Idol*,[5] *The Apprentice, The Next Food Network Star, Hells Kitchen*, and *Project Runway*. All of these formats provide the opportunity for human

---

[5] Shows such as *American Idol* and *Dancing with the Stars* call for variety-event and reality direction techniques.

conflict to occur, which makes this genre for television very popular. Some reality shows create minor celebrities of their contestants, and there is even a reality cable channel that is fueled by former reality shows.[6]

Though reality television is producer-driven, directors are required. In reality television, directors function more as coordinators for the cameras and camera people rather than as directors of the talent. They must anticipate what might happen and have coverage prepared for a variety of outcomes. They, along with the producers, analyze the personalities and foibles of the talent and attempt to determine where the tension or interest might come from. They then work with their camera team in a variety of ways, depending on the concept and logistics of the show. If the show is in a controlled environment, like *Starting Over*, they operate from an adjacent room in the location, speaking to each camera person through headsets. The cameras that are used can be anything from the smaller quality mini-DV cameras to larger, professional DV cameras. Some are self- or remote-controlled, recording sound directly on the tape. Or there may be a sound person working with the camera person on the crew. Directors determine how best to set up based on the characteristics of the participants and the elements of the show. Unlike event programming, the shows are not cabled to a control booth,[7] and directors do not call the show into a line cut. Instead, each camera records its own image, and the project is edited later.

On other shows like *The Bachelor* or *The Mole*, the director must make sure that the camera people know what the show is trying to achieve and attempt to communicate that to the crew before they go into the field to shoot the show. In these situations, and depending on the director, the crew is encouraged to look for moments of emotion from the participants. On some shows there is no director but instead a field producer who acts as the director, as in the cases of *Survivor* and *The Amazing Race*.[8] On other types of shows, such as *Starting Over*, the producer controls the show and the camera crew directs in the field.

Whether there is a director or a field producer-director, the direction tries to capture the overall action while looking for reaction and cutaway material for coverage. Cutaway coverage usually consists of the people who

---

[6] Portions courtesy of Wikipedia, September 2006.

[7] Portions of shows such as *Big Brother* are exceptions.

[8] The Directors Guild of America has recently recognized directors of this genre and has been working with some production companies to make sure directors are DGA members.

are not talking but who are part of the sequence nonetheless. Cutaway coverage can also mean insertion images, such as hands or other parts of the body, that would indicate a person's inner feelings. If the staging of any part of a reality-event calls for the participants to be observers, as in a competition or a game or a group of people waiting to see who gets voted off, as in *Survivor*, the camera operators (multiple) must make sure they get reactions of the people watching. Directors in reality television work at breakneck speed and sometimes under adverse conditions. There is no stage management when the reality unfolds. The stories are told on the fly.

The narrative and the drama for reality programming are determined together by the editor and the producer or story producer, although in some instances the director may be involved. They analyze the footage and create an outline of what the story of each episode should be. As in a drama, they consider the arc of the characters, especially if the series runs for an entire season. They look to have the characters play out the reality of the arc while hitting the story points in each episode. Story producers are writers, and they look to see whether these story elements exist in the footage so that the editor can work them into the show. Reality television is the closest thing to shooting a controlled documentary. Rather than a script being written, the reality of the situations and characters ensue and the script is developed from it. The director plays little or no part in this aspect. When a show is shot over many days, weeks, or months, the camera crew becomes invisible by maintaining the rule of never speaking to the talent and vice versa. This "wall" is very important. It is imperative to the human drama unfolding. There is a little bit of voyeurism in all of us, and this is what fuels this genre: watching real people in an unscripted drama. It has an appeal that will be around in television for a long time.

Directors are directors, no matter what medium they work in or the size of the screen. The processes may be different, but the basic underpinning is the same. The results may be different, but the origin of their creative approach is founded in concept, theme, and character (talent).

....

Award-winning documentary producer and director Robert Fiveson contributed the writing to the section Nonfiction: Documentary and Realism. His credits include *Escaping Death/Escape Tech*, *Red Space: The Secret Russian Space Program*, *The Mystery of Genius*, *The MIR Chronicles*, *Hiding Places*, and National Geographic specials for the Discovery Channel and *The Bloody Aleutians* and *Nazi Wine* for the History Channel.

Award-winning editor Barry Zetlin contributed to the section Reality Television. His credits include *Celebrity Mole: Yucatan, Starting Over, The Bachelor, TV Road Trip, High School Reunion,* and *Absence of Good.*

CHAPTER ELEVEN SUMMARY

➤ Variety or event television takes place in front of an audience and is talent-driven.

➤ The structure and logistics of variety shows require directors to work differently than for scripted narrative projects.

➤ Like scripted narrative, event television begins with a concept, and directors look for the concept when meeting or working with the talent.

➤ There is an immediate pressure in directing variety-event.

➤ When directing a multiple-camera variety project, directors lay out the camera positions for a shot pattern they can logically follow.

➤ Directors of event or variety must establish concept and theme with key personnel before rehearsal or taping.

➤ The first camera position to be set in variety-event tells the viewing audience *whom* they are seeing. The second tells them *where* that person is.

➤ The documentary director can be passive or active with the camera approach.

➤ In nonfiction/documentary, the director is often the producer.

➤ The nature of documentary requires the director to conceive the thread in postproduction.

➤ Reality shows appeal to the audience's voyeuristic side.

➤ Directors of reality shows encourage camera operators to look for moments of emotion.

➤ Directors in reality television work at breakneck speeds under adverse conditions.

➤ Drama for reality programming is put together by the editor and the producer.

*Creativity is discovering,
experimenting, growing, taking risks,
breaking rules, making mistakes,
and having fun.*

CHAPTER **12**

THE BUSINESS OF DIRECTING

The purpose of an artist is to uplift and fortify. Directing is an art and requires passion and vision. But calling yourself a director means making sure that you have the skills and knowledge for the business side of directing, because starting out professionally is always difficult. There is only one director per project, and that means you need to find a way to be that one. It is you and you alone who will ultimately face the producers, studio or network executives, and financial investors before you are hired as a director. That may be a surprise to you. Yes, television networks and film studios must approve the director. Financial investors must approve the director. Anyone who is on the fiscal side of the aisle will want to have confidence that the person directing the project can deliver the goods. They are businesspeople, so pay attention to some of the business aspects of being a director.

OVERVIEW

Always be yourself. Do not try to be someone you are not. The bottom line is that financiers, studio executives, and producers are investing in *you*, so be self-assured when meeting with them. If you are shy and withdrawn, you will not project the security that they need to see. Conversely, if what you think is self-assuredness is conceitedness and arrogance, you will not gain their confidence. Self-assuredness is the projection of a positive approach and belief in oneself without saying it. It is knowing, not wanting to know. It is confidence in who you are. If you are trying to get an agent or manager, self-assuredness will be very attractive. After all, that is what they will be selling when they speak of you and your talent to other people.

NEGOTIATING AND PITCHING

Learn some negotiating or pitching techniques, which are helpful in conversation and in encouraging people to see your point of view. Establish a rapport in informal conversation by talking about things outside of the project, such as sports, hobbies, or popular movies. This will make it easier when you get around to brass tacks. Let the people to whom you are pitching see how creative you are by painting a picture of the project you are talking about. Try to excite them and get them emotionally caught up in the vision. It is also probably a good idea to be humble about yourself and what you want to achieve; you don't want to appear to be arrogant, which can elicit a negative response. Once you start talking to someone about the project and you want to bring them unconsciously into it, refer to it as "our" project rather than "my" project. They will quickly feel a part of it and perhaps do something to help you with it.

RELATIONSHIPS, NETWORKING, AND YOUR EGO

Establish relationships as you travel up the ladder of your career. Relationships are very important, and you never know who you will meet going up the ladder that you may meet again later on or who may introduce you to their friends and colleagues while vouching for you and your talent. A talented student I know who is about to finish his film school degree took an internship with a well-known, well-established director and has shadowed him during preproduction and through production. The education he has received through this experience is one that his film school could never give, one that is teaching him the realities of the working profession while showing him both the pragmatic and creative sides of directing. He is also establishing a trusting relationship with the director and, as his friend, is meeting others (Morgan Freeman, for example) who are sharing their experiences with him. It is the nature of the industry to want to share and reach out to give someone a helping hand as long as that someone is genuine and does not appear to be "taking." This is called networking. Networking is very important, as relationships are the backbone of the profession. And with relationships, never burn a bridge, only reconstruct them. You will be surrounded with creativity, as creativity is the ability to see relationships where none exist. Maintain your integrity at all costs. You will at some time be faced with a choice of either jeopardizing or compromising your integrity. The business side of the profession seems to lead at some point to that quandary. This is something you must consider very carefully, as it is integrity that keeps relationships alive. Others will see your integrity and will come back to you and help you when you least expect it. Compromise is acceptable as long as you can retain some modicum of integrity within that compromise.

Keep your ego intact. Ego is a double-edged sword. The ego is the organized conscious negotiator between the internal person and the external reality. If it is out of balance and leaning toward the external reality, it can be perceived as pride, smugness, and vanity, which deflect confidence. But when in balance or leaning toward the internal person, ego will be perceived as a humble self-assuredness and attract others toward your convictions.

YOUR CREATIVE INTRODUCTION

Have stories you want to tell. Have projects you want to do. Have screenplays or books that you want to see on the screen. And have them all, because a small arsenal of projects shows that you are a visionary with passion. If you have a movie or a project or two that you have directed ready to show someone, all the better. But don't expect that person to fall in love with it. It is only an introduction to who you are and what you can do. It will be your self-assuredness regarding the new project that will sell you.

THE BUSINESS AROUND YOU

Be smart about the way the business works around you. Read the trade journals—*The Hollywood Reporter* or *Daily Variety*—and keep up to date with what is going on. Know the festival circuit and its value to you when the time comes. Visit the various film markets where movies are bought and sold, which may be tied to award festivals such as the Sundance Film Festival, the Toronto Film Festival, the Tribeca Film Festival, the American Film Market, and the Cannes Film Festival. You will network, be educated, and meet many people, some of whom are searching for directors for their projects. Directing is global, so don't fear working in foreign countries or in different languages. Gravitate toward your creative interests, whether they are mainstream or nonmainstream, and research opportunities in those directions. Be aware of or join organizations in which you will find other people to network with, such as the Television Academy (www.emmys.tv), Women in Film (www.wif.org), International Documentary Association (www.documentary.org), or the IFP (www.ifp.org). A journey on the Internet will identify more.

The Directors Guild of America (www.dga.org) has been referred to several times throughout the book. This is a professional organization in the United States made up of more than 13,000 directors, assistant directors, production managers, stage managers, and production assistants for features and television in all forms, including news and sports. The organization seeks to protect directorial teams' legal and artistic rights, contend for their creative freedom, and strengthen their ability to develop meaningful and credible careers. The Film Foundation falls under its umbrella. This is an organization whose educational programs, national campaigns, and public events provide support for preservation and restoration of projects at the Academy Film Archive, the Library of Congress, the UCLA Film and Television Archive, the National Center for Film and Video Preservation at the AFI, and the National Film Preservation Foundation. These cultural institutions are part of your legacy as a director and have mounted ambitious programs of preservation and restoration that enable public access to the United States' film treasures and the images we cherish most! Images that you should cherish most.

As stated on their website, the DGA is based in Los Angeles and New York City and neither solicits nor secures jobs for its members but is instead a bargaining organization whose primary jurisdiction is the United States.

Any production company is free to enter into an agreement with any director as long as it is not a signatory to the DGA. If the company has signed an agreement with the DGA, then it must only use members of the Guild, or the director it wishes to hire must join the Guild. DGA members are not permitted to work for a nonsignatory company. Minimum fees for DGA directors and other members are set by contract with the Guild, and the Guild makes agreements based upon a project's budgetary circumstances that permit DGA directors to negotiate their own fees (or work for free to exercise their egos if they want) below these minimums. The DGA is always headed by a president who is a working director in touch with the concerns—creative and otherwise—of other working directors. Do you need to be a DGA member to direct? Only for those projects of signatory companies.

BE PREPARED

Finally, be prepared to start at the bottom and work your way up. Take advantage of any opportunities, as they will always lead to something. Have a flanking expertise to directing so that you can work peripherally if you are not employed immediately as a director. Writing and producing are two good adjacent proficiencies. Many working people are writer-directors or producer-directors and function in either or both capacities on a project. What makes them better writers or producers is that when necessary they think like a director, and when directing they appreciate the creative responsibilities that are carried out by either the writer or the producer.

And experience life! Read the newspaper and magazines and discuss social awareness and humanity. Learn to laugh if you don't and cry if you want. Feel joy and sorrow and love what you do. And be prepared to be the director that you want to be. Strike that: *need* to be!

Stay in tune with technology, as it is ever-changing. It offers you new formats to direct such as video or Web games. Movies made for the Internet and video pods for your iPods, and mobisodes[1] for your cell phones are already here and increasing every year. Who knows what will happen in the next decade? Make no mistake: this is the visual century,

---

[1] A broadcast especially made for viewing on a mobile cell phone. The first mobisodes were launched in 2005. The word is coined by fusing together the two words *mobile* and *episode*.

and wherever there are moving visuals a director will be needed. It isn't the format that makes you the director; it is your ability to see the theme, the conflict, and the characters and to be able to weave them into a practical vision using your fluid imagination. And directors must dare to imagine! To quote George Bernard Shaw, *Imagination is the beginning of creation. You imagine what you desire. You will what you imagine. And at last, you create what you will.*

Now that you are prepared,
go out and direct!

AFTERWORD

There are many I things I could say about this author. Like the time he was invited to Kingston, Jamaica, to teach their theater directors how to direct their actors for the camera. Or the time he was invited to guide directors in India in the same way. But I won't. Instead I will tell you what it was like growing up with him as my father. When he took me to see a movie, I had the great pleasure of having them dissected piece by piece in terms of the acting, producing, directing, or the production. Forget about the endless questions (some of which I couldn't get into) about the impact it had on me. You could say laughingly that as a kid it kind of ruined it for me. Scary movies were no longer scary and action films were no longer exciting, but rather left me on the edge of my seat to see *where the director would go next* in the film. When I asked my father to explain the making of movies to me, he would say that in making movies, "Making the simple complicated is commonplace, but making the complicated simple—awesomely simple— is creativity. And making movies was awesomely simple." Many years later, when I finally knew what that meant, he told me that the first part of that statement he borrowed from Jazz great Charlie Mingus and that it applied wonderfully to making movies. Since I have grown up watching him direct or produce and having had the gratification of working at his side once or twice, I can attest that his passion is for actors, for directing, for producing, and for teaching and that it comes from his soul. And as a teacher, he places challenges on his students' passion not only to reach inside themselves for their voices but to do it in terms of what they will be asked for professionally.

I have a secret. I am my father's biggest fan. To me, this man has more knowledge and talent in his pinky toe than anyone I know. And he willingly shares it with his students. I have heard a couple of them say he has been their inspiration. Even saw a few come back with their successful careers and thank him. Yes, I am proud of him. But then again, I am his son.

—Eyan C. G. Schreibman

INDEX

RESOURCES

Daily Variety, December 6, 2005 – Eye on the Oscars: The Director
Daily Variety, January 26, 2006 – Director's Guild Awards
DGA Quarterly, Fall, 2005 – Raising the Tent Poles: 1st A.D.s at Work
DGA Quarterly, Spring, 2006 – The Straight Shooter: Interview with Clint Eastwood
Friendly Enemies, Maximizing the Director Actor Relationship, Delia Salvi, Watson-Guptill Publications (January 2003)
The Indie Producers Handbook, Creative Producing From A–Z, Myrl A. Schreibman, Lone Eagle Publishing, 2001
Elia Kazan, Richard Schickel, HarperCollins November, 2005
Brad Silberling Master Class, UCLA
Francis Ford Coppola Master Class, UCLA
Ben Peyser, www.standardquality.com

ABOUT THE AUTHOR

Myrl Schreibman's career is best described as an adventurous journey still in the making. His professional career as a producer and director has taken him to the concert stage, Broadway, movie studios, and network television. A professional well respected by both above- and below-the-line talent, Myrl Schreibman has been a member of the Directors Guild of America for thirty years and on the faculty of the UCLA School of Theater Film and Television for the past two decades. An innovator in the industry, he was one of the first directors or producers to marry hi-definition video with film before CGI, which is why he tells students not to think in the box with *what is,* but to think out of the box and say *what can it be?* His first book, *The Indie Producers Handbook: Creative Producing from A–Z,* is used by colleges and universities all over the United States. It has been translated into Chinese and is the text on producing at the Beijing Film Academy. *The Film Director Prepares: A Practical Guide to Directing Film and TV* follows in its footsteps.

www.indieproducing.com

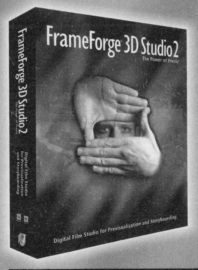

INTRODUCTION TO
THE COMPANION CD

The Companion CD in this book is a support CD for certain concepts discussed in the book. It contains all of the storyboard images created for the book in three different formats suitable for group or individual viewing and discussion. These formats are:

1. Individual color images (along with an overhead floor-plan view of the set at the moment the shot was snapped) in a Flash "slide-show" format.

2. The same color images in an HTML format which also includes technical information about the camera, its focal length, height, depth of field and so on.

3. The original FrameForge 3D Studio 2 files that were used to create the book images and that, with the supplied FrameForge 3D Studio 2 Demo, allows you to actually open the sets and further manipulate and explore the ideas and concepts that the images illustrate.

FrameForge 3D Studio 2 was used to create all of the images in this book because it offered the unprecedented opportunity to easily create the various scene illustrations to support the many story scenarios in the text.

And in a wonderful aspect of this software you will see how a sequence can be explored editorially once you have developed your coverage. Look for the "movies" of some of the scene scenarios.

ABOUT FRAMEFORGE 3D STUDIO 2

FrameForge 3D Studio 2 is the premier previsualization software program designed specifically for the director. It allows you to explore and experiment with shots, framing, and angles in an optically accurate 3D space while at the same time showing you such things as focal length and camera height.

3-D previsualization has long been used by the studios because it allows directors the ability to refine and discover the best way to approach a project prior to arriving on set. It does this in ways that simply cannot be accomplished with traditional 2-D or hand-drawn storyboards which come from an artist's imagination or which may be inaccurate when you actually get to the set. 3-D previsualization gives you the luxury to explore, expand, and develop your coverage while at the same time letting you exercise the "what if?" in the quiet of your own space so that when you get to the set you are free to think on your feet and find those "magic moments" that happen only on set.

I am pleased to be able to supply you with an extended demo version of FrameForge 3D Studio, available exclusively to purchasers of this book. This demo is available on this CD for both Macintosh OSX and Windows XP computers. It is the actual FrameForge 3D Studio 2 program, though it has several artificially imposed limitations. These include: (1) You can run it only 50 times; (2) While you can load all of the shots used to illustrate this book, you will be limited to having no more than 12 items on a set in shots that you create; (3) All snapped shots will have a demo "watermark" on them when you print or export; (4) The demo only has a subset of the object library available in the full version.

I highly recommend that you install the demo, as it is both a user-friendly program with simply astonishing capabilities for the director, but also because we have included the FrameForge source files that were used to generate all the images in the book. By having the demo installed, you can actually load the scenes that are being discussed at any point in the book, and you can both further explore them dynamically and actually put into practice the ideas and concepts that they are illustrating.

To install the demo, simply insert the CD and either click on the FrameForge 3D Studio 2 banner (if the CD interface automatically launches) or navigate to the folder FrameForge 3D Studio 2 Demo and run the setup application you'll find inside.

Frame Forge 3D is an excellent tool for a director's planning and previsualization, as it subtly shows you much more than just your storyboarded thoughts—it shows you how to get there. So enjoy!

—Myrl Schreibman

INSTRUCTIONS FOR THE COMPANION CD

1. Insert the CD

On Windows

- In most cases, it will automatically launch the Companion CD's graphical interface. If it doesn't, navigate to My Computer, double-click on your CD drive, and then double-click the file MENU.EXE.

On Macintosh

- It should automatically open a CD folder window.
- Double-click on the icon labeled DOUBLE-CLICK TO RUN.

In both cases you will see the following :

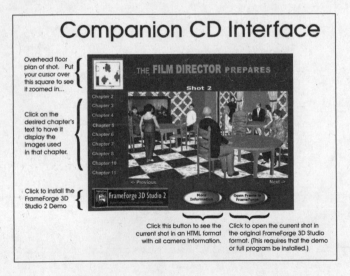

For further support, or if you wish to purchase the full program, go to: http://www.frameforge3d.com/